VOYA's

YA Spaces of Your Dreams Collection

Anthony Bernier

VOYA Press

an imprint of E L Kurdyla Publishing, LLC

Bowie, Maryland

ISBN 978-1-61751-011-3

Copyright © 2012 by VOYA Press

Published by VOYA Press, an imprint of E L Kurdyla Publishing, LLC

LCCN: 2012935470

The paper used in this publication meets the minimum requirements of the American National Standard for Information Sciences-Permanence of Paper for Printed Materials, ANSI Z39.48-1992.

Printed in the United States of America

Table of Contents

Acknowledgements vii
Introduction ix

Part 1 Small Teen Spaces Less Than 500 Square Feet

Cuyahoga County Public Library - Beachwood, Ohio
    Mina Gallo, October 1999 3

Sno - Isle Regional Library System (Edmonds Library) - Edmonds, Washington
    Tom Reynolds, August 2001 5

Swampscott Public Library - Swampscott, Massachusetts
    Vicky M. Pratt, October 2001 7

Houston Public Library, Texas
    Stacy L. Creel, October 2002. 9

Frederick County Public Libraries (C. Burr Artz Library) - Frederick, Maryland
    Natasha Stocek Carty, August 2003. 11

Rawson Memorial Library – Cass City, Michigan
    Kate Van Auken, April 2004 13

Wayzata Library - Wayzata, Minnesota
    Bethany Wagennar, August 2004. 16

Hammond Public Library - Hammond, Indiana
    Melody Scott, February 2006. 18

Lancaster Public Library (The Hub) - Lancaster, Pennsylvania
    Jennifer Fiene, Don Ankney, Jane Hannigan, and Kay E. Vandergrift, April 2008. 21

Fortuna Library (Tiny Space) - Fortuna, California
    Chris Cooper, August 2008 26

Crandall Public Library - Glens Falls, New York
    Frieda Toth, April 2010 30

Palm Harbor Library - Palm Harbor, Florida
    Katie Banks, December 2010. 33

Part 2 Medium Teen Spaces 501 to 1000 Square Feet

Waupaca Area Public Library - Waupaca, Wisconsin
    Kristen Anderson, August 1999. 39

Santa Cruz Public Libraries (Scotts Valley Branch Library) - Santa Cruz, California
    Janis O'Driscoll, April 2000 41

Cuyahoga County Public Library (North Royalton Branch) - North Royalton, Ohio
    Louise Miller, February 2001 43

Mastics - Moriches - Shirley Community Library - Shirley, New York
   Teri Germano, December 2001 45

Orrville Public Library - Orrville, Ohio
   Cindy Lombardo, February 2002 48

Bemis Public Library - Littleton, Colorado
   Jan Knauer, April 2002 50

Schaumburg Township District Library - Schaumburg, Illinois
   Amy Alessio, June 2002 53

Pinellas Park Public Library - Pinellas Park, Florida
   Patrice Dilley, August 2002 56

Cuyahoga County Public Library (Solon Branch) - Solon, Ohio
   Constance Dickerson, February 2003 58

Scott County Public Library - Georgetown, Kentucky
   Patti Burnside, April 2003 60

Glendale Public Library-Glendale Arizona
   Merideth Jenson-Benjamin, June 2003 62

Wadsworth Public Library - Wadsworth, Ohio
   Valerie Ott, February 2005 65

Leominster Public Library (Robert Cormier Center for Young Adults) - Leominster, Massachusetts
   Diane Sanabria, April 2005 67

Natrona County Public Library - Casper, Wyoming
   Emily Daly, August 2005 70

Middleton Public Library - Middleton, Wisconsin
   Rebecca Van Dan, October 2005 73

Harris County Public Libraries - High Meadows Branch; Aldine Branch; Barbara Bush Branch; Tomball
   College and Community Library; and Clear Lake City County Freeman Branch; Houston, Texas
   Sarah Booth, April 2006 76

William K. Sanford Town Library - Town of Colonie, New York
   Maureen DeLaughter, June 2006 78

Delray Beach Public Library - Delray Beach, Florida
   Lisa Kreutter, June 2007 81

Blue Island Public Library (Tech Annex) - Blue Island, Iliinois
   Darren Thompson, February 2008 85

Port Jefferson Free Library - Port Jefferson, New York
   Erin Schaarschmidt, June 2008 89

Hennepin County Public Libraries (Franklin Library) - Minneapolis, Minnesota
   Angela Fiero and Johannah Genett, June 2009 93

Hampton Bays Public Library (HBAY Teen Services) - Hampton Bays, New York
   Theresa Owens, October 2010 97

Part 3 Large Teen Spaces More Than 1001 Square Feet

Santa Cruz Public Library (Garfield Park Branch) - Santa Cruz, California
  Sandi Imperio, June 1999. 105

Los Angeles Public Library - Los Angeles, California
  Anthony Bernier, February 2000 107

Shaker Heights Public Library - Shaker Heights, Ohio
  Jennifer M. Asher, June 2000. 109

Los Angeles Public Library - Los Angeles, California
  Anthony Bernier, August 2000 112

Allen County Public Library - Fort Wayne, Indiana
  Sheila B. Anderson, October 2000. 114

Base Line Middle School Library - Boulder, Colorado
  Nancy Jane Moore, December 2000 117

Lindbergh Middle School - North Long Beach, California
  Helen Cox, April 2001 119

L.E. Phillips Memorial Public Library - Eau Claire, Wisconsin
  Kati Tvaruzka, October 2003 122

Phoenix Public Library - Phoenix, Arizona
  Karl Kendall, December 2003 125

City of Mesa Library - Mesa, Arizona
  Diane Tuccillo, February 2004. 128

Avon Lake Public Library - Avon Lake, Ohio
  Karen Scott and Jill Ralston, June 2004 130

Hays Public Library - Hays, Kansas
  Erin Downey Howerton, October 2004 133

Newport Beach Public Library (Central Branch) - Newport Beach, California
  Genesis Hansen, December 2004. 136

Southfield Public Library - Southfield, Michigan
  Shari Fesko, June 2005 139

Seattle Public Library (Starbucks Teen Center) - Seattle, Washington
  J. Marin Younker and Amy Duncan, December 2005 142

Carnegie Library of Pittsburgh (The Teen Space) - Pittsburgh, Pennsylvania
  Karen Brooks-Reese, August 2006 145

Waupaca Area Public Library - Waupaca, Wisconsin
  Peg Burington, October 2006. 148

Columbus Public Library (Teen Department) - Columbus, Georgia
  Brijin Boddy, December 2006 151

Palos Verdes Library District (Annex) - Rolling Hills Estates, California
  Alison Orr, February 2007. 154

Scottsdale Civic Center Library (Knowasis) - Scottsdale, Arizona
  Medina Zick, April 2007 158

Auckland City Libraries - Central Library - Auckland, New Zealand
   Annie Coppell, August 2007 162

Otis Library (Summers Young Adult Center) - Norwich, Connecticut
   Jennifer Rummel, October 2007 166

Pima County Public Library (Juvenile Detention Center Branch) - Tucson, Arizona
   William Bevill, December 2007 170

Elizabeth Public Library - Elizabeth, New Jersey
   Kimberly Paone, December 2008 174

Worthington Libraries: Northwest Library; Old Worthington Library - Ohio
   Sarah Cofer and Ann Pechacek, February 2009 178

East Meadow Public Library - East Meadow, New York
   Frances T. Jackson, April 2009 184

Oakland Public Library - Oakland, California
   Anthony Bernier and Nicole Brance, August 2009 188

McMillan Memorial Library - Wisconsin Rapids, Wisconsin
   Ron McCabe, October 2009. 193

Montgomery County Public Libraries: Bethesda Library; Quince Orchard Library;
   Chevy Chase Library - Maryland
   Kathie Weinberg, December 2009 197

Public Library of Cincinnati and Hamilton County (TeenSpot) - Cincinnati, Ohio
   Jennifer Korn, February 2010 201

New York Public Library (Battery Park City Branch) - New York City, New York
   Jeremy Czerw, June 2010. 205

Martin Luther King, Jr. Memorial Library - Washington, DC
   Elsworth Rockefeller, August 2010 208

Appendix: Resource List 213
Library Index 221
Author Index. 223
About the Author 225

Acknowledgements

I would like to extend gratitude to the current *VOYA* editor, RoseMary Honnold; publisher, Edward Kurdyla; and past *VOYA* editors who have continually supported this topic: Cathi Dunn McRae and Dr. Mary K. Chelton.

I would also like to acknowledge and thank Research Assistants Pam Okosun, MLIS; Collin Rickman; F. Joy Rodriquez; and most especially, Antonia Krupicka-Smith, MLIS, for their wide-open eyes and dedication; and to Dr. Mike Males for the constant march forward.

I would also like to express deep gratitude to the dozens of librarians who have, against assorted odds, continued to prosecute for the equitable sharing of the library's public space with young people. I would like to add the unsung Echo Park Branch of the Los Angeles Public Library and its staff, then managed by Sylvia Galan-Garcia. It was the experimentation cultivated there in the early 1990s that contributed mightily to my thinking about young people, libraries, and space.

This work was partially funded by an Institute of Museum and Library Services National Research Grant.

Anthony Bernier

Introduction

The June 1999 issue of *Voice of Youth Advocates (VOYA)* featured librarian Janis O'Driscoll's page-and-a-half descriptive profile of a young adult (YA) space modestly redecorated at the Garfield Park Branch of the Santa Cruz Public Library in California.[1] The profile inaugurated what thereafter became a regular column, initiated by then-*VOYA* editor, Cathi Dunn MacRae, who committed the magazine to featuring similar librarian-produced "YA Spaces of Your Dreams" profiles that have appeared in nearly every issue since. With six issues of *VOYA* per year, readers have seen descriptions and photos of nearly seventy-five different executions of YA spaces in public and school libraries throughout the country. These profiles forever connect *VOYA* with the advocacy of YA space equity.

After publishing more than ten years of these pioneering YA space profiles, it is time to ask what libraries have learned from them. Although we must qualify our current insights to the evidence before us, it is clear that some suggestive patterns have already taken shape. Among some of these preliminary insights, based upon the published profiles and a quick follow-up survey fielded from the libraries who published them, it is apparent that those institutions pursuing broader space equity for young adult users experienced a variety of demonstrable service outcome enhancements. More specifically, and sometimes contrary to our own legacy practices, values, and prerogatives, librarians report, for instance, that young adults emphasize and value their own experience and meanings of these public spaces over the library's commitment to collections and materials. Additionally, and perhaps also contrary to prevailing assumptions, the evidence presented here suggests that YA staff feel more supported institutionally than they did prior to offering a successful YA space.

YA Space and *VOYA*

In addition to being the inaugural profile appearing in *VOYA*, the Garfield Park branch was unusual because it was a branch dedicated entirely to young adult services. But the Garfield profile was conventional for more important reasons. Similar to most of the spatial profiles reproduced in this book, this YA space was conceived as an afterthought, a repurposing, or a renovation to a building's existing design. In this case, the original Garfield Park Branch was a 1919 Carnegie library. Thus, like most YA spaces, the project required creativity, resourcefulness, and an experimental spirit.

The Garfield Branch profile also provoked a long series of questions about YA spaces the profession has yet to address with evidence-based analysis. Should young adults be separate from the rest of the library users or should they be integrated? To what degree do young adults need special space of their own? How should that happen? Why? What are best practices? How should we proceed in answering these questions? These important questions are among the many for which we still do not have evidence and analysis when designing our future YA spaces.

Libraries still do not know for certain what to do with/about/for young adults when it comes to spatial allocation and design. As I have observed before, libraries devote more time and design energy to bathrooms than to teenagers.[2] The title of the *VOYA* column itself, "YA Spaces of Your Dreams," is instructive. Why is spatial equity for young people still only a "dream?" Whose dream is it? Why did the topic need this dream metaphor in the first place?

It is here that we must cast our minds back to the legacy of *VOYA* as an institution itself. Born out of 1970s movements to advance the civil rights of marginalized populations, the magazine's founders (Mary K. Chelton and Dorothy M. Broderick), as well as subsequent editors, advisory board members, authors, and readers felt themselves rather marginalized within the library and information science field in advocating for young adult services.

Thus, it is no accident that the magazine carries the name *Voice of Youth Advocates.* While a comprehensive history of YA librarians striving to gain and advance their specialization within the profession has yet to be told, such a narrative would necessarily need to include struggles for space as much as collections, resources and capacities for programming, outreach, YA courses in library schools, professional development, staffing levels, teaching faculty, and research, among other goals. The struggle to gain equitable space for young adults fits well within the broader *VOYA* context, mission, and legacy: *VOYA* and the advocacy for YA space are inextricably connected.[3]

An Early Struggle for Space

While very useful, this *VOYA's YA Spaces of Your Dreams Collection* of today's practice cannot responsibly claim to be everything the field needs on the topic of YA space. A selective collection of spaces cannot, for instance, serve as a history of the development of YA space in libraries, though such a history certainly would echo the struggle that originally gave birth to *VOYA*.

Ironically, my own original engagements with YA space began rather innocently in a tiny corner of a temporary bungalow building of a small Los Angeles Public Library (LAPL) branch located in a nearly hidden cul-de-sac between a baseball diamond and a pedestrian tunnel bordered on another side by a screaming interstate highway. Imagine a library hidden under a rock for an accurate picture. The only materials available were some leftover wall posters, torn-out pages from popular withdrawn YA magazines, some yellow "caution" tape from my garage, and the willingness of the library pages to "play" with unconventional shelving techniques. Posters on the ceiling certainly did raise eyebrows but the fundamental concern for enticing young people remained at the center. I gradually got a reputation for doing this "crazy" stuff. While my supervisor was hesitant at first, it was the evidence that persuaded her to endorse this experimental spirit. The shelving staff was gradually won over, and they began to take over, using their own creativity and familiarity with YA borrowing patterns to enact their own ideas.

The notion of YA space grew from there. That little collection began to generate dramatic circulation boosts in a community that had nearly been given up on for its lack of reading enthusiasm. The project caught the eye of an innovative city librarian, Elizabeth Martinez (later to become the executive director of the American Library Association), who asked me to consider developing a plan for the just renovated and massively expanded LAPL Central Library. The library had nearly doubled in size in the renovation following two arson-set fires that laid waste to much of the historic building on South Hope Street. The new plan had literally erased young adults and, instead, cynically integrated all YA materials into the library's massive collections.

I was asked to identify a partner to help with this notion of a YA space at the Central Library and was fortunate to recruit veteran LAPL YA specialist colleague, Ann Hoffman. Together we worked with willing library staff and groups of young people to develop the space and operation plan for what the young adults eventually named "TeenS'cape."

Thus, the first purpose-built YA space was initiated at the Central Library of the Los Angeles Public Library system, emerging from the embers of two conflagrations: the library's fires and the much larger 1992 civil disturbances in Los Angeles, that some may remember as the "Rodney King riots."[4] Amid the still smoldering fires in the riot's immediate aftermath I came to an increasingly clear interpretation that young people were unjustly accused of causing and perpetrating the violence. This view shook me into a new and more radical critique of LAPL's role with the city's youth.

TeenS'cape shared some commonalities with the Garfield Park Branch story. We, too, used existing (leftover) spatial resources. We, too, began with only the most modest of materials. And as I wrote in my August 2000 *VOYA* profile of TeenS'cape, the new space "received no redesign, no furniture, no permanent status, no direction signage, or even a place on the building directory."[5] Other than the city librarian's support, the institution's active resistance to incorporating young adults into the city's most cherished library space remains a deep bruise on my professional psyche. We faced active hostility and ostracism from colleagues and even more aggressive opposition from middle management. Some of that opposition included unilateral cancellations of *our* meetings and meeting rooms without notice. New YA space design processes today would not likely incur such hostility. And that *is* progress.

While libraries had offered shelving for housing YA collections in the past, what eventuated from those contentious early days at LAPL was the first purpose-built YA library space. The demonstrable success of that "first draft" TeenS'cape (an unbroken upward trajectory of performance measures in circulation, computer usage, class visits, and program attendance) attracted the attention of the library's foundation. It was the unlikely intervention and influence of the foundation that eventually vanquished what institutional opposition remained. The foundation subsequently and generously funded the build-out of the original design plan. And the profession began to take note.

In all these early stories, and to some extent in the hundreds I have learned about since, the theme of struggling to secure equitable YA space for young adults in public libraries persists. So it is both natural and reasonable that *VOYA* continue to promote these early pioneers in developing and executing YA spaces. After all, it was the struggle for equitable YA services that gave birth to the term "advocacy" in *VOYA*'s name in the first place.

Our advocacy for YA space may still encounter some opposition, though it is increasingly clear both that the opposition to spatial equity is not as pronounced as in the past and that advocates have successfully "nailed young adult spaces to the public library design agenda" in many instances.[6] Although we are only now beginning to examine actual data about new YA space design, it is rare today that a major new library construction project does not in some way attempt to deliver equitable YA space.[7] It took libraries about twelve years to begin incorporating separate children's spaces in libraries (1884-1896).[8] Incorporating children, of course, followed earlier battles to allow women— even middle-class white women—into public libraries. So, we should not be too surprised that it has taken about that long for the profession to recognize that young adults, too, deserve a place in their libraries. This represents progress for which YA librarians should take pride.

What We Know for Sure

After about ten years of pioneering and experimenting with YA spaces, what better time to ask what the profession has learned about YA spaces? Unfortunately, this still is not an easy question to answer. We don't know very much *for sure*, but we do have some resources. We have our continuing *VOYA* column regularly publishing individual descriptive profiles. We have several general YA resource guides that advocate for YA space. We have a few space resource manuals written by consultants; we have one doctoral dissertation and one master's thesis (both detailed individual case studies) we have two peer-reviewed research articles; and we have one significant historical document.[9]

The guides and manuals published thus far, while not reflective of empirical, evidence-based research, demonstrate both the capacity to attract and support the efforts of private consultants to focus on YA spaces. The degree to which libraries are keeping consultants busy proves a growing institutional capacity for realizing that libraries sometimes need specialized advice to compensate for the historic erasure of YA space considerations. The doctoral dissertation represents our first in-depth ethnographic study of one YA space. One of the two scholarly articles represents our first user-centered, post-occupancy evaluation of a branch's new YA space. The other article is my own synthesis of the early efforts of ten of the smallest YA spaces profiled in the issues of *VOYA*. Finally, the Institution of Museum and Library Services' (IMLS) National Leadership research grant, which I received in 2011 and on which I am currently working, is in the early stage of data collection and analysis. All of these efforts contribute to a growing base of knowledge and experience.

Overall, as Library and Information Science (LIS) scholar Dr. Christine Jenkins informed us not very long ago, the anemic research record of youth services in general remains a professional embarrassment.[10] Compared to the broader youth services research record, at least, the YA space topic now has a good start in building a respectable knowledge base.

Thus, we return to our *VOYA* profiles. Unlike any other continuing source of examples, ideas, creativity, enthusiasm, and experimentation, these descriptive views and images of new and renovated YA spaces represent the "pulse" of current practice and innovation.

About This "Collection"

This book organizes and reproduces the profiles of every YA space published in *VOYA* from 1999 through 2010. They appear in the Table of Contents, organized first by the reported size of the YA space and then chronologically by date of published *VOYA* article (from earliest to most recent). These accounts describe library spaces, executed within a broad range of resources and restraints, and are specifically designated to house materials, collections, and a variety of activities for young adults (library users roughly between the ages of 13-18). Some of these profiles portray, for instance, libraries luxuriating in lots of floor space for YA social experience. Others essentially hold little more than physical collections.

There are a number of important qualifications that readers should note about what this collection does not accomplish. As stated above, this is not a history of YA spaces in libraries. It is not a comprehensive collection of YA spaces in all libraries. Nor does it represent systematic, thorough, or universally applicable scholarly research. As a consequence, then, readers should be cautious about deriving notions that "best practices" applying to every library can be identified or extracted here. While there are, at times, non-spatial topics mentioned, these individual profiles do not explicitly address more conventional YA service topics like professional training, collection development, programming, outreach, etc. There are many current resource guides available for those purposes.

More than anything, however, the profiles in this scrapbook represent the efforts of pioneering and enthusiastic librarians to share their experiments in this new notion of YA space equity. The profiles offer readers the opportunity to learn about these early YA space concepts in some individual detail as well as the chance to compare and evaluate emerging notions and practices as they appear together.

Learning from the *VOYA* Space Profiles

As noted previously, this *VOYA's YA Spaces of Your Dreams Collection* contains all of the published profiles appearing in *VOYA* from 1999 through 2010 in one volume. This will help librarians, administrators from school and public libraries, teachers, youth advocates, library school students, and other interested readers draw their own conclusions in recognizing patterns and identifying advances they see developing over this eleven-year period.

In addition to gathering all of the published YA space profiles in *VOYA,* we also followed up with each of these libraries. In late March 2011, we contacted all of the sixty-one different library systems, profiling a total of seventy-two different library facilities with new YA spaces. We contacted these libraries by email and invited them to participate in a brief follow-up survey. We then circulated a six-item SurveyMonkey instrument that asked questions regarding some basic measures to complement the previously published YA space profiles. We asked them to reflect upon the following questions so we could offer readers updated and synthesized insights beyond what the individual descriptive profiles offer.

1. What is the name of your library?

2. From a librarian's point of view, identify the most popular features of your library's YA space appearing in the *VOYA* article.

3. What has changed in your library's YA space since the *VOYA* article?

4. What organizational changes have occurred since the *VOYA* article?

5. What is the total square foot area of your YA space?

6. What is the total square foot area of your whole library facility?

There are, of course, many additional questions we would like to ask, but we tried to balance the demands of busy librarians against our need for some basic follow-up responses. In other words, we wanted to avoid placing the profession's chronic lack of research capacity at the feet of practicing librarians.

As with any email survey, however, especially a survey employing contact information sometimes ten years old, the response rate was inconsistent. In the event of bounced-back email, we subsequently contacted the ranking youth services staff identified on respective library websites. We followed up with some libraries requesting clarifying information about the survey. A few libraries sent back email letting us know that they could not respond either for lack of access to information or did not have time to complete the survey.

Survey Results and Analysis

Our analysis of the thirty-five library responses provides suggestive and interesting insights for challenging some long-held legacy service assumptions as well as affirmation of several foundational aspects of library service.

Question 1: "What is the name of your library?" We asked this question so that we could be sure that we were surveying all of the YA spaces profiled in the regular *VOYA* column. We preserved anonymity by insuring that we would not identify their discrete survey responses.

Question 2: "From a librarian's point of view, check the *three* most popular features of your library's YA space appearing in the *VOYA* article." The choices were:

☐ Seating

☐ Technology

☐ Collection

☐ Different YA space identity (as opposed to children's or adult spaces)

☐ YA social experience

☐ Other

Among the thirty-five libraries responding, "YA space identity" received the largest support as the most popular feature with twenty-four votes. Librarians felt that the second most popular feature was "YA social experience," which received twenty-three votes. Significantly, the more conventional features of "technology" and "collection" were not identified as the most popular from the librarians' point of view, receiving nineteen and fifteen votes respectively. Seating was viewed as only slightly less important than library collections in the YA spaces, receiving fourteen votes.

Several important and suggestive concepts emerge from these results. Among the most interesting responses from librarians is that affording a venue for youth socializing and spatial identification with "their" area is among the most important benefits of having a YA space. This suggests that, contrary to the often-voiced view that librarians should anticipate behavioral issues in YA spaces, young adults using spaces designated for them do not present dramatic problems.

Also interesting is that library technology and collections are increasingly being recognized by library profession-als as not being among the most popular features of a YA space. These are the traditional features (size of collection, for instance, or the number of computer terminals available) libraries have promoted most about themselves for nearly a century. Together, these legacy assumptions represent the more classic "input measures" many librarians learned to value in library school programs of the past.

Instead, the librarians reporting on contemporary YA spaces are beginning to recognize that the spatial differen-tiation (achieved in many ways) and the social experiences that young people make for themselves in them (again, defined in various ways) are more valued by young library users. This could very well emerge as the most suggestive insight from the survey.

Further, it is fair to speculate that librarians may have placed "seating" further down on the list because they continue to connect current seating options more closely with task relationships (e.g., seating for computer use or studying), rather than as part of a wider variety of options for achieving stronger spatial identity and facilitating social meaning making.

The survey thus suggests the need for enhancing librarian awareness of the potentials inherent in exploring more varied seating options to improve YA space design success. As a consequence, we have emphasized creative seating options for libraries in the resources section of the book. (See appendix.)

Ultimately, it appears from these early findings that libraries should begin to imagine more complex ways to think about the nexus of space, function and access, materials, and the experiences that comes from their intersection rather than simply "offering space." Libraries experimenting with "gaming" and similar one-off events already have come to appreciate this space/function/experience nexus. The focus on space should better direct our attention to building and designing these features into original library designs rather than marginalizing these activities or risking competition with adult (or even children's) activities.

> Question 3: "What has changed in your library's YA space since the *VOYA* article?" Here, the respondents' choices shared similar criteria with Question 2: seating, technology, collection, and hours. Respondents were asked to assess if, for each of these criteria, their resources had "decreased, unchanged, increased." "Other" was also offered as an option.

The results from Question 3 also provide some instructive patterns among the thirty-five responding libraries. First, while collections increasingly demonstrate a lower importance when compared to separate space identity and social experience, the highest number of responders (twenty-six) reported that collection usage increased after opening their YA space. Only eight reported no change or a decrease. Use of technology was reported to have increased by twenty of the respondents, and seating capacity was reported to have increased by thirteen. Not surprising was the relatively low impact of adding a YA space ostensibly had on hours of operation—only three libraries increased their hours since opening a YA space. Indeed, as a sign of our current budget-constrained times, a full ten of thirty-five libraries reported experiencing a decrease in public service hours, though again, this was not correlated with the introduction of a YA space.

Alternatively, these preliminary answers could reflect librarians' efforts to maintain staff hours in the face of budget cuts that have otherwise reduced investments in seating, technology, and collections. Whatever the interpretation of the results, Question 3 generated significant positive narrative responses from several libraries as well. Here librarians added comments such as, "Programming continues to increase," "Outgrown space—new one is planned for 2012," "Expanded space (doubled our room size)," and, "We finally have a great teen sign above the door to the teen room." One librarian reported that, "Usage, access, outreach, and involvement has all increased over the past few years."

> Question 4: "What organizational changes have occurred since the *VOYA* article?" Here the choices were geared to four criteria, and respondents were asked to characterize the changes in one of three ways: "decreased/worse, unchanged, increased/better." The four criteria were:
>
> ☐ Staff hours
>
> ☐ Support for YA services staff - such as training, capacity building
>
> ☐ Young adult involvement in library affairs - such as YA advisory group participation, YA volunteerism, etc.
>
> ☐ Organizational perceptions of YA users
>
> ☐ Other

Several important and suggestive institutional results emerged from the responses. Fully twenty-one of thirty-five libraries reported either an increase in staff hours or no change. This must be noted as a tremendous advance and broadening institutional commitment in support of professional young-adult specialization particularly during a time of economic stress. While it would be unwise to draw a direct or causal connection between the introduction of YA space and increased institutional support for YA specialist librarian staff, the coincidence reported in these responses clearly hints at one.

A similar positive outcome emerging from Question 4 pertains to support reported for YA staff capacity development. While it is true that seven libraries reported a decrease or diminished support for YA professional staff training since introducing a new YA space, it is also true that twenty-seven of thirty-five reported an improved or unchanged condition. Again, this result must be viewed against the current backdrop of severe economic challenges to libraries in general, as well as another coincidental, positive pattern in the successful defense of existing or even increased staff development.

An even more positive pattern took shape on the matter of YA involvement in library activity. YA volunteerism and advisory group participation show particular promise. Of the thirty-five libraries responding to the survey, eighteen reported an increased and twelve reported an unchanged degree of YA involvement. Once again, while co-incidence does not prove causality, the overall pattern emerging from these reports connects consistent and positive outcomes for YA services after instituting a YA space. These responses indicate a trend toward libraries featuring YA spaces being increasingly sensitive to retraining and using staff to develop and supervise more YA volunteer contributions.

The final item from Question 4 enhances the previous three findings and represents perhaps the survey's most valuable learning for the profession as a whole. Of the thirty-five libraries responding, thirty-three reported that the organizational perceptions of YA users were either improved (twenty-one) or unchanged (twelve). Only one library reported a decreased perception of youth after the new YA space appeared. In addition to reported increases in circulation and general YA library use, both implying an increase of young people inhabiting the physical library, institutional perceptions of young people either improved or remained the same. *Thus, the more libraries were exposed to young people enjoying improved spatial equity, the more libraries viewed youth in a positive light and the less they regarded youth as liabilities.* Because apprehension toward increased numbers of youth in the library remains a common concern of library staff, this finding suggests a potential culture-change across the profession.

While the libraries surveyed were not required to provide narrative comments, Question 4 elicited more written detail than any of the other survey questions. All of the added comments reported on positive gains either in services or resources after instituting a YA space. One library commented, "Circ of YA materials has gone up 40-80 percent, hired two YS paraprofessionals." Another stated that, "Book budget doubled, space doubled." Still others reported, "Half-time teen librarian (with MLS) on staff now," "We have added YA programming and now have teen library volunteers," and, "I have been hyper-vigilant in hiring new staff who value the importance of serving the needs of teens." Thus, it is clear that libraries experimenting with YA spaces report uniformly positive gains in library resource inputs and service outcomes.

The next two questions asked about the actual physical space itself: Question 5: "What is the total square foot area of your YA space?" and Question 6: "What is the total square foot area of your whole library facility?"

The results of these last two questions represent perhaps the most provocative responses of this brief follow-up survey of libraries pioneering early YA spaces. Of the thirty-five libraries responding to the survey, thirty reported on this item. The average of the respective YA spaces was 2,024 square feet. Predictably, the range of YA space square footage was quite large: the smallest reported space was 96 square feet; the largest was 8,147 square feet. The average YA space, however, occupied less than 2 percent of the average total square footage (113,600) of the library facilities housing these spaces. These two figures help us begin to understand the percentage of YA space compared to overall library space, as well as ways, if any, in which library size relates to library perceptions and assumptions about YA space.

Methodological Concerns

As with any study, this one contained methodological challenges that, hopefully, future research on YA library space will better address. And while a full treatment of these issues is not possible here, it is important to at least disclose and note their existence.

Among the more challenging issues is, of course, the nature of the self-reporting survey. The survey asked only professional practitioners enthusiastic enough to have proudly published a profile of their recent YA space innovations. Clearly, these respondents would be enthusiastic to report ongoing YA services success. More independent verification methods would strengthen these claims. Further, due to time constraints, this survey did not include direct responses from young people themselves.

Of the seventy-two libraries contacted, thirty-five surveys were completed and returned. And not all of the thirty-five responded to all of the survey's questions. So while the information revealed provocative insights, the sample size would hardly qualify to identify patterns or results generalizable to large numbers of libraries.

Contacting appropriate staff was also challenging, as some of the YA space profiles were published ten years ago. Current email addresses were frequently difficult to establish. Many original *VOYA* profile authors had moved, transferred, or retired, and, predictably, some staff were too weighed down with day-to-day duties to respond.

Conventional challenges in studying YA services pertain to questions of space as well. Many of the study's terms can be interpreted differently by survey giver versus survey taker. Terms such as "staffing," for instance, can assume various definitions. Neither are librarians trained to estimate library square footage. Changes over time, concerning increased collection sizes, for instance, are difficult to verify with great certitude if baseline data were not collected and documented prior to instituting a YA space. Increasingly, digital or electronic collection circulation statistics risk skewing physical space measures.

Additionally, this modest attempt to re-connect with libraries that had pioneered and experimented with YA spaces in the pages of *VOYA* over the past ten years asked only six simple follow-up questions. Many additional and more complex questions about operating YA spaces deserve full scholarly treatment if those seeking YA spatial equity can ever expect to gain a firm foothold among library policy makers, administrators, space designers, and architects.

Finally, the generally positive findings should not exclude the exceptions. Not all libraries responded to the survey, and thus we must proceed without their contributions and without their insights. Also, not all libraries that responded reported positive findings. So we must be curious about any patterns embedded in those reports as well. We should be as curious about any patterns in circulation drops or youth participation decreases as we are in trumpeting the increases.

Conclusion and Discussion

As professional librarians we maintain an ethical responsibility to equitably serve young people just as we serve other populations in society. Equitable service includes providing spatial resources that invite and properly serve young adults. After over ten years of creative experimentation, it is time for YA specialists, designers, architects, administrators, and library school students to begin to critically evaluate and build upon what libraries have learned about instituting greater YA space equity.

This collection of YA space profiles published in *VOYA* attempts to inaugurate that critical conversation. For now, the question of what we have learned is provisionally answered with the response that while we are gradually overcoming a legacy of YA spatial marginalization and a continuing lack of evidence-based research, it is clear that, through this early period of experimentation and advocacy, instituting YA space equity demonstrably improves library service outcomes.

These improved service outcomes point to libraries' increasing willingness to accept that young library users value creating their own social experience in these public spaces as opposed to libraries simply maintaining their historic commitments to materials and collections. Further, librarians report that youth participation, which so challenges many institutions, appears to improve dramatically when libraries offer greater space equity. Among other suggested findings, young adult services are perceived in a more positive institutional light when libraries accommodate young peoples' spatial needs.

With such positive news we should only be encouraged to continue experimenting.

Notes

1. O'Driscoll, J. (June 1999). A place of our own. *Voice of Youth Advocates 22*, no. 2, 100-101.

2. Bernier, A. (October 1998). Bathrooms, bedrooms, and young adult spaces. *American Libraries 29,* no. 9, 52.

3. Jenkins, C. A. (2000). The history of youth services librarianship: A review of the research literature. *Libraries & Culture, 35,* 103-40.

4. While there is evidence that selected libraries did designate or re-allocate shelving space and some seating for young adults in the late 1940s and 1950s, called "youth quarters," these were on terms all set by the library, there was no research conducted on these areas, and they seemed to disappear after the mid-1950s. See American Library Association. (c. 1946). In every community a youth library. Division of Libraries for Children and Young People.

5. Bernier, A. (2000). A library 'TeenS'cape' against the new callousness. *Voice of Youth Advocates*, *23*, 180-181.

6. Bernier, A. (2000), page 181.

7. Feinberg, Sandra, and Keller, J. R. (2010). Designing space for children and teens in libraries and public places. Chicago: American Library Association.

8. Thomas, F. H. (Fall 1990). Early appearances of children's reading rooms in public libraries. *Journal of Youth Services in Libraries*, page 85.

9. Garrelly, M. G. (2011). Make room for teen! Reflections on developing teen spaces in libraries. Santa Barbara, CA: Libraries Unlimited.

    Feinberg, S. and Keller, J. R.. (2010). Designing space for children and teens in libraries and public places. Chicago: American Library Association; ALA Editions.

    Lee, S. A. (2009). Teen space: Designed for whom? Unpublished doctoral dissertation, University of California, Los Angeles.

    Pusey. A. E. (July 2008). Public library teen space design: An evaluation of theory in practice. Unpublished master's thesis, University of North Carolina at Chapel Hill, North Carolina.

    Bernier, A. (September/October 2009). "A space for myself to go:" Early patterns in small YA spaces. *Public Libraries 48*, no. 5, pp. 33-47.

    Bolan, K. T. (2008). *Teen spaces: The step-by-step library makeover!* published by ALA Chicago.

    Cranz, G. (2006). Body conscious design in a 'teen space: Post occupancy evaluation of an innovative public library. *Public Libraries*, *45*, no. 6, pages 48-56.

    American Library Association. (c. 1946). In every community a youth library. Division of Libraries for Children and Young People.

10. Jenkins. (2000).

Part 1

Small Teen Spaces Less Than 500 Square Feet

Teen Center

Beachwood Branch of Cuyahoga County Public Library
Beachwood, Ohio

Mina Gallo

Description: Part of a newly renovated library, the Teen Center of Cuyahoga County Public Library's Beachwood Branch occupies an airy space near Adult Fiction and the videos, tapes, CDs, at the opposite end of the building from the Children's Area. Perched high on a wall above shelves, a jazzy multicolored neon sign labels the space, flashing yellow bars and stars. Another sign saying "Young Adult" conforms to the system's name for all their YA areas. The roomy rectangular space measures approximately twenty by twenty-five feet, within sight of the young adult librarian's desk, which is separated from the Teen Center by a table and chairs between the adjacent Adult Fiction and media sections. Though not an enclosed room, the Teen Center feels like an oasis; its lounge area is in a sunny corner where walls of floor-to-ceiling windows overlook the Reading Garden. Under off-white walls, the patterned carpet features the decorator colors of plum, teal, salmon, and cream. Upholstery picks up the teal/green colors in the carpet. Bright posters of music groups add more color.

Furniture: Near the windows, four comfortable upholstered green chairs face a low coffee table; four more green chairs surround a higher round table of warm brown wood. A mix of shelving includes a wall unit about twenty-five feet long and over seven feet high, six swivel paperback stands, and a free-standing, face-out magazine/comic book rack with a flat all on one side holding a swirl-shaped acrylic book display unit. A free-standing pamphlet rack, labeled "Information Center," contains booklists, program flyers, and brochures on health, study tips, and community agencies where teens can go for help. Under the neon sign in the center of the wall shelving is a bulletin board with two surfaces, cork and marker board. Further afield behind the YA staff desk are more bulletin boards and a stand of metal grid shelving with baskets. A waist-high wood and glass display unit forms the front of the desk. Also near the staff desk are computers containing an on-line catalog, magazine and online reference databases, and unfiltered Internet access. Anyone under the age of eighteen needs parental permission to use the Internet. Word processing is available in a separate room. In the adjacent video/tape/CD section are five listening stations; headphones are signed out at the YA staff desk.

Collection: The YA collection contains about 11,000 volumes spread throughout the library. The Teen Center features mostly recreation materials in paperback and hardcover, including YA fiction, picture books for teens, adult books for teens, comics, graphic novels, audio books, magazines, and high school yearbooks. School-related items are test books, Cliff Notes, and college catalogs; the rest of YA nonfiction and reference is integrated with the adult and children's collections, with YA in the call numbers. Within the nearby media area are the YA videos, music CDs, and cassettes. Circulating CD-ROMs of interest to YAs are housed in the adult area. Young adult fiction is shelved alphabetically by author, with special genre sections for science fiction, fantasy, thrillers, movie tie-ins, TV tie-ins, and series. A large special collection of Holocaust books is integrated into YA fiction and labeled as Holocaust.

Young Adult Population and Community: Beachwood is a prosperous suburban community of just over 11,000 residents, with 9.4 percent minorities. There is a large Jewish population. The library branch serves one middle school and one high school with a combined total enrollment of 760 students. Beachwood's exemplary school system has an average class size of seventeen students and a 97.6 percent graduation rate; *Cleveland Magazine* rated its school as "A++." Students in sixth through twelfth grades use the library Teen Center both after school and weekends, with fairly steady traffic. Younger patrons read the Teen Center's comics. Beachwood Branch is one of twenty-two in the county library system, which also includes four large regional libraries and two mini libraries. Cuyahoga County Public Library is one of the ten busiest library systems in the United States, with the highest per capita circulation. Long known for its innovative and comprehensive young adult services, Cuyahoga County employs a full-time professional young adult librarian in a YA area in every library. As branches are renovated, each YA area is updated. Two regional libraries, Fairview Park and Maple Heights, feature especially large and snazzy new YA spaces.

Hours of Operation: The Teen Center is open during all branch hours: Monday to Thursday 9 a.m. to 9 p.m.; Friday and Saturday 9 a.m. to 5:30 p.m; and Sunday 1 p.m. to 5 p.m. during the school year only.

Staffing: The YA service desk is staffed by one YA librarian for forty hours a week. When the YA librarian is not there, children's and adult reference librarians cover the YA area.

Planning Process: The Teen Center replaced an older YA area when the Beachwood Branch was renovated. The library opened in 1982. Renovation planning began in the spring of 1997. The work actually started in November 1997 and continued until March 1998, with the branch closing for two weeks at the end of that period. A "Grand Re-Opening/Sweet 16 Celebration" was held in October 1998 featuring a jazz band, steel drum band, face-painting, bubbleologist, and a visit by the children's book character, Arthur. The mayor appeared for the opening ceremony, its festive atmosphere including refreshments and giveaways. All library staff had input in the planning process; Young Adult Librarian Paula Campanelli was involved in YA area planning. With her promotion to Regional Head of YA Services, new Young Adult Librarian Mina Gallo was hired during the renovation when all the planning was completed except for the signs and wall decorations. Gallo ordered the flashing neon sign and coined the Teen Center name.

Youth Participation and Programming: Gallo hopes to get a Teen Advisory Council started, and the branch uses teen volunteers whenever they are needed. The library system has extensive YA programming. Beachwood participates in the annual system-wide YA summer reading game, titled Extreme Reads in 1998 and Y2K Are You Ready? in 1999. There is an annual creative writing contest called Generation Next. Beachwood's other YA programs include crafts, SAT workshops, ghost storytelling, a Scary Movie Film Fest, and Mother-Daughter Book Discussions. Young adult programs throughout the system are posted on library's Web site at *http://clio1.cuyahoga.lib.oh.us.* From its home page, click "Programs & Events," and then click "Corridors," the title of the system's newsletter, for program listings by type. Selected teen Web sites from many locations are also linked to Cuyahoga's site.

True Confessions from YA Librarian Mina Gallo

This is the YA space of my dreams because…

"…it is a large, comfortable, B'cool' space that teens can call their own."

I still dream of these improvements:

"We need a new paperback shelving unit that would market the paperbacks better."

Teen Patron Comments

High school junior Naomi Glass is glad that the Teen Center is in a more distinct area than before and thinks the neon sign is cool.

Sixth grader Marie Daher likes the way the room is arranged and the view of the Reading Garden.

Ninth grader Libba Mendelson says it is easy to find books after the renovation, and she really likes the Teen Center.

Beachwood Branch, 25501 Shaker Boulevard, Beachwood, Ohio 44122-2398, (215) 831-6868, *http://www.cuyahoga.lib.oh.us/Branch.aspx?id=486*

Edmonds Library Sno-Isle Regional Library System
Edmonds, Washington

Tom Reynolds

Description: Heralded by four colorful banners high overhead that depict teen reading, the Teen Area occupies a large corner on the west side of Edmonds Library between the reference collection and the children's area. A bank of six computer terminals, four with unfiltered Internet access, sits in the center of the library between the reference desk and the teen section. (Teens also use the other thirteen terminals in the library.) Within a rectangle of about 450 square feet, the Teen Area features light blue walls, grey carpet with blue and salmon flecks, a large bulletin board, six comfortable upholstered chairs in blue tones, a round table with four hard chairs, book and magazine display racks, and shelving for about 900 catalogued volumes. Two large windows with a great view of Puget Sound give the Teen Area a light, airy atmosphere.

Collection: Young adult fiction fills 48 feet of shelving, including some adult novels for teens. On 18 feet of shelving, nonfiction focuses on teen lifestyle and issues books, contemporary biographies, and titles from "best" lists; most biographies and homework-related nonfiction resides in the adult area. Two paperback spinners and a rack attached to the side of the fiction bookshelves contain fiction and nonfiction paperbacks. The library's collection of music CDs, heavily used by teens, are shelved on the reverse side of the teen fiction bookshelves. A wooden magazine rack showcases eleven teen magazines with booklists and brochures. A freestanding unit topped by a cork board holds face-out display books. Circulation of teen fiction (4,638 in 2000) was slightly above the system average. Uncataloged teen paperbacks enjoy very high circulation.

Young Adult Population and Community: Fourteen miles north of Seattle, the city of Edmonds is a prosperous suburb covering almost nine square miles. Once mostly European American, it has a large Asian American minority. The 1990s brought more African American and Hispanic American residents. Going beyond the city limits to serve an estimated population of 38,858, the Edmonds Library is one of 21 libraries in the Sno-Isle Regional Library System that encompasses Snohomish and Island counties. Within the Edmonds service area are two public middle schools and two public high schools enrolling a total of 4,850 students. One private elementary school spans kindergarten to eighth grades.

Hours of Operation: The Teen Area is open during all library hours: Monday through Thursday from 10 a.m. to 9 p.m., Friday from 10 a.m. to 6 p.m., Saturday from 10 a.m. to 5 p.m., and Sunday from 1 p.m. to 5 p.m (school year only). Teens are its primary users, although it also attracts parents and older children.

Staffing: One full-time adult/teen librarian is in charge of the collection. Assistance to patrons in the Teen Area is provided by any librarian stationed at the reference desk.

Planning Process: The Edmonds Library has had an evolving young adult space since it opened in 1981, as do all Sno-Isle libraries. In June 1997, the staff invited a focus group of eight teens to answer a questionnaire about the YA area and collections. Their most frequent response: "Redecorate the YA area." Welcoming the opportunity for teen input, the library sought specific ideas for this redecoration from a new group of teens in the spring of 1998. The teen brainstorming group met twice to recommend these enhancements: (1) more comfortable and colorful seating, (2) new shelving to replace old small wooden bookcases, (3) a large bulletin board to display group projects and information of ongoing interest to teens, and (4) a teen volunteer redecoration project.

The fourth recommendation evolved into an art project for teens to create banners to brighten the young adult area. The adult/teen librarian identified an art class at Edmonds/Woodway High School to design and make the banners, working with the Edmonds Art Commission and the students to establish guidelines for colors and themes. Advised by their teacher, seven art students worked on the banners during 1999 as two other teen recommendations were fulfilled: new YA fiction shelving was installed and a large bulletin board was mounted. During a special ceremony in June 1999, the new banners were unveiled, hanging from wooden beams above the young adult area. A system-wide decision to change the area name from Young Adult to Teen was made a few months after the banners arrived. The final teen recommendation was slightly altered; the easy chairs already in the Teen Area were reupholstered in December 2000. The Teen Area facelift was completed over a three-year period, thanks to funding from the Friends of the Edmonds Library.

Young Adult Programming: Teens are involved in Edmonds Library's summer reading program and a biweekly summer reading group. The library presents two other in-library teen programs each year. The adult/teen librarian does extensive school visiting, booktalking to 850 students in 2000. The library system's Web site has a "Teen Connections" section (http://www.sno-isle.org/teen), where teens can post their book reviews and comments.

True Confessions from Adult/Teen Librarian Tom Reynolds

The most exciting part of our teen area redesign was . . .

". . . the approach we took to involve teens in the planning and implementation process. We attempted to accomplish each of the four goals of our 1998 brainstorming group. Although some were modified, such as recovering rather than replacing the stuffed chairs, we were successful in following through with the spirit of their recommendations to make this area more comfortable and teen-friendly. Our process of using teen input in stages could be a model for other middle-sized libraries on a limited budget."

I still dream of these improvements:

"Paint the walls a brighter color, add additional magazine displays, and enlarge the area to incorporate a homework center."

Edmonds Library, 650 Main Street, Edmonds, WA 98020, (425) 771-1933
http://www.sno-isle.org/?ID=1195

Teen Area:

Going a Long Way on a Short Budget

Swampscott Public Library
Swampscott, Massachusetts

Vicky M. Pratt

Fresh out of library school with experience only in a university library, in October 1999 I was hired as a Reference Librarian at the Swampscott Public Library in Massachusetts. Several days later, Library Director Alyce Deveau asked if I also would like to take on the challenge as the new Young Adult Librarian. I cautiously agreed, having had no experience working with teenagers.

When our 1915 building was renovated in 1997, no money was allocated for a separate teen room, but the director planned to assign a section specifically for teens. She showed me the corner of the first floor Reference Room set aside as a sanctuary for teens to read, socialize, and hang out. On heather-purple carpet beneath three large, arched windows, it consisted of three walls lined with YA books and magazines, some CDs in a cardboard box on a shelf, a study carrel, a wooden table with chairs, and two soft rocking chairs. This sedate and classic grey- and white-painted library space was in desperate need of some youthful pizzazz.

Within the next week, I bought a couple posters to hang in the area. I must have done a pretty good job of selecting them because a few months later, Britney Spears mysteriously walked away from the wall. She soon was replaced by Christina Ricci, and many other celebrities have since followed. Girls were begging to take home 98 Degrees, and one of them finally won the poster in a contest.

The next thing I did was to update the CDs; John Denver does not have quite the same impact as 'N Sync. With the director's go-ahead, I ordered about fifteen new CDs to get the collection rolling. I also felt that they needed a better display rack than a cardboard box. Thus began my history of stealing from other parts of the library. I absconded with a display table originally used for new reference books. I covered its corkboard with large clip art pictures of an electric guitar and amp, and tied pencil trays together with fishing line to make CD display baskets. We now own approximately eighty current, popular CDs.

Next came the creation of a video collection. I reasoned that since teens love music and movies, perhaps they might check out books located in the same area with other media that they enjoy. I began by ordering about fifteen VHS movies. The collection now consists of almost fifty videos housed on a tall metal shelf with audio books, magazines, and nonfiction of high teen interest, creating a border in the middle of the floor between the Teen and Reference Areas.

Another important part of making teens feel at home in their new space was to designate it as the Teen Area. The library did not have funds budgeted for a banner or sign, so I made one. Over several weeks, the library staff helped me to collect free CDs that we all receive in junk mail. I covered the backs of these CDs with plain lavender wrapping paper, strung them together with fishing line, and bought a few sheets of purple foam material from a crafts store to make huge letters spelling "Teens!"

At this juncture, I ordered new YA fiction and paperbacks. I also knew that health and social issues relating to teens needed attention, so I ordered quite a few nonfiction books on those subjects, shelving them beside the videos. I began making themed displays on the windowsills in the area, so that teens interested in a certain genre or author could find books they like easily. These displays are changed frequently to correspond with new collections and seasons.

In the summer of 2000, we asked teens to help redecorate two old, bright orange tables that had been in storage. The Friends of the Swampscott Public Library generously paid for the painting supplies as well as the reward of ice cream sundaes for the teens' hard work. We used black, gold, and silver paint, giving each table a different theme. The round table features cartoon characters, and the rectangular one has a space theme. These jazzy refurbished tables replaced the standard wooden ones in the Teen Area, seating four and five people respectively. The rest of the seating consists of four soft burgundy rocking chairs. In July 2001, teen painters worked their magic on our old spin-around paperback rack.

Most recently, the library purchased a CD-ROM game collection. Teens may check out up to two games for a one-week loan period at no cost. We currently own 25 games. This fall we opened a listening station where teens listen quietly to CDs as they do their homework.

At this writing, the transformation of the Teen Area has been over a year in progress. The library has spent less than $200 on posters and decorative improvements. On the Teen Comment Board, we often get requests for a larger space than our 162 square feet, and more "comfy couches." Nevertheless, we have done well to make our available space into a place where teens like to read, do their homework, and socialize.

Collection: About 1,200 books, magazines, and media materials reside on built-in wall shelving measuring approximately 48 square feet, a short wooden bookcase of 10 square feet, a spin-around paperback rack of 20 square feet, a metal stand-alone shelf of 72 square feet, and various small racks. Oriented toward recreational reading, hardcover and paperback books include YA fiction, adult books for teens, nonfiction on teen issues, and graphic novels. School-related YA nonfiction is shelved within the adult collection in Dewey order. Media items are described above. During 2000, materials from the Teen Area enjoyed a circulation of 1,800. Although there are no computers in the Teen Area itself, ten computers in the adjacent Reference Room contain an online catalog, unfiltered Internet access, reference databases, and word processing.

Young Adult Population and Community: On the North Shore of Massachusetts, Swampscott Public Library serves a primarily white middle- to upper-class suburban community of 13,464. The combined student population in one middle school and one high school is 1,340.

Hours of Operation: The Teen Area is open during regular library hours Monday and Tuesday from 9 a.m. to 9 p.m., Wednesday and Saturday from 9 a.m. to 5 p.m., Thursday from 1 p.m. to 9 p.m., Friday from 9 a.m. to 1 p.m., and Sunday from 1 p.m. to 4 p.m. The library is closed on summer weekends. During afterschool hours, ten to twenty teens can be found in the Teen Area; on winter weekends the average is lower, from eight to ten teens. The most frequent users are between the ages of ten and sixteen; parents and other age groups use the Teen Area occasionally.

Staffing: Two full-time professional Reference Librarians staff the entire Reference Room that contains the Teen Area. One of them is designated as Reference/Young Adult Librarian, but both librarians assist teen patrons.

Young Adult Programming: There is no official teen council. A teen book discussion group is currently in the launching stage, with members being sought through a registration form on the teen page of the library Web site—click "Teen Scene" at *http://www.noblenet.org/swampscott*. Individual teen programs have included a visit from the WFNX radio station staff with food, music, games, and book giveaways; a gaming night to preview the new CD-ROM game collection; a Teen Coffeehouse; a Poetry Slam; a Teen Advice Forum; Fingernail Art projects; and Groovy Movie Tuesdays on summer Tuesday afternoons.

True Confessions from YA Librarian Vicky M. Pratt

This is the YA space of my dreams because . . .

" . . . with very little money, the teens and I have created a space that is cool to hang out in."

I still dream of these improvements:

"Expand the space with room for more seating and materials, increase the materials budget, and install a really funky fish tank that would stand as tall as myself!"

Teen Patron Comments

"I like how the Teen Area has movies and books about teens who need help. I also like how they have lots of magazines for girls giving advice."—Kristen Lyons, 13

"We have tons of great books. The music at the Swampscott Library is awesome—we have great CDs."—Kaleigh Barbuzzi, 12

"I like the magazines. They are awesome because they have every kind made for teens. I like the biographies—they are wicked cool. There are a lot of books about puberty and hormones and stuff so you know the changes in your teenage years."—Matthew Keeney, 12

Swampscott Public Library, 61 Burrill Street, Swampscott, MA 01907, (781) 596-8867
http://www.noblenet.org/swampscott/

ConnecTeens

Houston Public Library
Houston, Texas

Stacy L. Creel

Most of us dream of the day when renovations will come to our library. For Houston Public Library, that day is on the horizon. With models and methods from Phoenix Public Library[1] and Los Angeles Public Library[2] to follow, our path to creating a great teen space is clear. But what do we do in the meantime?

More than a year ago, we surveyed the teens of Houston to find a name for the teen sections in all thirty-six Houston Public Library locations. The committee chose a write-in name on the survey, and ConnecTeens was born. Then we conducted a system-wide contest for teens to design our new ConnecTeens logo. Ruishi W., age fifteen, submitted the winning design and won $150. (For contest rules and the runner-up, see the library's teen page at http://www.hpl.lib.tx.us/teen/logo/htm.)

We now had a great name to go with our spaces, but were the spaces inviting, comfortable, and attractive to teens? The answer to that question at the Central Library was a solid "No." Knowing that renovations were on the way, we needed to do something relatively inexpensive to make our ConnecTeens more inviting. Here's what we came up with for Central Library's "in the meantime"—and all for under $600. (See the below budget.)

The teen area at the downtown Central library was formerly a place in which adults read newspapers. Although the section now housed teen materials, habit brought the adults back to the teen tables. Once they migrated to their spots, they monopolized the area by spreading out the newspapers and staying for hours. Of course, teens want a place designed specifically for them, not shared with adults. So we removed all tables from the teen area for more than six months, giving the adults time to develop a new pattern of use. Even now, we have only one round table in ConnecTeens, used for displays and crafts at designated times.

Houston Public Library's young adult collection focuses on entertainment, pop culture, and teen issues such as sexuality and beauty. Although our teen collection is not homework-related and our area lacks tables, teens are not deterred from doing their homework there. They often get comfortable in a beanbag lounge chair or floor rocker, and use the Bench for their laptops or for writing. The Bench is ConnecTeen's most exclaimed-over piece of furniture. It was purchased at a resale shop and decorated with stickers from Hot Topic, "a mall-based chain of retail stores that specializes in apparel, accessories, gifts, and music for teenagers" (http://www.hottopic.com). While some of the stickers might make parents cringe, the teens love them, exclaim how cool they are, and often ask where they can get their own.

Another step that we took to give the area less "adult appeal" was to convert to floor seating—most adults wouldn't be able to get out of our teen seats if they managed to get into them! The floor rockers and beanbag lounge chairs made the rug a necessity; an unexpected bonus is that the rug works well for overflow seating. We threw in some tube lighting and creative use of windows, and we were ready for teens.

Central Library's ConnecTeens Budget	
1 rug from Home Depot (on sale at half price)	$89.99
2 floor rockers, @ $79.95	$159.90
3 beanbag lounge chairs @ $64.00	$192.00
1 tube light	$35.00
1 bench (resale shop)	$35.00
50 stickers	$80.00
TOTAL	$591.89

Although the Central Library's teen area is not our ideal space, it has become a place where teens congregate. They're already calling ConnecTeens their own. In the meantime, it will definitely get us through.

Houston Public Library, Jesse H. Jones Central Library, 500 McKinney, Houston, Texas 77002, (832) 393-1313
http://www.houstonlibrary.org/central-library

Notes

1. Teen Central, *School Library Journal*, October 2001, 32.

2. Bernier, Anthony. Los Angeles Public Library's TeenS'cape Takes on the "New Callousness," *Voice of Youth Advocates*, August 2000, 180-181.

Teen Zone

C. Burr Artz Library, Frederick County Public Libraries
Frederick, Maryland

Natasha Stocek Carty

Description: Teens are beckoned upstairs to the second floor of the newly renovated C. Burr Artz Library by the royal blue and orange neon-like Teen Zone sign. They walk up the grand spiral staircase to find an orange lava lamp bubbling on a coffeehouse-style table, surrounded by funky low chairs. Internet access is a few steps away. The latest teen events are posted on the bulletin board. And of course, there are books—4,350 of them—selected just for teens.

In this central branch of Maryland's Frederick County Public Libraries, the Teen Zone is adjacent to the adult fiction collection. Within sight of the adult information desk, the rectangular space measures approximately 357 square feet. Its décor is understated yet eye-pleasing, with khaki walls and a carpet of mixed jewel tones. The custom-made Teen Zone sign highlights the orange and coordinates with the royal blue in the carpet. Located in an alcove, the Teen Zone's arrangement showcases the collection. The area is divided in half by low shelving that houses paperback series. On one side are two low, funky chairs upholstered in a geometric pattern of rusts and blues. Between them is a small round table with bookmark holders. On the other side is a larger table with two metallic chairs where teens do their homework. Shelving is a mixture of 87 feet of standard and universal shelving, with 9 feet of periodicals shelving. Several additional chairs sit right outside the Teen Zone.

Collection: Young adult materials are kept up-to-date with constant weeding. The collection includes YA fiction, paperback series, graphic novels, audiobooks, videos about teen issues, and teen magazines (*Mad, YM, J-14, Teen Ink, Computer Gaming World, ESPN, Teen People, Transworld Skateboarding, Tu, Electronic Gaming Monthly,* and *Seventeen*). Its nonfiction features high-interest topics, such as poetry, dating, and college, that do not support the school curriculum. School-related materials for teens are located in both adult nonfiction and children's nonfiction. New books, graphic novels, and paperback series are pulled from YA fiction as special collections. From its grand opening on May 3, 2002, through December 12, 2002, the Teen Zone circulated 5,948 items. Because the books fly off the shelves, the YA materials budget has been increased.

Young Adult Population and Community: In rural western Maryland, a land of rolling green hills and family farms, Frederick County Public Libraries serve a population of 192,703 with six branches. All branches have young adult collections and librarians in charge of teen programs. C. Burr Artz Library is the largest and central branch, serving the county seat of Frederick, a rapidly growing city of 52,767. Many residents commute for an hour or more to jobs in Washington, D.C. There are 8,991 middle school students in 7 middle schools and 10,985 students in 5 high schools. The student population is 85.5 percent white, with 14.5 percent minorities; 69% of high school seniors plan to continue their education at colleges, technical schools, or in the military.

Hours and Teen Traffic: The Teen Zone is open during all branch hours, Monday to Thursday from 10 a.m. to 9 p.m., Friday and Saturday from 10 a.m. to 5 p.m., and Sunday from 1 p.m. to 5 p.m. The area attracts teens ranging from grades six to twelve, with up to 75 crowding the space on weekends. Often there are teens reading magazines, perusing graphic novels, or studying at the table. During the summer, the Teen Zone is especially popular.

Staffing: There is no YA services desk in the Teen Zone, which is covered from the adult information desk nearby. A full-time librarian in Children's and YA Services maintains the Teen Zone space and does both local and county-wide teen programming. Another librarian does YA collection development.

Planning Process: Renovation planning for C. Burr Artz Library began in the fall of 1997. Construction started in June 2000, continuing until just before the weeklong grand opening celebration from May 4–11, 2002. Special teen programs featured internationally known slam poet Gayle Danley, an improvisation workshop, and a fabulous Teen Night with pizza, a live deejay, and a visit from Annette Curtis Klause, author of the YA horror novels, *Blood and Chocolate* and *The Silver Kiss*.

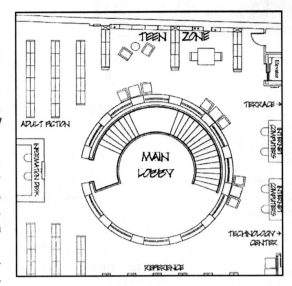

All library staff had input in the Teen Zone's planning process. When the renovation plans were well underway, Youth Services Librarian Natasha Stocek Carty was hired. She ordered the Teen Zone sign, helped to select shelving and furniture, and planned the area's layout. The Teen Advisory Group, still meeting monthly, helped to select Teen Zone as the name of the area, and suggested materials for purchase.

YA Programming: Regular young adult programs are scheduled at all Frederick County library branches, including mystery programs, book discussions, an anime film fest, a coffeehouse, and the statewide Teen Summer Reading program. Last year, the Maryland Division of Library Development and Services funded a grant to create a collection of quick, foolproof YA programs for all Frederick County libraries. A board games collection was developed, as well as boxed mystery programs and book discussion kits. Teen programs throughout the system are posted on the library's Web site at http://www.fcpl.org. A special teen page is currently being designed.

True Confessions from Youth Services Librarian Natasha Stocek Carty

This is the YA space of my dreams because . . .

". . . before the Teen Zone opened, we had no special place in the library for teens. The teens have really been enjoying this "cool" space. The circulation is way up—the teens are speaking with their library cards. After months of planning, scheming, and dreaming, we got just the response we had hoped for."

I still dream of these improvements:

"I wish we had our own separate room and a YA desk. We could use more graphic novels, more paperback series and a special shelving unit for them, a computer, and more display space, including a place to display teen art. Throw pillows, a place to listen to music, a teen music collection."

Teen Patron Comments

"I think it's very cool."—Tara Smeak

"There are a lot of good books for teens. It's easier to find the books we want to read."—Anna Morison

"Way awesome."—Audrey Conway

"It's nice, the way it's set up with the lights and everything. It's more open."—Laura Hutton

C. Burr Artz Public Library, Frederick County Public Libraries, 110 East Patrick Street, Frederick, MD 21701, (301) 600-1630
http://www.fcpl.org/information/branches/cburrartz/index.php

Rawson Memorial Library

Cass City, Michigan

Kate Van Auken

Description: Fueled by the ideas of an enthusiastic teen advisory group, small-town Rawson Memorial Library transformed a modest rectangular area of 170 square feet into an inviting environment for teens. When the 1970 library building gained a major addition in 1997, it contained no YA space until new library director Kate Van Auken spearheaded the effort that culminated in the opening of a teen-designed area in September 2003. Working within the building's existing layout, the new YA space incorporates one of the local school colors, maroon. At one end of the rectangle, a window ten feet long lights up the entire space. The walls around the window are painted maroon, with celebrity "Read @your library" posters on either side. Narrow magnetic word walls flank the window nook, which contains a high, black café table with two tall chairs, a paperback spinner, and a swivel rocker with an ottoman. Two other sides of the area are closed off with bookcases, one a single-sided shelf with four stools alongside, the other a double-sided shelf in a serpentine shape. The fourth side of the area is open to one of the library's banks of full-service computers shared with all patrons. The YA area's center floor space holds a round table with four chairs. On the tables are plexiglass display holders promoting YA books. The circulation desk faces the YA area, which sits off to its left side.

Collection: The opening of the teen space increased the recreational YA collection from fifty to five hundred volumes including YA fiction, science fiction, fantasy, nonfiction, and graphic novels housed in 384 square feet of shelving. Magazines reside in two wall racks.

Population and Community: Serving a population of 8,800 in an agricultural area, the district library is located in Cass City, a town of 2,500 people. In a tough economy, many residents travel to Saginaw, Bay City, or Detroit for work. The library is one of the community's greatest assets and is strongly supported by its users, 24 percent of whom are age eighteen or younger, attending one middle school and one high school.

Hours and Teen Traffic: The YA area is open during all library hours: Monday, Wednesday, and Friday from 9 a.m. to 9 p.m.; Tuesday and Thursday from 9 a.m. to 5:30 p.m.; and Saturday from 9 a.m. to 4 p.m. Its patrons range in age from ten to twenty, about five of whom visit the space each hour after school, increasing to ten or fifteen on Saturdays.

Staffing and Programming: Staffing is a group effort shared by the library director, a special programming librarian, and a catalog librarian. All staff members helped with the remodeling and serve patrons of all ages. Two librarians cover YA programming, starting with the YA area's Grand Opening on Saturday, September 6, 2003, featuring balloons, snacks, prizes, and a survey of teen interests. The teen advisory group that met several times to plan the new space continues to operate as the staff's sounding board for teen issues, a new YA Book Club meets monthly, and a teen summer reading program has long existed separately from the children's program. Teen programs are expanding with a recent urban legends program, a documentary film week, and a murder mystery night.

Find Inspiration in What Others Say and Do

As library director, one of my philosophies is to ask others what they feel about matters that pertain to the library—always including the library board and staff, and often patrons and voters of our district. I encourage all to voice their ideas, concerns, and suggestions. Through this positive interaction, many fabulous ideas have come about in the short time—less than two years—in which I have been director.

One major idea was to do something for young adults in our community. In a rural area such as ours, opportunities for outside activities are quite limited. I believed that we could help to change this situation by providing an area in the public library specifically geared toward twelve-to-eighteen-year-olds. My first step was to get support from my library board, which was very interested. The next step was to contact our middle school librarian to ask for help in forming a YA advisory group. We needed their ideas to visualize what they would want in a YA area at the public library.

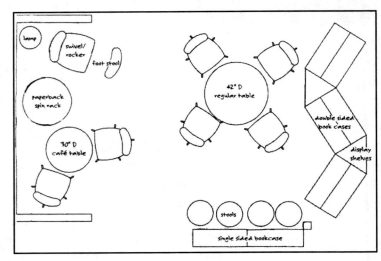

On October 24, 2002, we had our first meeting: seven middle schoolers and myself! We sat on the floor in the undeveloped area, and passed around library furnishing catalogs. We talked about lighting, shelving, and especially seating. Pondering all their ideas, I was looking at the Demco catalog when I saw its notice, "Free Design Service." I called Demco and a few months and faxes later, we had a floor plan! I met with the teens to update them on the progress and we were motivated to continue.

The Young Adult Advisory Group (YAAG) wanted to help in any way they could, so they decided to hold a bake sale in April 2003 (in conjunction with our Friends of the Library Annual Magazine Sale) to raise money for YA materials. It went so well that they did it again in August during our Annual Book Sale! They raised more than $500 for their own selections, each containing a book plate that reads: "Selected by the Young Adult Advisory Committee 2003." These teens kept the momentum going, and I wasn't going to let them down. They inspired me so much by their desire and willingness to help make this project a reality.

Next, I pored over issues of *VOYA*, turning to the YA Spaces of Your Dreams section to see what other libraries were doing with their teen spaces. I tried to visualize how our small area would be able to accomplish ample seating and privacy. As luck would have it, the February 2003 issue highlighted the teen area in the Solon Branch of Cuyahoga County Public Library in Ohio. The lucky part was that I was in the car with my family to visit relatives in . . . Solon! During this five-hour drive, I couldn't wait to arrive, breeze by the folks, and get to the library!

When visiting the Solon Library, I got a feel for what worked in their larger library, asking questions such as "If there was one thing you'd definitely tell others to do, what would it be?" and "What is the one thing you would not do if you had the chance to do it over?" I quizzed the librarian on YA programming and book selection, thanking her for submitting the story to *VOYA* because it really inspired me to order furniture, pick paint colors, and choose upholstery—with the counsel of my Solon sister-in-law, an interior designer!

Three weeks before our Grand Opening, my husband and I added suspense by hanging tarps that completely covered the teen area. We placed DANGER tape all over with signs that read "Dangerously New Material Coming September 6!" The evening before the opening, the YAAG enjoyed a special preview with eight members, eight nails in the tarps, and eight sets of pliers. Each member stood on a chair and pulled a nail so they could be the first to see the space that they helped plan, design, and finance. The staff enjoyed the preview as well, excited to see the teens poring over the new books for ages!

The next day, the Grand Opening was wonderful, and traffic has been steady ever since. Comments have been very complimentary, circulation continues to rise, and I am seeing faces in the library that I haven't seen before. Our new YA space is a great accomplishment for our library and our community. I encourage all who haven't done the YA thing in their libraries to do it—but seek ideas from others, especially teens. They have great ideas and boundless energy, and they bring inspiration to all they do!

True Confessions from Library Director Kate Van Auken

This is the YA space of my dreams because . . .

"Teens no longer have to venture into the Junior or Children's section to find good reads. They deserve a place of their own, especially in a small town—there are not many other places to go!"

I still dream of these improvements:

"Making the area a little bigger where laptops can be hooked up, CDs can be listened to, and all teens feel comfortable coming to the public library. I also dream of winning the Great Books Giveaway from the Young Adult Library Services Association (YALSA)."

Teen Patron Comments

"I thought there would be a shelf of new books. That's it. This is not what I expected."—Angela, 10

"It's a great place to work and it's great we have this place to read books."—Chelsea, 12

Heard from many teens who tested the swivel chair at the Grand Opening: "This chair is so cool. I want one for Christmas!"

Rawson Memorial District Library, 6495 Pine Street, Cass City, MI 48726, (989) 872-2856 *http://www2.rawson.lib.mi.us/nauken@rawson.lib.mi.us.*

A Room with a View

Wayzata Library
Wayzata, Minnesota

Bethany Wagenaar

Description: With its spectacular view from a large bay window overlooking Wayzata Bay on beautiful Lake Minnetonka, Wayzata Library's first teen space debuted in May 2003 when the new library opened on the same site as the old library. Teens enter the seventeen-by-sixteen-foot area, nearly square-shaped, through either of two entrances—one leading from the children's computer area and the other from the adult reference area and a quiet study room frequently used by teens. Spanning the space between the entrances is a wall-mounted work surface containing three black, flat-screen computers and a CD/cassette listening station. Computers feature Hennepin County Library's own *TeenLinks* Web pages (http://www.hclib.org/teens) with linked resources for teens to explore issues affecting their lives, get homework help, develop as lifelong readers, and have fun. They include word processing, database searching, filtered Internet access, and games.

Covered in golden beige metallic fabric, the wall above the computers is tackable for changing displays. Adjacent to the computer workstations and along two walls are eggshell metal bookshelves with cherry end-caps. Four paperback spinners divide the computer space from a lounge area with a coffee table and six lounge chairs on casters that are easily rearranged by teens or staff. These modern, square-shaped chairs are upholstered in bold purple, black, and gold fabric printed with large dots or squares, lending a hi-tech look that sets the teen space apart, although its green carpet and beige walls are shared with other spots in the building.

Collection: Sixty-three feet of shelving holds the 1,450-volume collection that includes fiction, audiobooks, magazines, graphic novels, and comics. A small nonfiction collection covers topics of teen interest such as college, employment, teen life, and health. Teens also use adult and juvenile nonfiction on the main floor, interfiled by Dewey number. Paperbacks are on spinner racks. Current magazines are displayed face-out on a flip-front panel with back issues in Princeton files whose labels are designed by teens. Teen videos and DVDs are interfiled with the adult collection. Some 4,941 teen materials circulated from May to December 2003.

Population and Community: The Wayzata Library is one of twenty-six libraries in the Hennepin County Library system, which serves the entire population of suburban Hennepin County, Minnesota, and the seven-county metro area. Wayzata is a suburb eleven miles west of Minneapolis with mostly middle- to upper-class families and some ethnic diversity. Along with other area libraries, Wayzata Library serves 5,270 middle and high school students in the Wayzata School District, most directly serving about 800 students in one public middle school and two private schools.

Hours & Teen Traffic: The library is open Monday and Wednesday from noon to 8:00 p.m., Tuesday and Thursday from 10:00 a.m. to 6:00 p.m., and Saturdays from 9:00 a.m. to 5:00 p.m. It is closed on Friday during the school year. During the summer, it is open from 10:00 a.m. to 5:00 p.m. on Friday and closed on Saturday. Typically fifteen to twenty teens ranging in age from thirteen to eighteen use the teen space after school and on weekends. The computers are heavily used by adults during school hours.

Staffing: The teen area is not staffed separately from the rest of the library. One full-time professional youth services librarian oversees its programs, displays, technology, and collection maintenance, along with her duties in the children's area. All staff, including an additional full-time senior librarian and a part-time paraprofessional associate librarian, answer questions and monitor teen behavior and usage.

Planning Process: The senior librarian, youth services librarian, and architect began the planning process for the new library by discussing how teens used the existing library as well as why and how a more teen-friendly space might be created. Teens were not consulted about the room configuration, but the youth services librarian worked with a high school staff contact to form a teen advisory board for furniture and fabric selection. About midway through the project, the senior

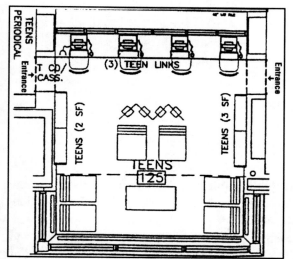

librarian accepted a new job. Shortly thereafter, the youth services librarian accepted a promotion and then the architect changed! Regrettably the teen advisory board was lost in the transition. Still the teen area has great bones. As the new youth services librarian, I rely heavily on teens for time, creative talents, and ideas to make their area really pop with teen-friendly signage, displays, and room enhancements. At the community celebration of the library's grand opening, more than twenty teen volunteers helped by assisting patrons with express checkout, dressing as storybook characters, taking Polaroid photos of children with those characters, painting faces, working at the Friends of the Wayzata Library table, preparing the library before it opened, and cleaning up at the end of the day. The high school jazz band and a quartet from the orchestra performed for crowds that gathered before the ribbon cutting.

Youth Participation & Programming: The Wayzata Library has a group of talented and motivated teen volunteers. Last summer, seventeen teen volunteers helped with shelving, checking in books, shelf reading, and filing reserves. Several helped with crowd control at live summer performances. Others enhanced storytime name tags, created flannelboards, assisted younger children at summer workshops, ordered material for live performances, created signage for the new library, and prepared displays. Several teens continued to volunteer throughout the school year or returned to volunteer over winter break. Libraries in the Wayzata School District also work with the high school's Youth Extending Service (YES) program.

Last summer, all Hennepin County Libraries featured a teen summer reading program in which teens entered to win books and gift cards to local bookstores. This summer the Wayzata Library also offers a summer teen book club in collaboration with a local middle school, and a beading workshop for teens. The library presents teen programs throughout the year, including booktalks and school visits, with special emphasis during Teen Read Month in October. Teen events at all Hennepin County Libraries are publicized on the library's *TeenLinks*, a nationally recognized Web site created with help from Teens Online, a teen advisory board. The eLibrarian in charge of *TeenLinks* works with a team of ten students to develop and maintain Web pages for the site's Free Time section. They review books, games, software, music, and Web sites, also offering advice on marketing *TeenLinks*.

True Confessions from Youth Services Librarian Bethany Wagenaar

This is the YA space of my dreams because . . .

"It's brand new. I love the furniture, and the tackable wall looks great, whether I've covered the whole thing to make a wall-sized graffiti board, have a book display, or feature only a simple quote."

I still dream of these improvements:

"I need a fun sign for the teen area that is visible the minute teens enter the library's front door, and I'd like more space for a TV/VCR/DVD player."

Teen Patron Comments:

"Every time you step through the door, there's something new on the wall or tables."
—Mary Ellen, 15

"Everything is so accessible and organized. It's very well decorated and changes all the time." —Michael, 15

"It's nice to have a place where teens can just hang out." —Zak, 12

Wayzata Library, Hennepin County Library, 620 Rice Street, Wayzata, MN (612) 543-6150
http://www.hclib.org/AgenciesAction.cfm?agency=Wa

Teen Scene

Hammond Public Library
Hammond, Indiana

Melody Scott

Description: Only teens are allowed in the teen room at Hammond Public Library in Hammond, Indiana. On the Main Library's second floor, near the stairway and elevator, the Teen Services Desk sits at the edge of Adult Nonfiction, about twenty feet from the glass door labelled "The Teen Scene," with special after-school and weekend hours posted. Inside this rectangular room of 351 square feet, a brilliant mural fills the entire back wall with swirling shapes in reds and golds and blues. Painted by local artist Candice Sagan, the mural is the room's focal point, setting it apart from the rest of the library and sparking comments from everyone who enters. In front of the mural are two black floor rockers with wood bases and cloth-upholstered foam. Scattered around are four large floor pillows in blue, beige, pink, and purple. Under two windows overlooking the parking lot are two round café-style tables with laminated tops, each with two swivel stools in red vinyl. Beige corduroy sphere chairs reside in two corners. Opposite the outer windows, an inner window looks into Adult Nonfiction. Below this window, blending with its frame and the mural is a double-sided booth bench in padded, wine-colored vinyl beside a laminated wood table and two upright chairs in mauve and beige fabric. The fourth wall features an alcove with two computer stations containing unfiltered Internet access, Word Perfect, and the library's catalog via its Web site. Magazine racks, a bulletin board, and READ posters decorate the white walls. Once a meeting room, it retains its original mauve carpet flecked with gold and teal. A small cabinet for board games and a listening station with six headphones complete the furnishings. Banquet tables are added for teen programs.

 Collection: One element missing from this small room is bookshelves. Aside from changing windowsill book displays, a few magazines, and a popular collection of 200 graphic novels on a shelf just outside the Teen Scene, the YA collection is in the Youth Department downstairs. The Teen Scene isn't big enough for 81 shelves of YA fiction and audiobooks, still housed near fiction for younger readers. Since the Teen Scene opened in June 2005, signs in the Youth Department have directed teens upstairs to the new space and its programs. Many teens check out materials in the Youth Department and take them upstairs to read in the Teen Scene. If they don't have a library card, they leave books with the Teen Librarian at her desk, where she holds them until readers return. Among more than 1,000 YA novels, 2005 teen circulation approached 5,000.

 Teens can find adult fiction on the second floor with genre sections for mysteries and science fiction. According to age level, YA nonfiction is either in the Youth Department downstairs for eighth grade and younger, or interfiled with adult nonfiction near the Teen Scene. All videos and music CDs are in the Audio/Visual Department. A college and careers section is located near the Teen Scene, general reference is in second-floor Information Services, and teen readers' advisory guides are at the Teen Services Desk.

 Library policy doesn't allow children under age fourteen upstairs in Information Services without a parent, so accommodation has been worked out for sixth and seventh graders using the Teen Scene. A Teen Room Club Pass is issued to teens of all ages for entry into the Teen Scene. (Children receive passes to the second floor if they need materials there, and they can check out items from any area of the library.)

 Young Adult Population and Community: Hammond is a multicultural city of 83,048 in northwest Indiana, about twenty miles from Chicago, Illinois. Its major industries include St. Margaret Mercy Healthcare, School City of Hammond, Indiana Harbor Belt Railroads, and Cargill. According to the 2000 Census, 12 percent of Hammond's families live below poverty level; 2,515 of them have children. The Indiana Department of Education reports that

38 percent of the total school population is white, 32 percent is Hispanic, 26 percent is African American, and 4 percent is multiracial. The Hammond Public Library serves this population with a Main Library and two branches. During the 2004–2005 school year, the library's target teen audience included 7,497 students in four middle schools, four high schools, one parochial school, and one bilingual department.

Hours, Staffing, and Teen Traffic: The Teen Scene is open only during the hours required by teens. Last summer, its hours were Monday, Wednesday, Thursday, and Friday from 12:30 p.m. to 5:00 p.m., Tuesday from 12:30 p.m. to 7:00 p.m., and Saturday from 9:00 a.m. to 5:00 p.m. When school began in late August, Teen Scene hours changed to Monday through Thursday from 3:00 p.m. to 9:00 p.m., Friday from 3:00 p.m. to 5:00 p.m., and Saturday from 9:00 a.m. to 5:00 p.m. The Teen Librarian works every Saturday, when the Teen Scene's hours match the rest of the library. Because the Teen Librarian works only one evening a week, a full-time "floater" or reference librarian covers the area on other evenings.

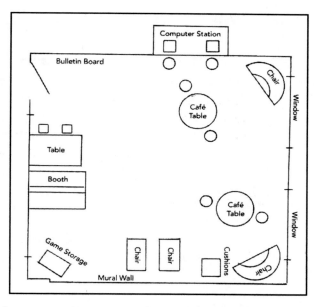

As part of Information Services, the Teen Librarian staffs the Adult Information Desk during morning hours while school is in session. She is stationed at the Teen Services Desk for after-school hours to supervise the Teen Scene and assist teen patrons. The Teen Scene's busiest times are after school when teens do homework, use the computers, play chess with their friends, read magazines, or just socialize. In its first year, word is still spreading about the Teen Scene, which is becoming the place to be for teens in Hammond. One-on-one interactions with teens allow the Teen Librarian to promote upcoming events, and program attendance is increasing.

Planning Process: Dedicated in 1967, the original Hammond Public Library began renovation in 2000, with a grand opening in 2002. Planning for a teen room waited until 2005, when the Teen Librarian met with the Library Director and Heads of Information Services, Technical Services, and Youth Services, as well as the Graphic Artist and the Maintenance Foreman, to plan the conversion of a meeting room to a teen space. Before the first meeting in February, the Teen Librarian researched other libraries' teen areas and asked her Teen Advisory Board (TAB) what they wanted. A large donation purchased many graphic novels. A small budget of about $2,500 for furnishings came from the Operating Fund. The library would have to manage the room without hiring extra staff. During each monthly meeting, the Teen Librarian presented the furniture she selected with teen input. In March, she ordered durable café-style tables and a booth from a restaurant catalog, a less expensive alternative to library furniture catalogs. In April, a trip to Target resulted in comfortable chairs and floor pillows. A local artist proposed three mural designs. After the TAB was consulted, the artist began to paint in mid-May, completing the mural by the first week of June. Then the furniture was put in place and computers were installed. The Teen Scene opened on June 11, 2005, the first day of the Summer Reading Program, Rock-N-Read. During the Grand Opening, teens enjoyed hourly raffles and refreshments.

Youth Participation and Programming: The eight members of the Teen Advisory Board (TAB) meet monthly to discuss library programs. They suggest movies for regular Teen Matinees and volunteer to help with programs. Among five teen programs a month, after-hours pizza/game nights are very popular. For craft programs, teens have made scrapbooks and CD holders. Other programs include Teen Open Mics, Battle of the Bands, and educational programs helping students with SATs, research papers, virtual college tours, and financial aid. The Teen Librarian also works regularly with VolunTeens for community service hours or work experience.

True Confessions from Teen Librarian Melody Scott

This is the YA space of my dreams because . . .

"I was able to create the room with the input of the Teen Advisory Board, however we wanted to do it. My director, Margaret Evans, and my supervisor, Rosalie Ruff, were very supportive and trusted my judgment for the teen room. They let me make all the decisions and did not turn down any wild idea I had. In the space given to me, I created a cool room for teens to use. I am very happy with the mural. It is amazing that with a limited budget, the room turned out looking great and I was able to purchase all the furniture we needed to make it teen friendly."

I still dream of these improvements:

"I wish we had a bigger space and that it was more visible to patrons when they get to the second floor. The room is slightly hidden behind shelves. I wish we could open up the space so that more people could see this great, colorful room."

Teen Patron Comments

"I like the wall, the chairs, and the whole room, because you can actually relax without anyone bothering you!"—Melissa, 15

"I think the Teen Room is cool. It has plenty of fun things to do."—Antonio, 14

Hammond Public Library, 564 State Street, Hammond, IN 46320, (219) 931-5100
http://www.hammond.lib.in.us/

The Hub:
An Unlikely Alliance of Young Adult and Senior Citizens

Lancaster Public Library
Lancaster, Pennsylvania

Jennifer Fiene, Don Ankney, Jane Hannigan, and Kay E. Vandergrift

Take a corridor/storage room, a Teen Advisory Board, a facilities coordinator, senior citizen volunteers, a grant from the H. W. Wilson Foundation, and a youth advocate within a library. Add mutual respect, a team approach, communication, and a lot of hard work. Combine all ingredients, and what can be accomplished? At Lancaster Public Library (LPL), in Lancaster, Pennsylvania, we built a successful teen center.

Recognizing the Need

There is little doubt that teen spaces are sadly neglected in many public libraries. Although we can point out some outstanding facilities for teens, many of which are profiled in *VOYA*'s *YA Spaces*, the sad reality is that the majority of teen spaces, if they exist at all, are a small appendage to the children's room or to the adult collection. Such spaces might house teen materials but too often do not provide a "home" for the young adult users of those materials. The lack of comfortable seating and workspaces for teens communicates to them, often in none too subtle a manner, that they are not valued members of the public library community.

Obviously limited resources are a key factor, and teens do not have either the political clout of adults or the "cute" marketability of children in libraries. They are, however, the near future of public library supporters. More important, young adults are deserving of the best possible support for learning and access to personal, informational, and recreational resources.

Another reason why many public libraries fail to provide YA facilities is because of the adult perception (librarians included) that teens are disruptive of the library's quiet decorum. The appearance of youth and their tendency to "hang out" in what seem to be constantly moving, eating, noisy congregations of hormonal activity make some adults apprehensive. Teens are not the only patrons that make quiet middle-class users of the library somewhat nervous; we need to find ways to make the poor, the homeless, and all those who proudly display their ethnicity, race, religion, political and social views, or their age welcome in what has always been considered "the free university of all people."

Two different angles display the roomy feel of the YA space, complete with computers, cafe-style seating, wall-art, and plenty of books.

21

It had been obvious for approximately six months prior to our involvement that a young adult space was needed to support and increase teen interest in the Lancaster Public Library. The YA collection was tucked into a small hallway adjacent to the children's room with no seating space, requiring teens to sit, or sometimes lie, on the floor when previewing books. In August 2006, several factors converged to make the establishment of this teen center a reality.

Building the Team of Unlikely Alliances

The Lancaster Public Library's teen center was created by the efforts of two non-teen service staff members and two groups of people who often avoid and are distrustful of each other—teens and senior citizens. The teens were wary of a group of old folks offering to do something for them, and retirees were somewhat apprehensive when faced with black-clad teens, some with multiple piercings. Initially most of the communication between these two groups took place through trusted staff members, but after frequent casual encounters, the teens and retirees gradually began talking with each other.

Jen Fiene, the library's Ready-to-Read Coordinator, assumed the responsibilities of being a young adult advocate because of her prior experience as a high school teacher. She organized a Teen Advisory Board, which coalesced additional support for a teen space, and was the liaison between the TAB and the rest of the team. It was immediately evident that Fiene needed a partner within the library to create the physical aspect of the teen space, and Don Ankney, Facilities Coordinator, had the necessary knowledge of the building to fit this role. In addition, his positive attitude and dedication to young adults were major assets to the team. Next on the team's to-do list was to find experience and to secure funding.

Seniors and teens admire the space they created with teamwork and perseverance.

Teens are ecstatic to finally have a space to call their own.

Former library educators Jane Hannigan and Kay Vandergrift had recently moved to Willow Valley Retirement Communities in Lancaster County. They initiated the Life of the Mind Consortium (*http://lifeofthemindconsortium. info*), a partnership among their community and three local higher education institutions to foster intellectual exchange between retirees and academics and to give back to the larger community. Local libraries, particularly facilities for youth, became a focus of the consortium's community service. After Hannigan and Vandergrift wrote a proposal, the consortium was granted $10,000 by the H. W. Wilson Foundation to continue its projects that improve library facilities for youth in Lancaster County. With this grant, several personal donations, the support of the Library System of Lancaster County, and the time, energies, and talents of retirees, library needs could be met. Consortium members visited the Lancaster Public Library where they saw teens sitting on the floor in that very small corridor connecting a spacious children's room, the Friends' Bookstore, and the Friends' Art Gallery. Young people trying to access the small teen collection were both disturbed and disturbing when other patrons tried to walk by. When Hannigan and Vandergrift met Fiene and talked with her about this situation, the first major project of the consortium was born.

Unlikely Spaces

The first challenge was finding an appropriate space that could be transformed into a vibrant teen center. A large passageway, also used as a storage area, was quickly identified as the only option. The five-hundred-foot L-shaped space had forty-five feet of useable wall space, with the longest continuous wall measuring eleven feet. To add to the challenge, there were seven doors, an elevator, an entranceway, a drinking fountain, a fire and burglar alarm panel, and an inset-mounted fire extinguisher that we had to work around. Obviously it was not the space we would have envisioned and it would lack the privacy required to create an area truly reflective of youth culture, but it was a start and would give teens a space they could call their own.

Teen Input

The teens immediately responded to the decision to establish a teen center. The TAB expanded to include eighteen diverse members representing five different high schools. City and suburban teens quickly meshed into friends who respected differences and supported each others' opinions. The teens learned that their opinions are important, but they also learned that working with a team means compromise.

Working in corners like this one provided a challenge to the creators in making everything fit.

Creating the Space

After removing sixty chairs from the area, we realized that the fire extinguisher had to be relocated, with the Fire Sheriff's approval, to open additional wall space. Repairs were made to the walls and a fresh coat of paint was applied. At this time, the youth advocate and facilities coordinator put on their carpenter hats and brought dismantled bookshelves into the space, reassembled them, and secured them to the walls. Because of the extensive work, it was necessary to complete it outside of the library's operating hours. The reference department's support of the project, coupled with the funding from the consortium, allowed for additional shelving to house the entire young adult collection.

As soon as their materials were moved to the space, teen library users claimed it as their own; however, the team was determined to do even more to identify this territory as a teen space. With teen input and the consortium's financial support, three stools, a café table and chairs, a bulletin board, a whiteboard, a clock, a wastebasket, and a magazine rack were added. The whiteboard has become quite a highlight—Fiene posts a weekly quote on the board, and the teens post their favorite quotes in return. Interestingly geometry proofs have also been solved on the whiteboard. Most important, though, it has become a forum and a place of self-expression for teens.

An essential component to any teen space is computer and Internet access. Many of these teens do not have computers in their homes, so LPL is a logical place for them to complete school assignments and communicate with others.

The senior citizens liked the students' artwork so much that they moved it to more prominent areas.

Because this corridor was not wired for computers, Ankney had to trace the closest wiring and drill through walls to redirect the power to the two computers currently in The Hub. Although full computer access was to have been made available, unfortunately this has not yet materialized.

Enhancing the Space

Everyone agreed that the new teen center should be as aesthetically exciting as possible. It needed to have teen appeal and reflect the diversity of the users. This territory "marking" is especially important in a space that serves as a high traffic area for library patrons.

A problem that arose was finding available wall space and art that would fit. Consortium members purchased a brightly colored ceramic sun from Mexico that originally hung above the two computer desks, and a long, narrow Indonesian mask to fit above the counter-height shelving that separates the teen space from the auditorium entrance. This art seemed to be appreciated by the teens, but we wanted to fully define the space by creating something dramatic for the ceiling overhang. A mural would have been ideal, but the area's layout made it impossible.

Hannigan and Vandergrift searched for a solution. They located 3D metal words and phrases (Celebrate, No Problem, Friends, Art Is Life, etc.) and asked one of the artists in the retirement community to create space-defining backgrounds that could be attached to the slanted overhang. The artist and her engineer husband created framed panels cut to match the angles of the overhang, and decorated them using soft, whimsical colors in random patterns. We placed the panels around the entire space to create the illusion of a "room" in this busy corridor.

During this time, the teens were busy agreeing upon a name for their new home. They considered other names for existing library teen spaces, proposed Latin names they were not sure the adults could translate, and finally decided on "The Hub." Another retiree immediately went into action, searching the Internet and locating very large, 3D wooden letters to spell "The Hub," and then sanded and prepared them for painting. After painting them a bright burnt orange to match other art in the room, we mounted the letters on separate panels in a central location. The TAB members were obviously pleased and saw it as an announcement that the space was their own.

Adult team members were unprepared for the quality of art created by the young people. On one occasion, a group of retirees walked into the library and saw a large, framed self-portrait of one of the TAB members on a wall where

Senior and Teen Cooperation Activities

Establish a Socrates Café that meets in the library with senior citizens and teens to explore issues and topics by questioning together. (See *http://lifeofthemindconsortium.info/Socrates Cafe.htm*.)

Offer qualified expertise from seniors to teens working on papers, assignments, and projects.

Share computer expertise. Teens may assist seniors who seek basic information about computer use. Senior computer users may share expertise with specific programs such as Excel.

Establish groups to explore film, television, art, drama, digital photography, local history.

Work together to establish a library garden or other "green" projects, where possible.

Establish brain games and puzzle sessions such as Chess, Bridge, and Sudoku events.

Develop literary events, like introducing each other to favorite genres, for example, teens: graphic novels and seniors: mysteries.

new shelving was to be installed. Fiene assured the group that the teen's drawing would be moved when the shelving was delivered. The retirees agreed that it should be moved but to a more prominent location. The young artist was so pleased that by the time The Hub officially opened, she had a second drawing framed and hung on the wall

We learned to seek out the unlikely, to embrace serendipity, and to thoroughly enjoy the process of making everything work together to accomplish a goal. Ours was an unlikely alliance of senior citizens, teens, and library personnel not directly responsible for young adults, who were well aware that sound vision, listening, planning, cooperation, and mutual trust are critical elements in team projects. Without this trust in each other, nothing would have been accomplished.

A key component of this project was the involvement of senior citizens, and this huge and talented group was eager to help. Senior citizens are among the strongest advocates of libraries, yet they are often overlooked as viable partners in such projects. Prior experience as librarians, teachers, artists, engineers, administrators, and other professions brought knowledge about the teen population and their need for an area in the public library. Other libraries might do well to look for similar local partners, not necessarily from large retirement communities but perhaps from senior centers or other places where retirees congregate.

We also began with a most unlikely space and converted it into a very comfortable and serviceable center for teens. Like many libraries, LPL had no teen center and no apparently viable space to create one. This group of teens, senior citizens, and library staff, however, refused to accept the obvious that had thwarted other staff members' good intentions for several years. Although we knew we would have to "make do," we resolved that we would make it work. The conversion evolved from sound planning, but serendipity also played a part. For example, when we were uncertain about what to do with the ceiling overhang, retirees discovered the metal sayings and had faith that other team members would figure out how to make them work. The process started in late September 2006 and was finished by early March 2007. Because of the immediate need and the fact that possibilities were extremely limited, we got right to work and finished the project quickly. It a testament that amazing things can be accomplished when people work together.

The cost of any such project is always a concern, and there is no question that having the grant from the H. W. Wilson Foundation was critical in the realization of this one. A local craftsman supported the project by cutting his prices considerably to build very sturdy shelving. Grant writing is an important skill for librarians, but it is also important to elicit both financial and other support from the local community. In many places, the locals are ready to help—they need only to be asked.

The creation of The Hub proved that seniors can work successfully with library staff and teens to reach mutual goals. With the cooperation of the Library System of Lancaster County, the consortium seniors are now working with additional public libraries and are also refurbishing a K-5 school library media center in Lancaster city. Young adults recognize that The Hub is their space in LPL and that it is vital to the culture they cherish. The words of the young adults testify that we achieved what we set out to do:

- "The Hub is building a foundation that will last for a long time. Before it was so boring and dull—now, there is life, colors, and activities."

- "I really like the Hub. I think the black frames, black leather stools, and black shelves for new books give it a more modern, updated feel. Overall I think it gives teens a place to get away from the younger kids and the [adults]. Also, I really like the artwork—I think it gives a cultural feel—great job!"

Lancaster Public Library, 125 North Duke Street, Lancaster, PA 17602, (717) 394-2651
http://www.lancaster.lib.pa.us/lcl/site/default.asp

Teenzone:
Tiny Space, Big Returns

Fortuna Library
Fortuna, California

Chris Cooper

A Space for Teens

Most honeymooners aren't thinking of ways to improve their hometown library. For me, Hawaii proved the perfect place to envision the idea of a teen space. I was on my honeymoon in 2004 and stopped in this amazing library in Princeville, Kauai. Immediately I saw that they had this special room for teenagers. In addition to comfortable furniture, they had a great collection of magazines, books, and music. I also noticed that it was located away from the children's section and that the teens there were proud of their area. This experience inspired me to convert my office at the Fortuna Library in Fortuna, California, into such a space. I determined that teens needed their own place in the library. As the supervising librarian, I valued my office for planning and working on projects, but the location seemed like an ideal place for a small teen room.

With doors removed, the wide entryway beckons teens to the tiny space with lots of heart.

Libraries in small communities like ours are readily responsive to the needs of seniors, adults, and young children and usually provide vibrant programming and colorful spaces. Teens can sometimes fall through the cracks, though. For instance, Fortuna youth don't have their own recreation center or skate park in town and funding for school programs has slowly been evaporating. Fortuna's Teenzone has not only become a safe haven for this overlooked group of library users, but it is also a vital component of after-school activities. It is truly surprising to everyone who enters the diminutive 8-by-12-foot space that a room could be so dramatically transformed. The teens who use the zone often come from homes without quiet places to study, read, or socialize. This room is their space, their safe place, their chance to explore what it means to be a teenager.

The Friendly City

Nicknamed the Friendly City, Fortuna is located on California's northern coast. Considered relatively remote—it is five hours away from a major city—Fortuna lies 253 miles north of San Francisco. Fortuna is situated near breathtaking natural beauty (the largest stands of the world's tallest trees, the coastal redwoods); Sasquatch country; the Lost Coast (the longest stretch of rugged, undeveloped coastline in the continental United States); and six of California's most scenic rivers. The rural town, which covers approximately five square miles, is bounded by the Eel River, mountains, bluffs, and scattered forests.

There are approximately 11,200 residents in the small town of Fortuna. Since 1995, there has been a generous influx of Spanish-speaking community members. As of 2005, approximately 25 percent of the Fortuna students spoke English as a second language. It's difficult to make a living in Humboldt County so the region attracts residents who have a spirit of resourcefulness. Residents are community minded and genuinely concerned with taking care of each other. Humboldt County has more artists per capita than any other county in California. Authors Roy Parvin and Cecilia Holland reside in Fortuna, and inspirational fiction author Jane Peart called it her home for more than thirty years.

Colorful shelves reflect the diversity of Fortuna's teen readers.

The Fortuna Branch Library

Fortuna is the busiest branch library in the Humboldt County Library System, which includes the main library in the city of Eureka, a book mobile, a large branch library in Arcata, and eight smaller branches throughout the county. The Fortuna Library is located downtown, within walking distance of Fortuna Union High School and Fortuna Middle School. The library serves the Eel River Valley where approximately 2,000 students, aged twelve to nineteen, are enrolled in twelve public schools, as well as students enrolled in charter schools, private schools, alternative schools, home schools, and independent study programs. The Fortuna branch is the only one in the county with an area designated specifically for teens. The library is open Tuesday from 12 p.m. to 5 p.m., Wednesday from 12 p.m. to 9 p.m., and Thursday, Friday, and Saturday from 10 a.m. to 5 p.m.

The Design and Remodel Process

Teen art, art deco, and funky displays cover the wall around the bar's work space.

In 2005, we were able to obtain approval and support from the City Parks and Recreation Department. After this hurdle, the transformation from office to Teenzone was smooth and quick, taking only eight weeks to complete. The first step in this broad collaborative effort was removing the room's only door to create an open entryway. The City of Fortuna Parks and Recreation staff helped paint, install light fixtures, and add additional shelving. They also resurrected an old study carrel from storage at the Eureka Main Library and converted it into a bar shelf. The project received support from Friends of the Fortuna Library, Fortuna Sunrise Rotary, Humboldt County (book budget), and the Rose Perenin Foundation. Two special Friends of the Fortuna Library, Ron and Judy Irvin, also made significant financial contributions to make the Teenzone possible.

The Teenzone is unique in that its design elements were chosen with input from then high school juniors and Youth Advisory Council members, Serra Gundlach and Elizabeth Clendenen. They selected cool mint as the paint color to replace sahara beige and whisper pink, designed mosaic switch plates, decoupaged bookshelf ends, advocated for mini-pendulum lighting, and chose the furniture. Other teen additions were overhead light fixtures covered with transparent photographic scenes, a lava lamp, and a glass display case featuring a dragon sculpture for the bar

Social networking enlivens the Teenzone while providing a haven for teen readers.

shelf. We embellished the walls with art created by the library's "Teenarts Program," paintings on canvas, and paper maché masks. A fluorescent-colored, boldly designed rug was chosen to cover the floor. Clendenen and Gundlach decided on black fabric canvas floor rockers, barstools, and giant pillows with shams sewn by Serra's mother, Sean. The teens selected a modern-looking, silver-framed clock, and chose black fabric to cover a bulletin board used for posting community events, book reviews, and library programs. Because of the space limitations, there are no computers in the Teenzone, but youth have unfiltered Internet access available from any of the five public access computers in the branch.

The room's design is different than what I would have done, but that's the point. The teens use their space to wait for available computers; they read, study, and work on reports. It is important that the Teenzone be what they want.

Located directly across from the circulation desk, the Teenzone is for youth aged twelve to nineteen. Curious adults and children who wander into this private area are politely reminded of this rule. This petite space is busiest after school on weekdays and can comfortably accommodate about five young people at a time.

The Grand Opening

The grand opening took place on December 6, 2005. The event featured live music from vocalist Mary Bonham and guitarist Josh Barry, members of the local teen band, Crossover. Susan Cooper, a Fortuna-based artist, led a free sculpting activity using Sculpey modeling clay. Guests of honor included former Fortuna Mayor, Odell Shelton, and Humboldt County Library Director, Carolyn Stacey. Many of the Friends of the Fortuna Library attended, including the Irvins.

Teen patrons Jeanette Schultz, Rachel Fouché, and Sarah Douglas voiced their opinions during the grand opening of Teenzone. "It's cozy in here. I could stay in here a long time," Shultz said. "It's awesome. I love the [psychedelic] rug," Fouché added. "This is what I want my room to be," Douglas agreed.

The Fortuna Youth Advisory Council

Students who participate in the Fortuna Library Youth Advisory Council are looking to improve their leadership skills, are passionate about literature, and want to make Fortuna a healthier community. They provide outreach and are community advocates on behalf of the library.

The Youth Advisory Council, which meets twice a month, was largely responsible for developing the collection for the Teenzone. Council members research and read reviews to make recommendations based on their own interests and what they think is appropriate for library purchase. Holdings include current fiction and nonfiction titles, magazines, zines, books on tape, and CDs. Uncataloged trade and mass market pa-

The designs seem far out and the colors bold, but teens loved deciding for themselves how the space would look.

perbacks are hung from special shelves attached to the outsides of two closet doors. A wide variety of music CDs, including rock 'n' roll, hip-hop, reggae, and country titles, as well as DVDs that appeal to teens are stored with the general collection.

Recent Programs

Members of the Youth Advisory Council design and develop library outreach programs. In 2007 and 2008, the Council organized several diverse programs including Making Books (presented by the North Redwoods Book Guild), Open Mic/Karaoke/Poetry Nights, Art Nights, Poetry and Writing Workshops for Teens, Summer Reading Programs, Wilderness Survival, Cooking Classes, and Altered Books workshops. Every other Saturday during the school year, members of the Council provide peer and cross-age academic tutoring in areas including Spanish, trigonometry, and calculus. The teens also provide assistance by leading craft projects and reading to groups of children at community health fairs, school literacy events, and Teenarts. These programs are supported by the Mel & Grace McLean Foundation, the Bertha Russ Lytel Foundation, Humboldt Sponsors, and Fortuna Sunrise Rotary. The Youth Advisory Council also maintains a Web site (*http://www. myspace. com/fortuna_youth*). We are fortunate to live in a community where young people are considered an important resource and are taken seriously. And the teens take their responsibility just as seriously.

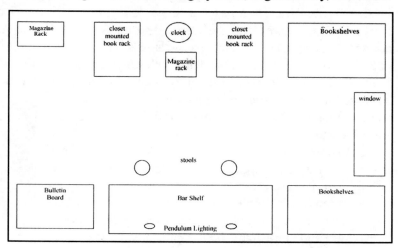

Final Thoughts from Supervising Librarian Chris Cooper

By fulfilling my administrative duties on a long table in the staff/archive room, I hope to show that no matter the size of a community or its library, you can always make space for teens. The staff, the teens, and the community of Fortuna have proven that even a tiny space in a small town library can have an enormous and powerful impact in recognizing teenagers' unique needs.

Teen Patron Comments

"It's a great environment and a comfortable space for reading! I'm really glad you put it in the library."—Cara Weare, 11th grade

"When I go to the library, I head straight for the Teenzone and stay there. There are excellent books and comfy chairs in the Teenzone."—Lucas Wennerholm, 11th grade

Fortuna Branch Library, Humboldt County Public Library, 753 14th Street, Fortuna, CA 95540, (707) 725-3460
http://co.humboldt.ca.us/library/branches/fortuna/

Teen Center

Crandall Public Library
Glens Falls, New York

Frieda Toth

Description: Sandwiched between the Children's Department and the 800s (literature section) on the second floor of the newly renovated Crandall Public Library is 90 square feet of glassed-in space known as the Teen Center. The area is full of windows and the green, gray-purple, and harvest gold color scheme works well to complement the nature outside in City Park. The area has a curved lounging couch, as well as four comfy purple chairs, two homework tables, two small round tables, and a reference desk that sits at the opposite end of the room from the lounge area. Teens have access to six computer workstations and are also encouraged to bring their laptops for the free wi-fi access. There is a total of 24,334 square feet of metal shelving with wood accents. The Teen Center is *nearly* soundproof—tested by five energetic teens—and located discreetly behind the couch is a "Hot Topics" section—items that teens need to know about but are embarrassed to ask for, such as dating, drug use, cutting, and subjects that are always on homework lists, such as global warming and vegetarianism.

Collection: The teen department is so new that librarians are still trying to figure out how to track YA circulation figures. The collection contains 2,500 fiction titles, including adult books for teens, paperbacks, and comics; 300 nonfiction titles, which include many career and homework help books; and more than 1,000 graphic novels. The books are arranged with the Dewey system except for graphic novels, which are shelved by author unless public demand requires something different. For example, Hulk is always found under "Hulk." Just outside the teen space is shelving for the audiobooks, CDs, and YA fiction. Board games are kept near the Hot Topics books. DVDs and magazines are found with the adult DVD/magazine collections because there is no room for more materials in the space.

One of the area's founding teens helps with RPG nights.

Young Adult Population and Community: Located on the Hudson River in the foothills of the Adirondack Mountains, Glens Falls (nicknamed Hometown U.S.A.) is home to 45,000 Upstate New Yorkers. The majority of the population is white and middle class, with one-fourth of the students in the school district receiving free/reduced lunch. Crandall Public Library serves two middle schools and one high school from the towns of Queensbury and Moreau and the city of Glens Falls, with a total enrollment of 5,265 teens. Average use of the teen center is approximately 1,000 teens a month. It is the largest library in the Southern Adirondack Library system, so even patrons living 45 minutes away, with their own libraries, choose Crandall over others.

The computer table in the teen center.

This tomato plant is part of a successful quiet activity that encourages teens to care for plants.

There is always a puzzle sitting out for teens to do at their leisure.

Hours, Staffing, and Teen Traffic: The Teen Center is open during regular library hours, Monday to Thursday, from 9 a.m. to 9 p.m.; Friday from 9 a.m. to 6 p.m.; Saturday from 9 a.m. to 5 p.m.; and Sunday (if school is in session) from 1 p.m. to 5 p.m. The area is popular among 13- to 19-year-olds, with up to 50 teens crowding the space on weekends. Older and younger patrons are welcome to browse the materials, but they cannot hang out or participate in programs. There is one full-time Teen Services librarian who maintains the young adult space, does collection development, and is in charge of teen programming. Luckily she is able to get help from a part-time library assistant and two part-time pages.

Planning Process: The current library building opened in 1931 and has been renovated twice; the latest renovation in 2008 included adding a new young adult space. This addition was achieved because area teens were their own advocates and successfully campaigned for their space. The renovations took a year and a half, during which a temporary space a few buildings away served as the library. During this time, the teens met and made recommendations. The founding teens are now too old for their room, but they are welcomed back any time they want to come, and some do occasionally stop by. The grand opening of the entire library was in December 2008.

Youth Participation and Programming: Teens can participate in two weekly programs: Confabulation, a book club with weekly themes such as "books that ended badly" and "my friends would be surprised I read this," and Reduced Teen Group, a social club with only two criteria, be a teen and respect your fellow members. Reduced Teen Group is teen directed, but the teen services acts as the facilitator to make sure programs can be done in a safe and inclusive manner. Some occasional programs the teens love are Origami Nights, Role-Playing-Game (RPG) Nights, and Podcast Nights, where teens learn how to podcast movie reviews. Teens started their own Teen Advisory Group (TAG) in November 2009, which has been responsible for voting on and implementing a puppet show for toddlers, a driver's education crash course for those getting ready to take their driving test, and writing workshops. Seventy-seven teens participated in a table top trebuchet game as part of the Summer Reading Program last year. The more books the students read, the more times they got to shoot the trebuchet. The library also offers tutoring for teens seven days a week. All teen programs and other pertinent information can be found on the Fans of Crandall Public Library Teen Group on Facebook.

True Confessions from Teen Services Librarian Frieda Toth

This is the YA space of my dreams because . . .

"It's respectful to the teens in its beauty and usability."

I still dream of these improvements:

"It's been so successful; I could use twice the space! And four times the staff . . . Homework at the high school level is intense; sometimes I can't give the attention I'd like."

Teens relax on the couch and read after Reduced Teen Group.

Teen Patron Comments

"Actually, it worked out great! We went from a dark corner where no one noticed us playing *Dungeons and Dragons* to prime real estate and a great collection! I mean, look at it!" —Curt Warrington, 22 (was on the Teen Planning Board)

"It's a great and comfortable place to come and read, or do work, or even relax. Great staff and friendly people. It makes you appreciate a library for what it's worth and enjoy coming here. It makes you want to come back more, not to mention the great view." —Cory Davis, 15

Crandall Public Library, 251 Glen Street, Glen Falls, NY 12801, (518) 792-6508
http://www.crandalllibrary.org/

Funky Town Teen Room

Palm Harbor Library
Palm Harbor, Florida

Katie Banks

Description: The Funky Town Teen Room is in the back corner of the Palm Harbor Library, adjacent to the study rooms, behind the nonfiction section, and next to the biography area. It is a glass-enclosed, wave-shaped, three-hundred-sixty-square-foot room that houses teen fiction, teen DVDs, teen music, and teen magazines, as well as study tables. The teen librarian desk is directly outside the front of the Teen Room, along with a black A-frame display shelf.

The library's Youth Advisory Board (YAB) chose the colors, accessories, and set-up of the room. The color scheme is red, turquoise, and charcoal gray. The carpet is a red and turquoise checkerboard design with a red and pink ocean wave accent around the border of the room. The walls are charcoal gray, and the shelving units are black. There is a neon "OPEN" sign reminiscent of a restaurant or diner hanging over the door. There is also a suspended sign in a wave shape that says, "TEENS."

The gaming nook features a large screen LCD TV.

Teens within the Palm Harbor community took part in designing and naming the Funky Town Teen Room. The Palm Harbor Library YAB met with the architect and interior designer at multiple planning stages and hammered out idea after idea until they came to what we now have.

The teens decided on a booth, round tables, and red sparkly chairs to mirror a diner-type atmosphere. A dry-erase board to put up announcements, poems, rants, and sketches was a must, so the construction crew added a long whiteboard on the end panel of the book shelves. The glass walls also make for a great space to draw and write with glass markers or dry-erase markers. The Funky Town Teen Room has a video-game nook in the corner of the room, where we have an Xbox with a large-screen LCD TV. The wave shape of the room is also a unique aspect that is very eye catching.

The Funky Town Teen Room has two round study tables with two chairs each, a booth that seats four comfortably, two videogame rocking chairs, four movable cushioned seats, and two bean-bag chairs. An additional set of stacking plastic chairs can be moved around where needed.

Three computer workstations are available on a high-rise bar with three plastic barstools. The workstations have the online catalog, databases and CD-ROMs, word-processing programs, _Microsoft Office_, unfiltered Internet access, and computer games.

The room has thirty-nine feet of YA fiction and manga, two free-standing shelves for three-and-a-half feet of YA paperback series, two free-standing shelves for three-and-a-half feet of YA DVDs, a magazine rack, and a spinning comic book rack. Fiction and manga are arranged alphabetically by last name of author, DVDs are arranged alphabetically by title, and music is arranged alphabetically by artist. Paperbacks are shelved alphabetically by series name. In the 2008–2009 fiscal year, eighteen thousand teen materials circulated. In June 2009, 1,505 fiction materials, 150 nonfiction materials, 375 teen DVDs, and 245 manga/graphic novels circulated.

The YA nonfiction is shelved within the adult nonfiction. This is due to space constraints but also because the librarians found teen materials to be useful for adults and vice versa.

Young Adult Population and Community: Palm Harbor, Florida, is an unincorporated entity of Pinellas County. The population as of 2007 was sixty thousand, 95 percent of which was Caucasian, and the median income was $50,000. Twenty-seven percent of households had children under the age of eighteen. Palm Harbor Library has 2,951 registered users aged thirteen to eighteen. We serve a total of 5,100 students in two middle schools and one high school.

Hours, Staffing, and Teen Traffic: The Teen Room is open during all library operating hours: Monday through Thursday 9 a.m. to 8 p.m., Friday 12 p.m. to 5 p.m., and Saturday 9 a.m. to 5 p.m. An average of thirty teens use the Teen Room during the after-school and evening hours, and an average of fifty teens use the teen room on Saturday. The age range is thirteen to eighteen. We strictly enforce this rule, as it is our strong belief that teens should have their own space, uninterrupted!

There is one teen librarian who monitors and provides reference service during heavy traffic hours. The teen librarian is full time and is also the sole provider of other teen services, including collection management and programming.

Planning Process: The Palm Harbor Library building opened on July 5, 1988, and was renovated from December 2007 to January 2009. We wanted the teens to have a say in *their* space, so we had each of our YAB members, who are teens ages thirteen to eighteen, draw and list everything they wanted and hoped for in a teen library. We

The wave-shaped glass wall showcases the YA room.

The diner theme is exhibited in the restaurant style booth and tables and chairs.

then narrowed down the suggestions by lots of voting and discussing. The interior designers, architect, and library director worked very well with the teens and accommodated most of their wishes. The library renovation took place in four phases, and the Teen Room was completed during the third phase. Prior to the renovation, the Teen Room was in a 226-square-foot room, which has since been turned into an office. The new Teen Room is three-hundred-sixty square feet.

Since the Teen Room was finished during the third phase of the renovation and the library was in operation during the entire remodel, the Funky Town Teen Room was opened in October 2008. The room then underwent minor additions, such as furniture and wall hangings. The official library re-opening was January 10, 2009, and the Teen Room was a major player in the festivities. As folks explored the new library, they participated in a scavenger hunt to collect stickers from each department. Since the patrons were required to visit the Funky Town Teen Room, the YAB set up our Nintendo Wii and instructed children, adults, and senior citizens on using the video game. The teens handed out candy and small giveaways and promoted the YAB to other teens. The teens also set out the glass markers and dry-erase markers for folks to doodle or write on the glass walls.

Youth Participation and Programming: The YAB discusses things teens want to see in the library, plans programs appropriate and timely for teens, creates children's programs sponsored by the board, and raises funds for the library and teen library services.

The Funky Town Teen Room accommodates teens' needs for entertainment and study.

The Palm Harbor Library also has a Computer Squad to assist patrons in our computer lab. They answer basic questions regarding printing operations; creating e-mail accounts; using disks or USB drives; accessing, downloading, and editing digital photos; and other basic tasks.

During the summer of 2010, the teens participated in the Make Waves @ Your Library reading game consisting of a bingo card with activities and games.

The information technology team at Palm Harbor Library designed the teen page, which is available at *http://www.tblc.org/phl/ library/teens.html.*

Area high school teens provide homework assistance to elementary school children in the Children's Room of the library.

Our most popular and successful program is our annual haunted house. The YAB creates, designs, and performs this very fun event. The library partners with the local community center for their Halloween carnival. The teens set up their haunted house in the community center rooms and hallways. Some recent themes were Haunted Pirate Ship and Haunted Circus. This one-day event is a fund-raiser; over the years the teens have raised an average of $500 per year at a cost of $1.00 per entry. It is a very popular and extremely fun event!

Another popular program is our Parents' Day Out. The YAB hosts a day of fun for kids ages five to nine. Parents drop off their children in the afternoon and pick them up in the evening. This is especially popular at Christmas time, when parents can get some extra shopping done. The teens plan reading games and crafts, show a movie, and eat lots of snacks.

True Confessions from Teen Librarian Katie Banks

This is the YA space of my dreams because . . .

The Funky Town Teen Room has everything the teens are interested in: a TV where they can watch movies or play video games, lots of popular teen fiction, computers with research databases for homework, and board games. It's just a nice place to relax. Plus it's a cool layout. We've gotten a lot of comments from adults that the teen room is really the showpiece of the new library!

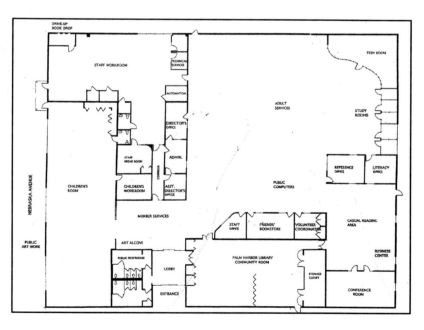

I still dream of these improvements:

Though the teen room allows for many things, we still have to provide our programs in the library's larger community and program rooms. Someday we'd like to be able to have more space to expand the collection and really spread out for fun events.

Teen Patron Comments

"The old teen room was nice, but it was quite small. It was cozy, though; you could sit around and hang out with your friends, but I love the new teen room even more. It has a lot more space, can fit more people, and there's more room to sit around and do homework or even play video games. The bright carpet colors bring a lot of fun to the room. The wide selection of books, movies, and video games specific for teens is awesome. The old-fashioned, diner-style booth is really great for doing group projects. The new room is such an improvement; it's great."— Ryann, 15

"The Teen Room is a nice, relaxed environment for studying or having some fun."— Kristin, 16

"I love the video games provided in the Teen Room." —Tasha, 13

Palm Harbor Library, 2330 Nebraska Avenue, Palm Harbor, FL 34683, (727) 784-3332
http://www.palmharborlibrary.org/

Part 2

Medium Teen Spaces 501 to 1000 Square Feet

Best Cellar

Waupaca Area Public Library
Waupaca, Wisconsin

Kristen Anderson

Description: Located in the basement of the Waupaca Area Public Library, the Best Cellar is a separate room of 616 square feet designated for young adults, adjacent to the Youth (Children's) Department. Its name is emblazoned on a blue neon sign that hangs on the wall, with a matching neon clock. Dark blue is the prominent color, complementing the rest of the library and yet remaining distinct. Overstuffed chairs are covered with a teen-selected fabric, a colorful pattern on a dark blue background. On the walls are inspirational and movie posters, bulletin boards, and an annual youth are a exhibit. A wall mural by teen artists may be added. In order to avoid the sense of a "desk boundary," there is no staff area. The atmosphere is laid back and relaxed. Teens choose from a selection of music CDs to play on the radio/CD player, and snacks are sold for eating and drinking within the room. The Best Cellar allows teens the freedom to laugh, talk, snack, and listen to music without disturbing others.

Furniture: There's lots of lounging room in six easy chairs and five beanie chairs, with three small tables. There are four wooden chairs at each of the two work tables. The sole computer workstation has two chairs and contains word-processing software and CD-ROMs with games and education programs. Internet access is planned as soon as possible. On-line catalogs are right outside the door in the Youth Department; an extra catalog license would be costly and unnecessary when the catalog becomes available through the Internet. Large wooden bookshelves cover 219 square feet, with small shelves of 22 square feet for new books and career materials. Video and board game shelving takes 11 square feet and the magazine rack is on the wall.

Collection: The collection of 2,565 items includes YA fiction, non-fiction, graphic novels, adult books for teens, magazines, audio books, videos, and board games. Both recreational and school support materials are offered, with reference, study skills, and college and career information. Though teens use materials from other parts of the library, all items purchased for teens are housed in the Best Cellar.

Young Adult Population and Community: Waupaca is a small city of just over five thousand people in central Wisconsin. It has several large industrial employers, and also serves as a bedroom community for nearby larger cities of Stevens Point and Appleton. The Waupaca Area Public Library has a service area of over 13,000 people, and is part of the innovative Outagamie Waupaca Library System (OWLS). Only one other library in the system has staff exclusively dedicated to working with young adults, many system libraries are extremely small.

There is little ethnic diversity among the 1,520 students in one middle school and one high school. After school, fifteen to eighteen teens can usually be found in the Best Cellar, ranging in age from twelve to sixteen. It is more crowded on weekends, with up to twenty-five teens. The Best Cellar's video collection has been attracting users outside the teen age range, and adults also use the career materials. In actuality, the collection serves anyone from ages seven to seventy.

Hours of Operation: Monday to Thursday 9 a.m. to 8 p.m.; Friday 9 a.m. to 5 p.m.; Saturday 9 a.m. to 4 p.m. in winter and 1 p.m. in summer; for a total of 56 to 59 hours a week.

Staffing: Two part-time paraprofessional Young Adult Coordinators staff the Best Cellar, helping teens with homework, organizing programs, shelving, and doing whatever is needed. Staff is scheduled only when public schools are not in session, from 3:30 p.m. to 8 p.m. weekdays and all day Saturdays, summers, and school vacations. The coordinator positions are usually filled by education majors from the University of Wisconsin in Stevens Point. The Best Cellar staff is supervised by the Young Adult Librarian, who does all YA collection development. Because she also serves as Assistant Library Director, she does not regularly work in the Best Cellar.

Planning Process: The current library building opened in October 1993 without a special space for young adults. A Young Adult Advisory Committee (YAAC) was started to discover what teens needed from the library; their overwhelming concern was for more and better space. By the summer of 1996, YAAC was brainstorming their dream space with the librarians, becoming very instrumental in its planning. The Library Foundation was supportive when they were approached for funding, and the Friends of the Library purchased the neon sign. A separate room was created by enclosing a portion of a storage area off the Youth Department Making the Best Cellar a reality—with its name chosen by YAAC—was a collaborative effort among the YAAC, the Library Foundation, the Library Board, Library staff, and Friends of the Library. Posters in the schools and community advertised the space, and newspaper articles covered its creation. The Best Cellar celebrated its grand opening on May 13, 1998, with an open house for teens, the community, staff, Friends, Foundations, Board, and City Council. Taco dip and nachos were served as people explored the new space.

Youth Participation: With eight to ten members ranging from ages thirteen to seventeen, the YAAC, who consulted on Best Cellar planning still meets monthly to plan programs such as a movie night, an author visit from Alden Carter, a cake demonstration, a scrapbook program, and a Mehndi demonstration. In the summer of 1998 they held their first teen book discussion group, reading five mysteries and ending with a "murder in the library" party. Elsewhere in the library, teens volunteer to help with children's story time and summer reading.

True Confessions from YA Librarian Kristen Anderson

This is the YA space of my dreams because . . .

"...teens can gather and study here without worrying about disturbing other library patrons. The space meets their needs and caters to specifically them. They no longer have to try to fit into an adult space. They have a space of their own."

I still dream of these improvements:

"We are still waiting for an Internet connection and a phone. We held off on Internet wiring because we were hoping to fund it along with a larger project, which fell through. I can see that we will need to find more spaces in a few years. We have already had to move in more shelves. We may also need to consider expanding our hours of service."

Teen Patron Comments

"I like the wide selection of books. One of my favorites is *Avi's Nothing but the Truth*. The Best Cellar has a great selection of movies and also a good amount of magazines."—Scott Grob, grade 7

"In comparison to where the young adult books were, I have seen a definite improvement. The Best Cellar has more room for the increasing number of books being published for young adults. They have had to add shelving. In my opinion, this is a good sign. The youth have a place to go and more reading at their disposal. We can find books on colleges that we may be interested in attending sometime in the future, and other reference material useful to our age group. In addition, we are able to receive help from the young adult staff on homework problems and such. The youth of Waupaca have a room all to ourselves, like the children's department and adult section of the library."—Jenny Abrahamson, grade 10

Waupaca Area Public Library, 107 S. Main Street, Waupaca, WI 54981, (715) 258-4414
http://www.waupacalibrary.org/

A Recipe for Young Adult Spaces and Services

Santa Cruz Public Libraries
Santa Cruz, California

Janis O'Driscoll

I'm a terrible cook. Any warm memories my college student daughter has of meals with me are of a great restaurant in San Francisco, not of wonderful smells coming from my kitchen. It isn't that I can't occasionally prepare something that tastes pretty good. I just can't repeat the experience the way a good cook could. For me, it's hard to follow recipes the same way twice. In the kitchen, this is bad. In the library, this is actually good.

In 1995, the Santa Cruz Public Libraries in California had the opportunity to explore ways of developing effective library service to young adults by devoting the Garfield Park Branch Library to this focus. (See "YA Spaces of Your Dreams: A Place of Our Own, Garfield Park Branch," *VOYA*, June 1999, page 100-101.) Two years later, we came up with this list of essential ingredients, but we weren't sure we had a recipe.

1. **Youth Participation:** It should start with a needs assessment, and continue in meaningful ways through analysis, design, development, and operation of an effective plan.

2. **Community:** Partnerships with community organizations strengthen the library, while young people become aware of the network and how groups work together to solve problems.

3. **Build on what you have:** Spend the time to make an honest evaluation of what the library already offers in YA services.

4. **Technology:** The way to a teenager's heart is through a T-1 line.

5. **Experimentation:** An expectation of the unexpected is an asset to the library staff who wants to expand YA service.

6. **Keep asking:** Even when things finally seem routine, keep assessing: YA service always has late-breaking developments.

The combination of these ingredients in a tiny Carnegie building produced a vigorous branch library with an electric Homework Center, a Teen Advisory Council, and teen library users with a passion for HTML. "Very tasty, " said the Director, "the public likes it. Do it again, but in a full-service branch this time."

Do It Again?

So we took our list of ingredients to the Scotts Valley Branch Library. Scotts Valley is home to Silicon Valley commuters and their families. Unlike the young people in Garfield Park, most Scotts Valley teens have computers at home. The middle school is within walking distance of our storefront library, and the new Scotts Valley High School opened nearby. There is just a freshman class, and no school library yet. Guess where they go after school?

What is developing at Scotts Valley is different from Garfield Park. Peer tutoring in math was the first project at the new site; now HTML classes are also very popular. Teenagers fill the Homework Center—as well as the whole branch—to overflowing from after school until about 6 p.m. when parents start returning home. Students take access to computers for granted. They are more project-oriented and less focused on the technology itself, as we see in Garfield Park. Classic and contemporary YA fiction is read at Scotts Valley, while science fiction and pop culture reign at Garfield. Both branches have fully functioning homework centers/YA areas, computer software and hardware, a teen advisory council, YA activities, and an electronic newsletter. Garfield Park's newsletter is *What's Next.* (the period is important). Scotts Valley's is *The Digital Marmot.* Vigor is at a very high level at both branches!

So the list of ingredients has been successfully combined in Scotts Valley. With the Director's blessing, more branches will have the chance to work out creative combinations for young adults spaces and services. The most astonishing news is that Santa Cruz Public Libraries are recipients of a generous Gates Foundation grant that will expand Garfield Park and add new homework centers to our Central, Branciforte, and Live Oak branches. Five of our eleven branches will feature expanded YA spaces.

The teenagers at another branch in the mountains, the Boulder Creek Branch, are not waiting for us to expand services. There is an alcove where we use to keep all the media. But teenagers like to study there. Eventually, the staff gave in and moved the commuters' audiotapes around the corner, replacing them with a YA collection. Now we have a group of fabric mâché artist and graphic novel mavens as active parts of Boulder Creek's library community. This development seems akin to self-rising flour, or some new kind of popcorn that pops itself.

As we plan new Homework Centers, the list of ingredients remain the same, with a possible addition: the physical space should be small. I'm not kidding. The Garfield Park's library is tiny (1450 square feet), the Scotts Valley Homework Center is 600 square feet, and the Boulder Creek alcove is smaller than that. In small areas, teens feel comfortable, getting to know the staff and each other.

We began to suspect that size may matter when Garfield's Park's branch manager, Sandi Imperio, and I brought a panel of teens to a California State Library workshop in September. When asked if they use any other branch libraries, the teens said, "No they're to big. They don't know me there. *They won't be able to help me as much.*" No one mentioned the larger collections at other branches. We're not sure about the significance of size. Maybe it just happens that our spaces so far have been small. Maybe the space should "feel" small, encouraging the staff and young adults to interact easily.

A list of ingredients doesn't need a recipe as much as it needs a good cook. We have four-star chefs in Sandi Imperio at Garfield Park, Ann Young at Scotts Valley, and Laura Whaley at Boulder Creek, with more waiting to get into the kitchen. As far as we can determine, you need the list of ingredients, no cookie cutters, and the willingness to make up your own recipe.

Santa Cruz Public Libraries Administration Headquarters, 117 Union Street, Santa Cruz, CA 95060, (831) 427-7706
http://www.santacruzpl.org/#

Teen Reads

North Royalton Branch, Cuyahoga County Public Library
North Royalton, Ohio

Louise Miller

Description: When teens open the door of the North Royalton Branch of Cuyahoga County Public Library, one of the first things they see is a huge rainbow neon sign mounted near the ceiling, proclaiming "Teen Reads." If they are unable to resist its allure, they need only step to the right immediately inside the library entrance to enter a teen realm. Two large windows lend cheerful brightness to a square-shaped space of 576 square feet. Though the space is self-contained, it blends in with the rest of the newly renovated branch library with the same color scheme of patterned carpet in blues, grays, and greens, with misty gray walls. The huge custom-made half-moon service desk that sits in the center of the library serves the whole branch; the young adult librarian sits on the side that faces the Teen Reads area.

In the teen space are three group tables and one table set apart for quiet study—each table seats four. Posters of popular rock artists adorn the wall above the music CDs. The U-shaped fiction section has shelves four feet high with display space on top, featuring changing topics and seasonal displays such as "Reads to Make You Scream," draped with a large spider and his web. Nonfiction covers the wall opposite the fiction section. Further into the space is a Career, College, and Test Guide section. Comics, graphic novels, and magazines reside in clear plastic ascending cases. There is also a separate area for series. Two computers for teen use offer unfiltered Internet access, word processing, various information databases, and an online library catalog. E-books are also available, and patrons may set up personal e-book accounts to view at home. Computer games are for loan only.

Collection: The 8,000 volumes in the young adult (YA) collection include YA fiction (shelved in 144 square feet), series (20 square feet), nonfiction (19 square feet), career/college/test guides (32 square feet), music CDs (54 square feet), and magazines (9 square feet). In a collection covering both recreational reading and study needs, there are also adult books for teens, comics and graphic novels, audio books, videos, and a reference section. Standard Dewey and alphabetical order is used for most materials, though series and special sections are grouped by topic. Few YA materials are housed in areas beyond Teen Reads, and the annual 35,000-item YA circulation reveals interesting teen usage. Almost half the circulated items are audio books, a third are hardcover books, and over 2,500 magazines are checked out.

Young Adult Population and Community: Ohio's Cuyahoga County Public Library has long been known for exceptional young adult services. (**NOTE:** Its Beachwood Branch's Teen Center was featured here in YA Spaces in October 1999.) Once a department of the Cleveland Public Library, it opened in 1922 and became an independent system in 1942. On the south side of Cleveland not bordered by Lake Erie, the county surrounds the city. Today the Cuyahoga County Library System contains four large regional libraries, twenty-four branches, and an administration building. Each library has a young adult area with a full-time professional YA librarian. The North Royalton branch is in a southwestern suburb of Cleveland with mostly middle- to upper-class families and some ethnic diversity. It serves a total of 2,945 students in one public middle school, one Catholic middle school, and one high school.

Hours of Operation and Teen Traffic: Teen Reads is open the same hours as the rest of the branch: Monday through Thursday from 9 a.m. to 9 p.m., Friday and Saturday from 9 a.m. to 5:30 p.m., and Sunday from 1 p.m. to 5 p.m. during the school year. After-school hours draw from twenty to thirty teens a day to the YA space, with heavier traffic on weekends of thirty to fifty teens a day, ranging in age from ten to eighteen.

Staffing: The forty-hour young adult librarian position in this branch is job-shared with two twenty-hour professional degreed librarians. At this writing, one of the positions was open.

Planning Process: As in all Cuyahoga County libraries, there has always been a well-stocked separate YA area since the branch opened in 1978. During branch renovation, the YA area was moved to a different part of the building. Renovation planning for Teen Reads was part of a two-year process for the whole branch, with input from the branch manager, the YA librarian, and the architect. Major features added were the YA display areas and the neon sign. Although the branch renovation was completed in March 2000, the grand reopening ceremonies were delayed until January 2001 due to the construction of the new service desk. Festivities included all-day food and entertainment. To win the music posters on the Teen Reads wall, teens competed by listening to a tape of misheard lyrics to figure out the correct words. In place of the posters will be an original work of art picturing musicians by local artists.

Youth Participation and Programming: A teen advisory council is in the planning stages, and should commence once the remaining YA librarian position is filled, as will a teen volunteer program. Because the county system's young adult programming has long flourished, the branch participates in the system-wide young adult summer reading program each year, has a book discussion group meeting monthly (some as mother-daughter meetings and others open to all), and offers many YA programs including craft projects, babysitting workshops, computer classes, Monopoly® tournaments, chess and Pokemon sessions, open plays, passive programs, booktalks, and school visits. All branches' YA programs are listed in *The Teen Times* newsletter. A committee of YA librarians from several branches is adding a Teen Web site to the county library's main page; it should appear soon at http://clio1.cuyahoga. lib.oh.us. Homework Help also will be available online.

True Confessions from Young Adult Librarian Louise Miller

This is the YA space of my dreams because . . .

"It's brand new, it's self-contained, it has a nifty sign, a great collection of materials (especially music)—and I have a good budget and control over purchasing materials."

I still dream of these improvements:

"I would love to have a listening center, an area of more casual seating, and personal computers for word processing and game-playing."

Teen Patron Comments

"The posters are really cool."—Cathy Lee Pfeffer, 15

"I love the sign—it lets me know right where to go."—boy, eighth grade

North Royalton Public Library, Cuyahoga County Public Library, 14600 State Road, North Royalton, OH 44133, (440) 237-3800
http://www.cuyahoga.lib.oh.us/Branch.aspx?id=648

Teen Services Department

Mastics-Moriches-Shirley Community Library
Shirley, New York

Teri Germano

When the Mastics-Moriches-Shirley Community Library opened in 1981, it had no space especially for teens. In our 1994 renovation that doubled the size of the library, we compensated for that lack by planning two teen spaces, the librarian from each area working directly with the architect. Serving children from birth through eighth grade, our Children's Department devoted an alcove to "Young Teens" in grades six through eight with comfortable seating, neon lights, magazines, music, and a TV/VCR. Librarian Mary Maggio obtained design input from her Young Teen Advisory Board (YTAB).

As the young adult librarian working with older teens in ninth through twelfth grades in the Adult Services Department, I was responsible for their space on the library's new Lower Level, adjacent to the adult nonfiction collection. The focal point of our trapezoid-shaped 875-square-foot space became a Media Bar seating five teens on upholstered swivel stools at computer workstations and music listening stations with CD players and headphones. When it didn't disturb anyone, a TV/VCR could be used. The area also contained book stacks, seating for fourteen, ample display space for posters and program announcements—and neon lights for pizzazz. In the 140-square-foot Teen Study Pit, a sunken semi-circular room four steps down from floor level, we placed eight wooden carrels with lights for individual study. Our chrome ceilings, white walls, and gray/brown tweed carpet match the rest of the library.

During a three-year process, the two areas achieved the mall look envisioned by the teens. In July 1998, we merged services for seventh through twelfth graders in our new Teen Services Department. As an autonomous department with our own budget and real estate—all on the Lower Level—we spent five months making minimal renovations. We installed clear plexiglas paperback shelving on the ends of the stacks. We removed shelving on one wall to make room for six additional computer workstations, painting the wall bold purple, our department's signature color.

We removed more stacks to create seating areas. Two round library tables each seat four. Two formica tables with slatted oak, park-style benches seat eight. Recently we purchased lightweight, inexpensive solutions to our seating shortage: four folding canvas lawn chairs in bright colors—with rockers!—and two metal bistro tables with chairs. They're movable and holding up amazingly well. A couple of umbrellas create an instant lounge for programs in our community room; we stow them away when not in use.

Most importantly, we designed a Teen Reference Desk at the threshold of the room, creating a true hub of activity for and about teenagers. Teens must walk past the desk to enter or leave, allowing the staff to greet them. Of course the top of the reference desk is purple—and we even found a purple three-drawer file cabinet.

We brightened the Teen Study Pit by painting its walls brilliant teal, adding life-sized artificial trees. We mounted a verse of Henry Wadsworth Longfellow's poetry on the wall in six-inch white lettering: *"The love of learning, the sequestered nooks, / And all the sweet serenity of books."* The Study Pit became an oasis of calm and quiet in the midst of a busy and often noisy Teen Services Department. (See color photos on our Web site at *http://www.communitylibrary.org.*)

After just three years, the Teen Services Department is ready to grow again. We are planning a library-wide interior renovation to reapportion space. Doubling the size of our department, it will enable us to create separate but contiguous areas for reference/academic activity and recreational activity. We hope to add a food service or café, convertible meeting space, and a comfortable lounge area. Our present Teen Advisory Board (TAB), advised by Mary Maggio, will help to plan our expanded space.

Recently we surveyed the entire teen population for their wish list of entertainment in the community. Results overwhelmingly indicated that they want a place to hang out with friends, eat, and attend activities. Because our community is sorely lacking in such places, our library will offer a neutral, safe, and inviting space for teens.

Collection: On 636 linear feet of white metal shelving with oak end-panels reside almost twenty thousand items, including young adult fiction, graphic novels, audiobooks, magazines, biographies, college and career guides, Cliff and Monarch Notes, test study guides, reference books, videos, music CDs and cassettes, and board games. Three racks hold about a hundred paperbacks each. Young adult nonfiction is interfiled within the adult collection, the first Dewey half on the library's Main Level, and the second half on the Lower Level near our area. YA circulation in 1999–2000 totalled 24,170 items.

Computer games are available both in-house and for circulation; some of the most popular games are *The Sims, Top Gun, Star Wars Monopoly,* and *Michelle Kwan.* Each of our nine computer workstations (with color printers) contains unfiltered Internet access, Microsoft Word, Excel, Publisher, PowerPoint, and FrontPage; PrintArtist and PrintShop; and Barron's Regents Reviews for several subjects. A dozen databases range from *Searchbank* and *World Book Online* to *Poemfinder* and *Newsday.*

Young Adult Population and Community: On the south shore of Long Island, sixty miles east of Manhattan, our library serves a semi-suburban, semi-rural population of approximately 46,000 in the hamlets of Mastic, Mastic Beach, Shirley, and Moriches. We also contract with 1,600 to 1,700 out-of-district patrons in a nearby community without a library. Our population is 79.66 percent white, 7.76 percent black, and 11.56 percent Hispanic, with 1.12 percent classified as "other." The median income is $52,807, with 8.7 percent below the poverty level. Most families live in single-family homes. As a school district library, we are funded almost exclusively by the taxpayers of the William Floyd School District. District statistics list 4,176 teens in grades seven through twelve. Another two hundred students attend private schools or homeschools.

Hours of Operation and Teen Traffic: The Teen Services Department is staffed during all library hours, Monday through Thursday from 10 a.m. to 9 p.m., Friday from 10 a.m. to 6 p.m., Saturday from 9 a.m. to 5 p.m., and Sunday from noon to 4 p.m. (October through May). We conduct much of our teen programming on Friday evenings after the library is closed, so we don't compete for meeting space with other groups. During afterschool hours, an average of thirty-five to forty teens can be found in the teen area, increasing to fifty or sixty during the evening; even more teens overflow into other departments because we don't have enough seating in Teen Services. On weekends, about forty to fifty teens use the area. Most patrons are in grades seven through twelve. Younger and older patrons use our Teen Study Pit as well as our music and computer games collections. Only teens may use our computers.

Staffing: The Teen Services Department has sixteen employees, three full-time and thirteen part-time. Professional staff is the equivalent of four and a half full-timers, with one full-time Department Head, two full-time Librarians, three part-time Librarians (thirty-five hours weekly), and two part-time Librarian Trainees (twenty hours weekly). Non-professional staff consists of one full-time Clerk, two part-time Clerks (sixteen hours weekly), and five teen Pages whose work totals fifty-five hours per week.

Young Adult Programming: A color brochure reveals a rich and diverse array of summer 2001 programs: a summer reading club with a scavenger hunt and auction, a book discussion group, coaching sessions for the county Battle of the Books game, "Dinner & a Movie" nights, field trips to a Broadway show and an amusement park, workshops on old-time radio drama, photography, beauty, and babysitting; and ongoing Internet Café and Homework Help sessions. Other programs throughout the year include PSAT/SAT review classes, job fairs, fashion shows, a Girl Power Club, and a Camera Club. A department brochure lists its many programs and services.

True Confessions from Teen Services Department Head Teri Germano

This is the YA space of my dreams because . . .

" . . . it is fully staffed with YA specialists and dedicated support staff. Everyone who works in our department has chosen to be here. The staff is our most important feature. As soon as we launched the Teen Services Department, we felt the immediate demand for the same level and components of services enjoyed by children and adults. We were able to promote ourselves to teens as a unique agency and garner the support of parents. We were more visible to the school district administration and teachers, and to public officials who love to hook up with us in order to demonstrate their concern for teenagers. It didn't happen when we just had attractive space—the real estate isn't enough. Consistent service by a caring and focused staff, whenever the library is open, has made the difference."

I still dream of these improvements:

"More space for seating, computers, an eatery, and a supervised, neutral area for teens to gather for nontraditional library activities, such as listening to music, holding meetings, game clubs, etc. For our portable lounge programs, we are requesting a foozball table, air hockey, a ping pong table, lava lamps, a black light, and a popcorn popper."

Mastics-Moriches-Shirley Community Library, 407 William Floyd Parkway, Shirley, NY 11967, (631) 399-1511
http://www.communitylibrary.org/

Young Adults Area

Orrville Public Library
Orrville, Ohio

Cindy Lombardo

Description: Immediately to the left of the main entrance to Orrville Public Library, teens enter a 612-square-foot corner that belongs to them. From one side of the Young Adults area, steps lead up to Adult Fiction. Open on three sides, the YA space is also adjacent to the audiovisual area and visible from Circulation and Reference. The fourth side contains a floor-to-ceiling window. Filled with natural light, this airy space gives teens a place of their own for studying, talking, dreaming, and reading while still feeling connected to the rest of the library. Three overstuffed chairs upholstered in a bright geometric pattern of blue, violet, and gold lend an aura of comfort, punctuated by two small round occasional tables. On a raised platform underneath a large picture window, booth-style seating attracts an after-school crowd to two three-by-six-foot tables surrounded on three sides by a long, padded wooden bench. A bulletin board is also on the platform. The Young Adults sign repeats the style and colors of the chair fabric, blending with the burgundy carpet containing flecks of blue, grey, and brown. Warm classic oak woodwork adds to the ambience of the room, in shelving and other touches from the stair bannister to the windowed divider separating the upper adult section from the lower YA area. The metal shelving below the divider features a wooden countertop for displaying fiction titles. A freestanding wood-encased waist-high shelving unit in the center of the floor contains face-out magazines, reference, and more fiction. Oak shelving lines the entrance to the area with special displays and audio books.

Collection: Emphasizing recreational reading, 2,521 items include hardcover and paperback young adult fiction, paperback series, selected nonfiction display books, comics and graphic novels, and magazines. Audio books include 22 on CD and 28 on tape. There is a small YA reference section. Most young adult nonfiction is shelved within the adult section, with constantly rotating display titles pulled for the YA area. The nearby audiovisual section shared by all patrons includes videos and music CDs purchased for teens. Although no computers reside within the YA space, teens use nine terminals located nearby that contain the library catalog, several databases, and unfiltered Internet access. Some terminals may be used for chat, and all are open for e-mail. No separate YA circulation figures are tabulated.

Young Adult Population and Community: Orrville is a rural community of 8,423 residents in northern Ohio; 2,001 of those residents are between the ages of five and sixteen. The median age is 32.4 years. The 1989 median household income was $28,399, with 10.5 percent of families falling below the poverty level. High school graduates comprise 75 percent of the population, and 14 percent have college degrees. The library serves 850 students in one junior high school and one senior high school, also offering services for homeschooled students and those attending Christian academies.

Hours of Operation: The Young Adults area is open during all library hours: Monday through Friday from 8:30 a.m. to 9:00 p.m., Saturday from 8:30 a.m. to 5:00 p.m., and Sunday during the school year from 1:00 to 5:00 p.m. After school, anywhere from twelve to twenty teens ranging in age from twelve to seventeen can be found in the YA area, and twenty to thirty teens crowd the space on weekends. Other users of the area include adult fans of YA literature and parents looking for books for their children.

Staffing: No staff member is located in the YA area or designated specifically as a young adult librarian; all reference staff are trained in readers advisory for teens. The library director orders YA print materials, with input from both adult and children's staff in nonfiction. The head of the children's department orders videos and DVDs, and a reference technician orders music CDs.

Planning Process: During a renovation of the 1941 building (renovated once in 1977) starting in March 1998, the library moved to a temporary location. It reopened in an expanded building of 25,000 square feet in July 2000, with a grand reopening celebration including group tours of each area. To plan the new YA space, a teen group was gathered to give suggestions and ideas for its design and interior decoration. All staff were heavily involved in each iteration of the architect's drawings.

Young Adult Programming: Two reading programs for teens include a summer program in conjunction with the children's program that offers thematic prizes. Year-round, teens also keep track of the pages they read as they collect Dairy Queen coupons. Occasional YA programs have featured yo-yo maintenance and tricks, Car Care for Teens, a Celebrity Disguise Game, and a Masterpiece Match game. Class projects are supported with special areas set aside for Assignment Alert materials, a Science Fair Help program, and a college math tutor. Teen volunteers help with summer reading, paging, and special projects. There is no separate teen Web site, but recommended sites for teens appear as links through the "Internet Favorites" heading on the library's home page at *http://www.orrville.lib.oh.us.*

True Confessions from Library Director Cindy Lombardo

This is the YA space of my dreams because . . .

"It clearly gives the impression that we value and welcome young adults to the library. The books are up-to-date and displayed attractively, and we provide a comfortable space for lounging, talking, and browsing."

I still dream of these improvements:

"More space so we can include computers, listening stations, video stations, etc. I'd also love to start a teen advisory council and a book discussion group. We just received a Drew Carey grant for $25,000 to implement a collaborative project on photography and writing that will involve the library, the junior and senior high schools, the boys and girls clubs, the local paper, and a publishing company. (***Editor's Note:*** *For information about Ohio's Drew Carey grants, see* Who Wants to Be a YA Librarian? . . . in Ohio? *by C. Allen Nichols in* VOYA's *June 2001 issue on page 110.*)

Teen Patron Comments

"I like that we have our own space separate from the Children's Department!"—Larry Wright, 13

"The benches are a neat place to come after school to sit and look at magazines."—Corey Bukovitz, 13

"Before, in the old library, I didn't even know there was a place for young adult books—it was down in the basement in a corner. Now we have our own space with cool chairs and a lot more books. It's neat!"—Derek Bukovitz, 15

Orrville Public Library, 230 North Main Street, Orrville, OH 44667, (330) 683-1065
http://www.orrville.lib.oh.us/

Teen Central

Bemis Public Library
Littleton, Colorado

Jan Knauer

Description: A large solarium just inside Bemis Public Library's main entrance has been transformed into bright and inviting Teen Central. Its name beckons in large yellow letters over a design of teal, red, and purple spirals painted on a glass panel beside the door. Teen Central's space was once outdoors; it was enclosed during the library's 1982 expansion. Its south-facing floor-to-ceiling windows look out upon a garden and circular driveway. (The space is so sunny that the staff had to wait until a rare cloudy day to take indoor photographs!) Opposite the windows on the other long side of the 52-by-14-foot rectangle are alcoves in the white brickwork that was once the outdoor wall. Each four-foot-wide alcove contains oak shelves or cabinets below windows that look out from study booths on the other side of the wall. Large bulletin boards with colorful posters hang from the top of each alcove. Contributing to the almost-outdoors ambiance is the red tile floor, reminiscent of a patio.

Teen-friendly seating lines the windows in the 728-square-foot space. Two horseshoe-shaped booths feature fabric backs with dancing Matisse-like figures in teal, purple, red, and gold on a black background. The benches of these real restaurant booths have been recovered in black vinyl, holding up to six people. Teal tabletops in the booths pick up the upholstery color. Between the booths is a large foam floor mat (six feet by eight feet) covered in non-fading teal fabric, custom-made by an outdoor furniture manufacturer. A dozen pillows in four contrasting colors are scattered on the mat, offering an irresistible invitation to lounge. Beyond the second booth, a counter-height round chrome table has four matching diner-style high stools with black vinyl seats. Right next to the magazines, the high table is a perfect browsing spot. On the other side of the glass wall at the far end of the space is a hallway leading to restrooms and stairs to meeting rooms and the children's library. The Teen Central entrance is to the left of the front door and across from the circulation desk.

Collection: Two free-standing shelving units, six feet long and five feet high, contain magazines, Cliff Notes, teen fiction paperbacks, and graphic novels. Four shelving and three storage units in the alcoves contain topical displays and the Teen Self-Esteem collection. A cabinet in the first alcove holds a TV with a VCR. CD-players are available for in-library use. The rest of the young adult collection is outside the Teen Central area: Hardcover YA fiction is shelved at the beginning of adult fiction, and YA nonfiction is interfiled with adult nonfiction. Items in the YA collection have not been counted; from a total library collection of 135,000 items with a circulation of 276,500, annual YA circulation is over 5,000.

Young Adult Population and Community: The City of Littleton is a suburban community of Denver at the southern edge of the metropolitan area. Littleton's population is about 43,000, but Bemis Public Library also serves commuters and people from neighboring counties. Littleton's median household income is $51,000 and its average household size is 2.27. The largest ethnic population is Latino, at 8.4 percent. In a single building with no branches, the library serves four public high schools and five public middle schools that include an alternative middle and high school. Of the 10,161 students in all these schools, 9,243 are white, 524 are Latino, 239 are Asian, 109 are African American, and 46 are Native American. School district boundaries extend beyond Littleton's city limits, and there are also private and charter schools in Bemis's service area.

Hours of Operation: Teen Central is open during all library hours: Monday through Thursday from 9:00 a.m. to 9:00 p.m., Friday and Saturday from 9:00 a.m. to 5:00 p.m., and Sunday from 1:00 p.m. to 5:00 p.m. The space is in use all day by a variety of patrons. In the mornings and early afternoons, tutors and their students often use the booths. Small children wait on the mat for their parents to check out books after story time. Seniors wait for the bus. People of all ages chat with friends for a moment before entering the rest of the library. From 3:30 p.m. into the evening on school days, teens use the booths or spread out on the mat. They study, browse magazines, or chat in groups. Groups from the alternative schools use the space for study during the day. Weekend use is also mixed.

Staffing: The full-time Young Adult/ Outreach Librarian maintains the displays and collections in Teen Central and runs teen programs, but no service desk is located in the space. Readers advisory and reference services are provided elsewhere in the library by ten adult services librarians and five children's librarians.

Planning Process: Bemis Public Library has a long and fascinating history. Begun with funds awarded to the fire department for putting out a fire in a train wreck in 1892, the first library in Littleton opened in 1897 on a single bookcase in a Main Street drugstore. It soon moved to the Town Hall, but did not have its own building until 1917, when a Carnegie library was built on Main Street. In 1965, the current modern building opened on South Datura Street, named for Edwin A. Bemis, Littleton's newspaper publisher.

By the 1970s, the library had one of the few young adult areas in Colorado. A corner near the circulation desk contained young adult fiction, a few tables and chairs, and giveaway booklists and brochures. A 1982 addition to the library more than doubled its capacity, but the young adult books lost their area and were moved to shelving near Adult Fiction. The YA area revived in 1991 in a large space on the mezzanine. With funds donated by the Friends of the Library, sixteen wooden shelving units, carrels, special seating, and tables were purchased. The YA librarian was available at a service desk on the mezzanine, with a small reference collection, YA fiction, spinner racks of paperbacks, a career pamphlet file, a play file, and Cliff Notes. Dedicated to Dr. Ralph Shugart, the Friends group founder, the space was called the Shugart Young Adult Area.

When the mezzanine was needed for periodicals during the most recent renovation, the solarium was selected for the new teen space. Ad hoc groups of teens met over the course of a year and a half to brainstorm ideas for the space, which they named Teen Central. The teens participated in a state-funded focus group to generate funds for furniture. The Friends of the Library gave another generous donation of $7,000 for furnishings, shelving, and the Teen Central door sign. In the summer of 2001, armed with the teens' ideas, Young Adult Librarian Jan Knauer and Head of Adult Services Phyllis Larison went shopping for furniture in a store that sold all types of seating, new and used. They were excited to find just the right diner-style tables, stools, and booths that the teens visualized. The mat and the alcove units were custom-made. During Teen Read Week in October 2001, Teen Central opened with a Book Swap and an appearance by young adult author Todd Strasser.

Young Adult Programming: BIBLIOMANIA is a game-show-style competition in which teens form teams to answer questions about books. There's a mother–daughter book group, and both a general YA book group and writers group are being recruited. Teen Summer Reading encourages teens to earn prize points by writing reviews of books, magazines, Web sites, movies, and music; reviews are available for others to read in Teen Central. Summer programs in 2001 included a Sun Watching Party and workshops on juggling and writing hieroglyphics. During the 2002 spring break, a series of anime/animation/cartooning workshops were held.

Movies are co-sponsored with Adult Services on some Friday nights when the library is closed. In Memories of World War II, a 2001 intergenerational project run by Adult Services, teens interviewed war veterans about their wartime experiences and placed veterans' biographies and photographs on the library Web site. In VolunTeens, a cooperative project with the Parks and Recreation District, teens doing community service in the library garden come into the library to work with the YA librarian on learning experiences related to what they did outdoors.

True Confessions from Young Adult/Outreach Librarian Jan Knauer

This is the YA space of my dreams because . . .

"It is visible, near the main area of the library, apart from the very quiet study sections of the building, interesting-looking, and a place where teens meet and greet one another."

I still dream of these improvements:

"Providing a coffee/snack area within Teen Central for all patrons, having ongoing media available (music, video, computers), and providing more information about local services and events that concern teens, their teachers, and parents."

Bemis Public Library, 6014 S. Datura, Littleton, CO 80120, (303) 795-3961
http://www.littletongov.org/bemis/

Teen Center

Schaumburg Township District Library
Schaumburg, Illinois

Amy Alessio

Description: Named to resemble the United Center, home of the Chicago Bulls basketball team, the Teen Center at Schaumburg Township District Library in Illinois might be the first YA space with a sports theme. On both ends of a concourse connecting the Adult Fiction and Youth Services areas, a marquee Teen Center sign welcomes its audience with electronic banners that announce upcoming teen events. The two entrances are modeled after the famous Cubs' Wrigley Field signs, with fake turnstiles and four ticket window/display cases on each side. Because the neighboring departments also connect through the lobby, this 750 square-foot space enjoys a semi-private location.

Astroturf with white lines and hash marks covers the floor. Logos and jerseys from three high schools and the local minor league baseball team decorate the wall and display cases amid the shelving. Red and blue mini-lockers line the top of the shelves, labeled with the names of Teen Advisory Board members. On the opposite faux brick wall is an ivy-covered chain-link fence, where clear magazine racks are mounted. High school art decorates other walls. A listening station in the corner contains an audiodome reminiscent of the Cone of Silence from the TV show, *Get Smart*. Ten CDs are listed on the top, and teens play it like a jukebox. The sound does not carry outside the Teen Center.

Four moveable comfy armchairs sit by the audiodome. Three large circular tables have embedded board games (Sorry ™, Monopoly ™, and chess/checkers) under their surfaces. Because teens have access to more than sixty Internet/ Microsoft Office computers throughout the library, the Teen Center features two computer stations just for fun, with CD-ROMs such as *The Sims* ™, *Groovy Games*, *Midtown Madness* ™, and *Tony Hawk* ™. Twenty black chairs go with the tables and computer stations.

Thirty-three 3-foot shelves cover the south wall. A freestanding shelving unit with a half-circle bulletin board as its end-cap blocks off the audiodome corner. A mailbox in another corner makes passive programming easy; teens "post" contest entries, surveys, suggestions, and forms requesting program information.

Collection: Mainly recreational, approximately 2,000 items include fiction arranged by author on the south wall, and freestanding shelves with face-out graphic novels in series order, nonfiction in Dewey order, and new fiction. A Teen Readers Choice section contains multiple copies of ten popular fiction and nonfiction titles. Magazines, audio books, and music CDs round out the Teen Center. Reference and research materials for high school teens are upstairs in the Adult Services Department; junior high teens go to Youth Services Reference. Readers Advisory reference materials for teens are located next to the Teen Center in the Adult Fiction Department. The large Audiovisual Department has many displays geared to popular music, and requests from teens are respected. Since 1998 when the library started emphasizing teen programming, teen circulation figures have increased on an average of seventy percent each year. Nine hundred titles are circulated each month from the Teen Center.

Young Adult Population and Community: Schaumburg Township District Library (STDL) serves 150,000 people in three towns and parts of other towns, making it the second largest public library in Illinois, after Chicago Public. Schaumburg is home to Motorola, Sears, and other corporations. The community is extremely diverse, with Asian, Indian, and Hispanic populations increasingly prevalent. Its citizens represent all economic ranges, living in government-subsidized housing, middle class, or expensive homes. More than 15,000 teens hold STDL library cards. Three public and one private high school, plus five public and three private junior high schools feed into this central library and its two branches.

Hours of Operation and Staffing: The Teen Center is open during library hours: Monday through Friday from 9 a.m. to 10 p.m., Saturday from 10 a.m. to 5 p.m, and Sundays from noon to 9 p.m. during the school year and noon to 5 p.m. in the summer. After school, about ten to twelve teens hang out in the Teen Center, usually junior high people actually reading. Numbers surge up to 25 in the evening, when teens overflow available seating—they double up in dating/homework groups. Even adults try to find room!

The Teen Coordinator's office is a small room in the Teen Center; its window displays posters and trivia contests. When the full-time Coordinator is not on duty, two cameras keep a watchful eye on the area, their monitors located at the adjacent Readers Advisory Desk, where teens often come with questions.

Youth Participation and Programming: The Teen Advisory Board has 25 active members who meet each month to help plan teen events at the library. They also go on outings to ball games, celebrate holidays with parties, and hold an annual Lock-In.

Because the local high schools require twenty hours of community service, the library employs more than 25 teen volunteers each semester in almost every department.

Established reading programs are getting a facelift this summer. In Teen Invasion, teens get points for going to events throughout the community, including performances at the Arts Center, Park District Programs, getting their bikes registered with the police, climbing the rock wall at the mall—even finishing the reading program. Teens who accumulate 200 points enter a raffle for $200 at the mall. Teen summer reading incorporates a BINGO card of books and library programs with prizes for completing a row of events, genre or suggested books, or free-choice reads.

A variety of other teen programs occur throughout the year. A recent issue of *Teen Happenings* (a newsletter on the teen page of STDL's Web site) featured the Teen Writing Club and a writing contest, coffeehouse poetry readings, college financial aid information, a "Bored" game tournament, and a Graphic Novel e-Club.

Pitfalls of the Planning Process: Finding the Right Fit

Teen Services are new to STDL, a library system that began in 1962 and now has a large central facility and two branches, soon to add a third. There was little programming for teens before the 166,000 square-foot central building opened in the fall of 1998. At that time, there was no Teen Coordinator position, just a part-time high school liaison in the Adult Services Department who managed teacher and student reference needs along with basic reading programs. The new Teen Corridor contained comfortable chairs, paperbacks, and magazine racks—but teens did not like to sit there because it was too open and looked like an extension of the children's area. The YA collection held only 600 titles.

As a Youth Services librarian, in 1998 I petitioned for the creation of a staff teen advisory group and a Teen Advisory Board (TAB). Book circulation increased steadily after TAB's first meeting, when teen input on the collection and programming began to attract the interest of more young people. In late 1999, the library board was asked to create a Teen Coordinator position. I became the Teen Coordinator and with TAB, lobbied to remodel the teen area to reflect teen needs. TAB chose the sports theme, name, and several design elements, which became selling points with the library board. A local designer incorporated all teen suggestions into the new area, which was closed for almost two weeks for remodeling. Not one teen commented on not having access to the books! Only staff and adults complained about not being able to cut through the Teen area from Youth Services to Adult Fiction.

The Teen Center opened in early March 2001. To promote the new space, trivia games and events were held each week during the first month, with snacks. I incorporated the Teen Center into programming, such as using the Astroturf for mini-golf and holding writing club meetings there. Within seven months, a few electronic components such as the CD listening station and the electronic marquees broke down. The company that installed the Teen Center was out of business, and the manufacturers were across the country, so it has been difficult to make repairs. Local carpenters will soon address the sign problem, and I have become a decent electrician repairing the listening station's wiring. A new CD changer is budgeted for next year. Advice for anyone using a designer for your teen space: Consider purchasing the plans or sketches and finding local manufacturers and fixtures yourself.

Our library experienced growing pains *after* moving into the new building. Months of planning cannot anticipate the response of the public after the move. Two areas that were not popular or well developed in the old building—Readers Advisory and Teen Services—experienced increased demands in the new building. No staff were allocated to these areas before the move, but such staffing quickly proved essential. Within two and a half years of moving into the new facility, both the fiction room and the Teen Center were remodeled.

Lessons learned: (1) Moving into a new house with old furniture never works; (2) Don't open a new teen space without teen input. The participation of TAB in the remodeling of our Teen Center transformed our YA space from an underused hallway to a busy recreational and educational hub.

True Confessions from Teen Coordinator Amy Alessio

This is the YA space of my dreams because . . .

"It is heavily used and enjoyed. I have to move adults out of here!"

I still dream of these improvements:

"Adding more book display space and graphic novel shelving, and increasing the number of trivia contests. I would also like to see more teen help with the display cases. The high school volunteers do some, but it's hard to keep up with eight cases!"

Teen Patron Comments

"It's a Kool place to hang out, just for teens."

"I feel relaxed and good—I can do whatever I want."

"I like the new Teen Center because there's so much to do in it."

Schaumburg Township District Library, 130 S. Roselle Road, Schaumburg, IL 60193, (847) 923-3191
http://schaumburglibrary.org/

Teen Lounge

Pinellas Park Public Library
Pinellas Park, Florida

Patrice Dilley

Description: Hanging from the ceiling in a corner on the east side of the library building, a sign in yellow, white, and green neon announces the presence of the Teen Lounge. Occupying center stage beneath the sign is a huge, soft, chocolate-brown sectional couch or pit group, with two ottomans. In this corner is a floor-to-ceiling window, four round wooden tables with chairs, and low display shelving for new YA titles. Young adult shelving extends into a long, narrow area. Opposite the children's area and between adult nonfiction and periodicals, this 750-square-foot space is integrated with the rest of the library, while arranged to give the feel of an enclosed space. It echoes the newly renovated library's color scheme of green and beige as it proclaims its special function for teen comfort and appeal. Teen-oriented accents include rope lighting surrounding a bulletin board mounted on a square pillar, a plasma ball, and a glitter lamp. Although there are no computers within the teen area, fourteen computers are available to young adults, ten near the reference desk and four in the children's area. All computers have Internet access (filtered only in the children's section) and a Microsoft Office package with Word, Excel, PowerPoint, and Publisher. The computers in the children's area also contain educational CD-ROM games. Online library catalogs are housed in six separate terminals throughout the library.

Collection: The young adult collection contains 4,200 books and no media, with a circulation of 690 books per month. New YA fiction and nonfiction is highlighted on a display shelf. Paperback fiction occupies 72 square feet on wire racks, series reside on two spinners, and hardcover YA fiction takes about 115 square feet of standard wooden library shelves. Graphic novels and a sizable anime collection are magnets for teens. Young adult nonfiction older than six months is moved to adult nonfiction, where teens also find homework help, college and career materials, and Reference. To serve a substantial homeschool population, the large homeschool collection emphasizes the library as homeschool-friendly. Magazines, music CDs, CD-ROMs, audio books, and videos of teen interest also are shelved within the adult collection.

Population and Community: Pinellas Park is a city of 45,000 in the Tampa Bay area on the west coast of Florida, part of the St. Petersburg metropolitan area. It has a suburban atmosphere and a median household income of $26,109 (1990 census). Its largest ethnic groups are Hispanic (6%) and Asian (4%). Young adult residents of Pinellas Park number 5,017 in the 10 to 17 age range, but teens from neighboring cities also use the library. Registered library card holders from two middle schools and one high school number 5,381, which does not include students bussed to two other high schools and those attending five private schools for middle and high school students.

Hours and Teen Traffic: The Teen Lounge is open during regular library hours of 9:00 a.m. to 8:30 p.m. Monday through Thursday, 9:00 a.m. to 5:00 p.m. Friday and Saturday, and 1:00 p.m. to 5:00 p.m. Sunday. Thirty to forty users ranging from ages ten to eighteen occupy the space after school, increasing to fifty on weekends.

Staffing: No library staff are designated as serving young adults alone. All seven Children's Department staff work with teens: two professional librarians, three library assistants, and two clerks. There is no staff desk within the Teen Lounge.

Planning Process: The original Pinellas Park Library opened in 1969 in the current location. Still a single building, it is part of the Pinellas Public Library Cooperative of fourteen libraries, two of which have several branches each. When a new building was planned, a two-year process of designing its first teen area began. Staff input and teen surveys sought elements that would appeal to teens. The three members of the library's Teen Advisory Board (TAB) were consulted for their ideas on the décor of the Teen Lounge. When the thoroughly renovated and enlarged building opened on April 1, 2001, week-long grand opening festivities followed a genre theme. On mystery day, the library hosted a teen murder mystery program.

YA Programming: The Teen Advisory Board (TAB) has grown to fifteen middle and high school members who meet once a month to advise the library on YA collection development, teen programming, and the library's Web site (*http://pppl.tblc.fl.us*, click on Teen Zone). Teens enjoy ten lock-ins each year, usually three-hour programs with food, crafts, and games, held on Friday evenings after the library closes. There is a teen penpal program, and summers feature a teen reading program for sixth through twelfth graders who complete short review forms about books they have chosen, entering a weekly prize drawing. In the summer of 2002, the library hosted a series of movies paired with books, called Never Judge a Book by Its Movies. An ongoing teen volunteer program assigns twenty volunteers to work two hours a week on programs, shelving, or reading to younger children.

True Confessions from Youth Services Librarian Patrice Dilley

This is the YA space of my dreams because . . .

"It is a place where teens really feel at ease. It has the most comfortable furniture in the entire library. The neon sign is a real attractor—its green glow can be seen from most areas of the library. Little touches such as the plasma ball also make a difference."

I still dream of these improvements:

"I would like to continue to expand the YA collection. It would be great to have a CD listening station and a mural in the teen area."

Teen Patron Comments

"It's pretty cool. I like the books over there, the couch, and the lights."—Jacqueline, 15

"It's a really good spot to read books and the couch is really cool."—Amanda, 13

Pinellas Park Public Library, 7770 52nd Street, Pinellas Park, FL 33781, (727) 541-0718
http://www.pinellas-park.com/Departments/library_and_recreation_services/pinellas_park_public_library.asp

Teen Area

Solon Branch, Cuyahoga County Public Library
Solon, Ohio

Constance Dickerson

Population and Community: Suburban Solon's population of 21,802 contains African American (5.6%), Asian (3.5%), and Hispanic (.5%) minorities, serving significant Chinese and Indian populations. The library's Chinese New Year celebration last February attracted two hundred people. Our middle and high schools contain 1,600 students at each level; Solon schools are rated by the state as excellent, meeting all twenty-seven standards.

Collection: Because the Teen Area borders the library's main computer area, we only have two catalog computers in our own space, with a dedicated Internet station coming soon. Young adult items number 3,300, including YA fiction, adult books for teens, audiobooks, videos, magazines, and nonfiction. Special sections feature college and careers, new books, short story collections, series paperbacks, and comics and graphic novels. Music CDs and Reference are nearby. In 2001, YA circulation topped 36,000 items.

Hours and Teen Traffic: The Teen Area is open along with the rest of the library, from 9:00 a.m. to 9:00 p.m. Monday through Thursday, 9:00 a.m. to 5:30 p.m. on Friday and Saturday, and 1:00 to 5:00 p.m. on school-year Sundays. Additionally, each year we offer four or five after-hours teen programs from 7:00 to 9:00 p.m. After school, Teen Area seating is usually filled, and we have steady traffic all weekend, with an age range of eleven to eighteen.

Planning Process: Our library building is new; it opened in September 1998. One of the former librarians had input on the arrangement and size of the YA space, making sure to add extra display units of bulletin boards and slatwalls.

YA Programming: Although our teen advisory council has dwindled and there is no current group, we offer at least one teen program per month, such as poetry cafes, bake-offs, teen writing workshops, crafts, and an annual mystery night. A mother–daughter book group has been meeting monthly for the last year, and we plan a series of book discussions that target boys next summer. Our low-key summer reading program allows teens to fill out entry forms with titles they have read, which are entered into a weekly prize drawing. The teen page on our updated library Web site, *http://www. cuyahogalibrary.org*, is a work in progress.

True Confessions from the Teen Librarian

My dream space. Right now it's littered with bits of paper, remainders of a big school project. A while ago four teens plotted their project, straddling a poster board on the floor with markers and other paraphernalia fanning out around them. In our backwards L-shaped space, measuring about thirty feet on either leg, there's enough room for that plus two four-chair tables, a long bench seat in front of the windows, three easy chairs, ample shelving, a couple of slatwalls, a traditional bulletin board, and a cube bulletin board. It is, indeed, a dream space—and my memory is not too short to remember my first professional job, when among my duties as youth librarian, I selected YA literature and hoped that teens would find it among the children's and adult shelves. I used to wonder if there was something deliberate about not giving teens furniture or space of their own, signaling that we didn't want them to stop and "set a spell," get rowdy, smoke in the bathroom.

So I am most appreciative of my current digs, especially because it has been enhanced by art selected by my jobshare partner and me; Nancie Sknonezny and I split the full-time professional position. We had the windowed west wall painted buttery yellow to offset four prints by B. Andrea, titled "Run Proud," "Secret Heart," "True Things," and "Hindsight." Brightly colored, abstract figures accompany meaningful text. For example, "They came to sit and dangle their feet off the edge of the world and after a while they forgot everything but the good and true things they would do someday," and "I didn't listen to her because she was my mother and wouldn't know anything till I was much older."

Bright purple, blue, red, and green corkscrew ornaments hang in the corner, swinging in constant motion. They complement the Alternative Alphabet Poster for Little and Big People, purchased from the Syracuse Cultural Workers, who offer a variety of interesting, inspiring posters. (See their Web site at *http://www.syrculturalworkers.org*.)

We are proud of our latest enhancement, a magnetic wall. We purchased magnetic paint from Highsmith and several sets of magnets including the classic magnetic poetry set, signs and symbols, face-making, funny faces, Margaret Bourke-White photos, and inspiring quotes. The wall attracts adults and children as well as teens. It seems that no one can pass by without pausing to express their creativity. Their words are smart, funny, painful, and provocative. "Worship me," demands one sentiment. Proclaims another: "I trudge deliriously out to dream, garden, think, swim, produce." A good example of terse verse: "Drive car, hit, run." A poignant arrangement grouped Bourke-White's photos of New York City with the words: "ache," "moan," and, "why?" Inviting speculation: "Water has the most light @ the pole."

My job-share partner is a genius at creating eye-catching displays. At the end of February, posters and books celebrating Black History Month complement a map of Africa draped in an American Flag on the slatwall. Angel-hair snowy mountains stand behind the Olympic Rings on the main bulletin board, serving as a backdrop for a display of books on the theme. A Lucite cube sporting a shamrock garland sits beneath a sign that says, "Luck of the Irish: In March read a book with green in the title or with a green cover." A selection of green books sits atop the cube.

The teen advisory group made a poster from comic book cutouts, which hangs above a trunk-sized basket filled with comics. Information about colleges, contests, and news are posted on the cube bulletin board. Lucite pamphlet holders full of flyers and booklists are attached to the two pillars that separate the Teen Area from the rest of the library. Our area is off the main concourse, to the right of the computer bank, adjacent to the audio-visual section, and bordering the reference collection.

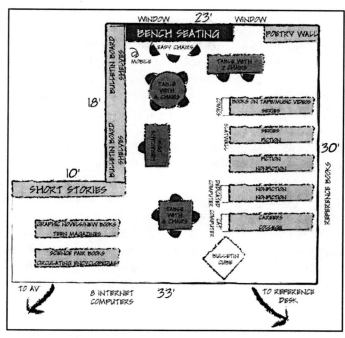

During the winter holidays, a group of college students met at the library. They gravitated to the Teen Area. Sprawling on the bench seat and easy chairs, they reminisced about high school days, rearranged the things on the magnetic wall, and chatted with me. One said, "I never knew libraries could be so comfortable."

"This is not your parents' library," I said.

Bright, light, comfortable, roomy, with lots of eye candy, ours is truly a library teen dream space.

Solon Branch, Cuyahoga County Public Library, 34125 Portz Parkway, Solon, OH 44139
(440) 248-8777
http://www.cuyahogalibrary.org/SolonBranch.aspx

Teen Area

Scott County Public Library
Georgetown, Kentucky

Patti Burnside

Description: Visible from the library's main entrance, a blue-green neon sign proclaiming "teens" draws those targeted patrons into their own square-shaped space. The area has sightlines from the Circulation Desk and is adjacent to a computer lab containing seven non-filtered Internet and word-processing stations, an individual study room with a word-processing computer, and the library's media collection of videos, audiobooks, and CDs and CD-ROM software. Occupying about 800 square feet, the Teen Area ties in with the color scheme of the rest of the library. Heathery multi-colored tweed carpet, purplish jewel-toned stained-glass transoms at the tops of the windows, cherry wood shelving and furniture, and upholstered chairs in geometric prints of blue, fuchsia, and black give the space a relaxing atmosphere. A special touch for teens is the tackable wall surface for displaying teen artwork and posters, which are changed frequently. Four round wooden tables—one with four chairs and three with two chairs—encourage individual or group study. The three easy chairs sit alongside wooden end tables. Slanted magazine shelving along the wall below the neon sign takes 27 square feet, with current issues for in-house use and back issues underneath for circulating. Book shelving for paperbacks and hardcovers takes 350 square feet.

Collection: The young adult collection includes 1,758 paperbacks, 2,549 hardcover YA fiction titles, 311 YA audiobooks, and 11 teen magazines. New titles are marked on their spines and displayed separately. Graphic novels have their own shelves, and music CDs and CD-ROM software also reside in the Teen Area. One OPAC computer is located in the teen space, with other full-service library computers and extensive media nearby. Nonfiction and reference for teens are interfiled in the adult collection. In the library's first year in its new building (July 2000–June 2001), about 10,000 young adult items circulated, showing a 78 percent increase from the old building.

Population and Community: The single-building Scott County Public Library in downtown Georgetown, Kentucky, serves not only the town's population of 18,000, but also the county population of 33,000 (with a bookmobile for outlying areas). Semi-rural Georgetown is on Interstate 75, 15 miles north of Lexington, Kentucky, and 55 miles south of Cincinnati, Ohio. Since a Toyota Motor Manufacturing plant was established twelve years ago, the county has experienced tremendous growth. Its residents' median age is 32.4 years. Two middle schools and one high school contain a total of 2,902 students, and a significant number of families homeschool their children.

Hours and Teen Traffic: The Teen Area is open during regular library hours from 9:00 a.m. to 9:00 p.m. Monday through Thursday, 9:00 a.m. to 6:00 p.m. Friday and Saturday, and 1:00 to 5:00 p.m. Sunday. Forty to fifty teens visit the library every day, after school and on weekends. Many come to use the Internet, browsing in the Teen Area while waiting for a terminal to become available. Because all Scott County schools use *Accelerated Reader*, the library keeps copies of each school's list of titles; librarians often help students find enjoyable books to read for the program. Students in grades six through twelve are the Teen Area's primary users, but patrons of all ages visit its graphic novel and magazine collections.

Staffing: There is no staff assigned to the Teen Area alone. All staff assists teens from the Information Desk in the center of the floor near the Teen Area: four full-time professional librarians, one full-time paraprofessional, and four part-time paraprofessionals. Young Adult collection development is handled by a professional Adult Services Librarian, and the paraprofessional Educational and Outreach Services Coordinator does teen programming.

Planning Process: The library's original 1928 building of 9,000 square feet was used until June 2000, when the library moved to its new 28,000-square-foot facility with greatly expanded services and space. As plans developed for the new building, data was gathered from a youth focus group. With this teen input, the librarian planners knew they needed a teen area large enough for students to work together on group projects, and shelving that would allow the collection to grow. They specified that the teen space be placed away from the Children's Area in a location convenient for supervision from both the Circulation and the Information Desks. The glorious new Children's Area, with fantastical storybook décor, is at the opposite corner of the library from the Teen Area. One of the most important lessons that the librarians learned while planning the new building was the importance of space and location of particular areas within the overall layout.

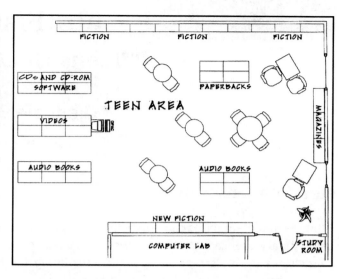

YA Programming: A teen book discussion group meets every other month. All ages participate in a summer reading program in which individual readers set their own goals, winning coupons to area attractions (furnished by the state library) and other special prizes. Summer programming for teens includes sessions on self-improvement (such as hair and nail care), crafts, game nights, and computer workshops. Summer teen volunteers aged thirteen and up assist with registration for the summer reading program and arts and crafts projects for small children. A teen volunteer program runs year round for students aged fifteen and up.

True Confessions from Adult Services Librarian Patti Burnside

This is the YA space of my dreams because . . .

"We have the space and funding to grow!"

I still dream of these improvements:

"Organizing a Teen Advisory Council and adding some sort of listening station."

Teen Patron Comments

"This new teen area is great. We're not treated like little kids!"—girl, 14

"I'm not really a teenager yet, but I come over here all the time. I like the comics [graphic novels] a lot. My school library doesn't have those. I also get to read magazines that help me with my video games."—boy, 12

Scott County Public Library, 104 South Bradford Lane, Georgetown, KY 40324, (502) 863-3566
http://www.scottpublib.org/

Club Fishbowl:
Teens Under Glass

Glendale Public Library
Glendale, Arizona

Merideth Jenson-Benjamin

Club Fishbowl might be the only teen space developed as the result of a library security system upgrade. Since the main library opened in 1987, teen materials were housed in two alcoves off the circulation and adult reference desks. Drawbacks to this arrangement included splitting the teen collection in half, shelving YA nonfiction in the adult stacks, and a location far from the youth desk, where the YA librarians work. To accommodate the new security system's demands, many areas of the library would be shifted. With no remodeling budget, a YA area would be created from existing library space.

I hoped that the space originally designed as the library gift shop—now housing the audio-visual collection—could be turned into an inviting teen space. I got my wish. Measuring 850 square feet, this room is glass-enclosed on three sides, looking out to the library's garden, lobby, and checkout desk. A red brick wall is its fourth side. Directly inside the library's front doors, its proximity to the youth and checkout desks make it an ideal teen spot. (A minor disadvantage is the large utility room within it, consuming floor space and dividing the room into a U-shape.) To free the room for YA use, we would shelve nonfiction videos in adult nonfiction, and place the rest of the AV materials in the former teen alcoves and Youth Department.

Our parameters for the YA space were strict. No remodeling or renovation of the space could take place. The lighting, carpeting, and entrance would remain as is. No new shelving could be ordered; the A-V shelving would be retained for the teen room. Limited funds were available for furniture and signage. To start the process of creating the teen room, we circulated a survey in May and June 2002 to teens participating in the Summer Reading Program. From more than 190 surveys returned, the teens' wish list for their space contained everything from couches to catered meals.

Instrumental in the design of the Teen Room was the Teen Library Council (TLC), formed to provide input on the teen space design. Through applications and interviews, we chose fifteen teens to serve on the TLC. They met in June to begin designing the space with the survey results as their guide, mindful of the limitations. The library staff had an open invitation to attend TLC meetings and many did, participating in the planning process firsthand. Although the teens always listened to the adults' suggestions, they often overruled adults' ideas. With direction from YA librarian Kathy Pastores and me, the TLC met monthly until September to select a color scheme, furniture, posters, and a name for the room. Inspired by the glass walls,

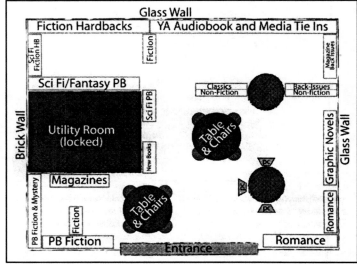

they christened the room Club Fishbowl. With the library's graphic designer, they designed a neon sign to hang over the entrance of Club Fishbowl, featuring its unofficial mascot, the angelfish.

Given the high ceilings and brick and glass structure of the room, the TLC decided to go with an industrial look, using chrome and black accents. We ordered furnishings in August 2002. Then we waited for the AV shelving to arrive; no work could commence on Club Fishbowl until the AV collection moved out. After countless delays, new video shelving was installed in November 2002, and work on the teen space proceeded rapidly. The walls were painted, the glass windows were tinted, and shelving was installed. In December, the computer workstations were connected, the YA materials were shelved, and the furniture was arranged.

Club Fishbowl is decorated in shades of red, black, and gray, coordinating with the shelving and black metal framework of the window walls. Two inner walls (outside the utility room) are painted vivid red; a shelving unit is framed with a gray and red checkerboard pattern. The industrial feel is carried out with track lighting and furnishings. Shelving has black wire end-pieces with gray melamine shelves. Two black melamine and chrome café tables are matched with four black leather and chrome chairs each. Five oversized beanbag chairs are in the same vivid red as the walls or gray of the shelves. Three computer workstations—with filtered Internet access, the library catalog, and Microsoft Office—continue the black-and-chrome motif. Teen magazines attract attention in a Lucite shelving unit. Above the magazines are displays.

When Club Fishbowl opened at the end of December 2002, its target audience found it immediately. Club Fishbowl has accomplished many goals. It consolidates all YA materials into one browsable area and creates a welcoming environment for teens. Most importantly, the creation of Club Fishbowl put a spotlight on teens, a neglected user group. Invited to be part of the process, staff members grew more comfortable dealing with teens, and have become enthusiastic supporters of the Young Adult Department.

Collection: All Teen materials are housed in Club Fishbowl, 6,817 pieces on 543 feet of shelving. Nonfiction (780 items) is shelved by Dewey number, with paperbacks and hardbacks interfiled. Fiction totals 5,674 items. Teen fiction paperbacks are under these genre headings: Romance, Mystery, Graphic Novels, Fiction, Science Fiction, Fantasy, and Media Tie-In. Hardcover fiction, new fiction, and audiobooks round out the collection. From July to December 2002, 14,918 young adult books circulated. The only YA items outside Club Fishbowl are music CDs housed in the Youth Department, moving into the teen room soon.

Population and Community: Over the past three decades, Glendale has been one of the fastest-growing cities in one of the fastest-growing metropolitan areas in the U.S., with a population of 218,812, 16.21 percent of whom are between the ages of ten and nineteen. The community is predominantly Caucasian with a growing Latino population. Glendale is also home to a bustling international community, thanks to the Thunderbird American Graduate School of International Management. The median age of "Glendalians" is 30.8 years, and more than 54 percent are college-educated. The average annual household income is more than $49,000. In the Phoenix metro area, Glendale has the largest percentage (32) of households with children under eighteen years old. We serve a total of 2,695 students in four junior high/middle schools and 12,653 students in seven high schools. These figures do not account for seventh- and eighth-graders enrolled in K-8 schools, or patrons from elsewhere in the metro area.

Hours and Teen Traffic: Club Fishbowl is open with the rest of the library from 9:00 a.m. to 9:00 p.m. Monday through Thursday, 9:00 a.m. to 6:00 p.m. Friday, 9:00 a.m. to 5:00 p.m. Saturday, and 1:00 to 5:00 p.m. Sunday. On most afternoons or evenings, five to fifteen teens at a time browse, read, use computers, or just hang out in Club Fishbowl. Weekends see a burst of activity from ten to twenty-five teens at a time, with the computers in use all day. The area is open to patrons aged twelve to eighteen; most are on the younger end. We aggressively enforce age restrictions, asking people under twelve or over eighteen to use another area of the library.

Staffing: The room is not staffed. From the youth desk, three full-time YA librarians include Club Fishbowl in their normal rounds.

Youth Participation and Programming: Creators of Club Fishbowl, the Teen Library Council (TLC) has fifteen members aged twelve to eighteen who meet monthly to advise on programming and collection development. Fantastic Fiction, a science fiction/fantasy book group, discusses books chosen by teens with teen discussion leaders. Annual Teen Summer Reading Programs attract at least 700 registrants. For every four hours of reading, teens earn a small prize or enter a drawing for movie passes or gift certificates. We offer at least one teen program a month from August to May and one teen program a week in June and July. Planned for 2003 are an after-hours program with trivia and library skills games, a forensics program presented by our Department of Public Safety, and a chocolate-making workshop. Periodically we designate certain YA books as "Instant Winners." When a teen checks out the book, he or she wins a prize.

Our Teen Volunteer program invites teens aged fourteen and up to volunteer in the Youth Department. It includes Community Service Saturdays and a Book Buddies program that matches little "buddies" (aged five to eight) with teen readers.

True Confessions from YA Librarian Merideth Jenson-Benjamin

This is the YA Space of my dreams because . . .

"It puts the entire teen collection in one place. It manages to feel private while being visually open. And its planning process helped staff members become involved with teens."

I still dream of these improvements:

"Converting the utility room to a group study space. Installing a music sound system and more computer stations. We would like to have a YA desk in the room at some point."

Teen Patron Comments

"It's great [to have] a teen room, because teens are in the in-between stage, both in the library and out. They don't belong with adults, but they're not children either."—Sarah, 13

"The room looks so cool! It's classy and a good place to hang out."—Liz, age 16

"More libraries should have places like this; it's neat and the computers are just for teens."—Zach, 14

"I like how Club Fishbowl is away from the other parts of the library. It gives me and my friends a place to read and talk away from the little kids."—Josie, 12

"It's really easy to find books now because they're all in one place and they're kept in better order."—Levi, 17

Glendale Public Library, 5959 W. Brown Street, Glendale, AZ 85302, (623) 930-3537
http://www.glendaleaz.com/library/

The Loft

Wadsworth Public Library
Wadsworth, Ohio

Valerie Ott

Description: Partially enclosed with glass and slightly elevated on a platform, this new teen space is situated right in the middle of the library. Sliding glass doors that separate the room from the audiovisual department remain open unless there is a program in progress. At the other end of the room, a ramp and two steps connect teens to the adult fiction area. The square-shaped, 840-square-foot LOFT (Library Outlet for Teens) is a hub of activity. Its décor coordinates with the rest of the library but is kicked up a notch for teen appeal. Multicolored tweed carpeting complements the four easy chairs that are upholstered with a fun, geometric pattern in blue, green, gold, purple, and red. These chairs cluster around a small, round coffee table. Two tables with four chairs each are available for studying or socializing. The Teen Services Librarian's desk is in one corner of the room beside a hutch that stores art supplies, board games, and a sound system. The hutch has magnetic poetry all over it. Nearby is a teen bulletin board and a glass display case where passive programs, contests, and teen artwork are displayed.

The room is bright and cheerful because of the borrowed light from the glass partitions and the clerestory windows along the top of the wall. Most of the wall space is covered with shelving—approximately 280 linear feet. Posters decorate the back of the waist-high magazine rack in the center of the room, which separates the reading area from the LOFT's two computer workstations. One computer is devoted to gaming, containing games such as *Backyard Baseball, The Sims, Monopoly Tycoon,* and *Rollercoaster Tycoon.* The other station offers the online catalog, Word, Excel, PowerPoint, filtered Internet access, and resumé-writing software. A large, green neon Howard Miller clock is a unique feature of this space, hanging above the glass doors to the audiovisual department.

Collection: The LOFT's collection holds 4,227 items, including 1,286 hardbacks, 1,811 paperbacks, and 31 magazines. In YA fiction, hardbacks and paperbacks are shelved together by the author's last name. Nonfiction is shelved in Dewey order. A paperback literature collection is shelved separately for ease in locating books for school assignments. The YA Reference collection near the librarian's desk contains school textbooks and general reference sources such as dictionaries, a thesaurus, titles from the Opposing Viewpoints series, and science fair resources. Comic books are kept in colorful milk crates near the seating area. Graphic novels and audiobooks have their own shelves. A free-standing unit contains a special collection of financial literacy materials. In the adjoining A/V room are the library's video and music CD collections. The LOFT's sound system usually plays special mix CDs created by Teen Advisory Board members. Circulation figures for the young adult collection keep rising. In 2003 when the new LOFT opened, YA items circulated about 11,315 times, a nine percent increase over the previous year. Incomplete figures for 2004 already show another four percent increase since 2003.

Young Adult Population and Community: Fifteen miles west of Akron and forty miles south of Cleveland off Interstate 76, Wadsworth is a semi-rural, middle-class town in Medina County with a population of about 19,000 people. Its residents enjoy a small-town feel in proximity to two cities. The Wadsworth Public Library is an independent library serving the citizens of the Wadsworth area, city and township. An intermediate school, a middle school, and a high school are all within walking distance of the library, with a total enrollment of 2,724 students. One parochial school for grades K-8 is also nearby.

Hours and Teen Traffic: The LOFT is open during regular library hours from 9:00 a.m. to 9:00 p.m. Monday through Thursday, 9:00 a.m. to 6:00 p.m. Friday and Saturday, and 1:00 p.m. to 6:00 p.m. on Sundays during the school year. Thirty to forty teens visit the LOFT every day after school and on weekends. Many come to use the Internet, but the lounge area has become a favorite spot just to hang out after school with friends. The reference staff near the LOFT answers several homework reference questions and directs teens to the paperback literature collection

65

for reading or English assignments. The LOFT's primary recreational users are in grades six through ten; older teens check out books from the collection or gather materials for school. Surprisingly adults also enjoy the space to read the newspaper in the morning and early afternoon.

Staffing: One full-time, professional Teen Services Librarian and one part-time paraprofessional monitor the teen room and handle collection development and teen programming. Although no staff is solely assigned to the LOFT's desk, the reference desk is just a short distance from the space. The reference staff consists of four full-time professional librarians, one full-time paraprofessional, and two part-time paraprofessionals.

Planning Process: The library's original 19,000 square feet did not include a space for teens. One bulletin board tucked away in a corner and a very small amount of shelving was carved out for teen fiction. Nonfiction was interfiled with the adult collection. In August 2001, ground was broken for a 12,000 square-foot addition which included plans to turn the old magazine and adult reading area into a spot just for teens. The Teen Services Librarian gave her input to the library's director, the architects, and the interior designers throughout the planning process. The library's Teen Advisory Board (TAB) was surveyed for their opinions about what they wished to see in the new space, and a contest was held to name it. The idea was to create a space with plenty of shelving for the entire teen collection plus room for growth. Display space was a must, as was furniture for studying and relaxing. The new library addition opened on March 9, 2003.

Youth Participation and Programming: The Teen Advisory Board (TAB) meets twice a month, once for a monthly meeting, and once for an after-school program such as a holiday-themed party or an arts and crafts workshop. The TAB plans future programs and publishes a bimonthly newsletter called *Keeping TABs*. Its officers accompany the Teen Services Librarian on a book-selecting trip to a local bookstore each fall. There are several ongoing programs. A chess club and a knitting club meet on alternating Mondays throughout the month. Pizza & Pages, a book discussion program that meets after school, involves lively discussion about the monthly book selection over a pizza snack. One meeting is for fifth and sixth graders and another is for seventh and eighth graders. Thursday Theater takes place the last Thursday of each month when the Teen Services Librarian shows a feature film and serves popcorn.

LOL @ Your Library was the theme for the 2004 Teen Summer Reading Program, which drew 157 participants. Prize drawings occurred each week; three grand prizes went to the teens who read the most over the summer, and there were plenty of programs designed for comic relief. A new theme is picked by the TAB every year, with coordinating activities.

True Confessions from Teen Services Librarian Valerie Ott

This is the YA space of my dreams because . . .

"I am able to show off the great collection of fiction and nonfiction books that were virtually hidden before."

I still dream of these improvements:

"There is still a lot of white space in the LOFT, but we're hoping to commission an artist to paint a mural on the wall above the shelving, which will incorporate the name of the room. In terms of programming, I'd love to increase services to homeschooled teens."

Teen Patron Comments

"Not very many libraries give teens their own room. Now that we have one, it's an honor."—Heather, 15

"The LOFT is a great place to go just for teens, with limitless things to do."—Andy, 16

Wadsworth Public Library, 132 Broad Street, Wadsworth, OH 44281, (330) 334-5761
http://www.wadsworthlibrary.com/

Robert Cormier Center for Young Adults (The BOB)

Leominster Public Library
Leominster, Massachusetts

Diane Sanabria

Description: The Cormier Center is a separate room on the Leominster Public Library's second floor, with one entrance into the adult nonfiction/study area. A second door in a glass wall leads downstairs to the foyer. Mounted on the glass is a neon sign that announces the "Robert Cormier Center for Young Adults," incorporating the famous local author's actual signature. Above the YA fiction shelves, a long mural created by Leominster High School Art Club students is inspired by Cormier's life and work.

This rectangular room of 768 square feet (24 by 32 feet) is cheerful and crowded. In the 2001 renovation, its repainted walls changed from light blue to a yellowish "sand." The lounging area contains a big brown couch and two overstuffed green easy chairs. An end table holds board games and magazines. An oak table with four Sauder Ply-Lok (rocking) chairs occupies the space between the soft furniture and the new computer (from a Gates grant), which contains Microsoft Office, *Infotrac* and *Novelist* databases, and unfiltered Internet access. It has no online catalog or games. A CD player with wall-mounted speakers *always* plays music when the Center is open.

In the center of the room is the YA librarian's desk, cluttered with amusing toys and souvenirs collected by several generations of teens, starting with a "California Snowman" water globe brought back from vacation by one teen as a gift to the librarian. Other teens added more water globes, a Big Ben pencil sharpener, official water from Niagara Falls, a telephone booth bank from the island of Malta, and more—a tacky but fun collection crowned by a lavender lava lamp. Beside the desk is a bubbling fish floor lamp.

On the other side of the room, steps lead up to a reading loft that holds three or four people overlooking the entire area. Littered with big comfy pillows, the loft features a magnetic poetry wall made of two panels of sheet steel sprayed with black automotive undercarriage paint. A small shelf holds books about teen sexuality. Twined around the loft railing is white rope lighting. The teens love the loft so much that they insisted that a similar area be incorporated into the new library building—it's in the architects' plans.

Collection: Approximately 3,700 items include YA fiction, adult books for teens, and nonfiction on fixed-wall shelving, science fiction and fantasy paperbacks on 2 small and 3 large bookcases, and 4 paperback spinners holding general YA titles plus horror, romance, classics, series, and sports. Magazines reside on a spinner and wall unit. Four display book trucks near a butterfly chair contain Japanese manga, and 2 trucks hold anime DVDs. Music CDs live on 2 movable racks. Since 2000, Cormier Center circulation has tripled; in 2004, 16,660 items circulated.

Furniture is portable to make room for programs. Wheeled paperback racks are easily moved to accommodate long tables for craft/game programs in *very* cozy seating for 12 to 14 teens. Book and writing groups meet in the lounging area; the table is moved against the wall for snacks and chairs are added as needed.

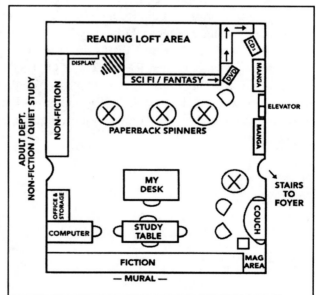

Young Adult Population and Community: The 2000 U.S. Census counted 41,303 Leominster residents. Long known as the "Pioneer Plastic City" to reflect a blue-collar workforce engaged in plastics manufacturing, Leominster now promotes its image as "The Birthplace of Johnny Appleseed." Skyrocketing housing prices magnify Leominster's increased role as a bedroom community for suburban Boston. There's a sizeable Puerto Rican population and increasing Asian, Brazilian, and Portuguese immigrants. The library's downtown location in an ethnically diverse neighborhood is reflected in frequent use by minority teens. The library serves 2,853 students in one high school and three middle schools.

Hours, Staffing, and Teen Traffic: As a separate room staffed by one young adult librarian, the Cormier Center is open for limited hours: Monday through Friday from 2:00 to 5:00 p.m., and Wednesday nights until 7:00 p.m. Unlike the rest of the library, it is not open weekends and twelve-hour weekdays.

Center hours have fluctuated throughout its history. When the Center opened in 1978, a library assistant kept it open evenings and Saturdays, while its founder, Nina Crowley, worked weekdays. In 1981, state budget cuts eliminated the YA assistant's position. Then Crowley left, and the library offered her full-time job to the assistant, Diane Sanabria, who had just graduated from college with a teaching degree. Sanabria remains as Young Adult Services Coordinator—and the only Center staff member—24 years later. In 1991, further budget cuts reduced several full-time librarian positions to part-time, including Sanabria's—further limiting Center hours. Not until 1998 was Sanabria's position restored to full-time. Between 15 and 35 teens in grades 7 through 12 use the Center each day after school; Reference staff escorts teens to retrieve materials after hours.

Planning Process: The original Carnegie building opened in 1910, with an addition in 1966. The Young Adult Center was created in 1978 with a $20,500 LSCA grant to furnish the room and YA materials. The grant was the culmination of attempts to increase services for teens, starting with a second-floor area with beanbag chairs, a listening station, paperbacks, and magazines. It proved popular, but too noisy to co-exist with adults nearby. Trust funds were used to wall off a portion of the second-floor nonfiction/study area, creating a self-contained room for teens. Crowley, the Center's first director, recruited teens to paint the room and choose furnishings and materials. A September 1978 opening featured a dance with a live band.

Soon the Young Adult Center became known by its acronym, the "YAC." Its teen advisory council planned programs, drew art and wrote copy for the Center's newsletter, and provided "muscle" for many projects. Budget cuts in 1990 curtailed hours, staff, and programs. When the YA librarian's hours were restored to full-time in 1998, the popular REACT teen book discussion group and the Red-Eye Writers group served the function of an advisory group. These teens helped to redesign the YAC from 2001 to 2002. On April 7, 2002, the Center was formally dedicated in memory of Cormier as the Robert Cormier Center for Young Adults. Its patrons felt strongly about naming it for young adults instead of teens. Now they look forward to a space tripling in size in the new building.

Youth Participation and Programming: Two groups meet monthly in The Bob. The REACT Book Discussion Group gives an annual REACTOR'S QUEST AWARD to their favorite book that year (in 2004 it went to R. A. Salvatore for *The Highwayman*, CDS Books, 2004). The Red-Eye Writers meet for Saturday breakfast and an opportunity to share their work. The group is working on a page that will be linked to the library's Web site (*http://www.leominsterlibrary.org*). Other teen programs include a summer reading game, crafts projects, and manga drawing workshops.

True Confessions from Young Adult Services Coordinator Diane Sanabria

This is the YA space of my dreams because . . .

"When teens enter The Bob, they know instinctively that this is *their* space. The funky décor, the music, the neon, the toys, the loft, the comfy furniture, and the diverse, high-interest collection all combine for an atmosphere that says, 'You are welcome here. We value your input, and respect and respond to your opinions and choices.' If teens are looking at it or listening to it or reading it, I like to think that they can find it here."

I still dream of these improvements:

"*More hours!* The Center should be staffed and open all evenings and weekends that the library is open. *More space!* I'd like to expand the manga and DVD areas, and introduce new collections like YA Books-on-CD. *More computers!* I'd love workstations loaded with CD-ROMs and computer games like *The Sims.* I am hopeful that the expanded facility will address these issues."

Teen Patron Comments

"The Bob is a comfortable place to get books, look at books, read books, or look at all the gadgets and gizmos on Di's desk! With comfortable couches and the loft, it's nice to relax at The Bob. I think it needs to get a little larger but don't lose the style!"—Cassie, 13

"The Bob . . . a place where teen lovers of books feels like they're at home. From the luxurious comfy couches to the magnetic poetry alcove, you always have fun!"—Nancy, 17

[In regard to the manga collection:] "You guys have saved me *so* much money!"—Olivia, 13

Leominster Public Library, 30 West Street, Leominster, MA 01453, (978) 534-7522
http://www.leominsterlibrary.org/

Teen Zone

Natrona County Public Library
Casper, Wyoming

Emily Daly

Description: The Teen Zone beckons from the mezzanine floor of the Natrona County Public Library's three-level Main Library. The raised, rust-colored lettering of the Teen Zone sign, a free-form shape held by suspension cables, is visible both from within the area and from the library's first floor. Approached by a wide stairwell from the main floor or a short staircase down from the reference section, the Teen Zone is the only public area on the mezzanine level. The 628 square-foot rectangular space exudes an eclectic coffeeshop feel, with a muted color palette of earth tones including plum, rust, artichoke, pale yellow, and grey-blue, pleasingly mixed throughout the area in walls and furnishings. Because the original ceiling height made the room feel cramped, some tile was removed to reveal painted pipes and electrical wiring. Recessed canned lights and chunky, round hanging fixtures provide a pleasant glow and serve as task lighting for browsers and readers. Low bookshelves (four feet tall) and countertop desk spaces have a wavy edge that contributes to the theme of rounded lines and objects repeated in the lighting fixtures, furniture, and carpeting. The floor is covered with two different colors, one a solid burgundy and the other a subtle pattern incorporating four colors used on the walls. The two carpets are seamed together in an eye-catching design. Several houseplants and a betta fish contribute to the area's warmth.

The center of the Teen Zone is filled with comfy butterfly and upholstered chairs for reading or chatting with friends, a game table and four chairs for doing homework or playing cards, and a café table with tall chairs. A countertop desk contains three flat-screen computers, each equipped with Telus (time and print management software), word processing programs, Internet capability, and computer games. An additional computer is devoted to library catalogs and databases. A Movie Lounge in one corner features an oversized bean bag chair and cushioned wedge bench seats for viewing a TV and VCR/DVD player. Teens may watch a movie from the Teen Zone's non-circulating collection of DVDs and videos or opt for one that they have checked out from the library's audio-visual section. Also in the lounge are a spinning magazine rack and a CD listening station.

Back in the main area, teens may study quietly at countertop desk space that lines portions of two walls, with nine chairs in three different colors. The remaining wall space is devoted to shelving. A small hallway leading upstairs to the reference section is home to three vending machines and another café table and chairs, where teens eat and drink. A public service desk, staffed during after-school hours, weekends, and school holidays, is positioned on the other side of the main stairwell, adjacent to one of the quiet study spaces.

Collection: The Teen Zone's 4,100 items for recreational reading and school support include YA fiction shelved in 6 tall wall units of 6 shelves each (108 square feet) and 10 short units of 3 shelves each (90 square feet). Two tall wall units of 5 shelves each (30 square feet) contain nonfiction. Paperback series fiction resides on 2 tall wall units of 6 shelves each (12 square feet) and graphic novels live on 2 wall units the same size as the paperback shelves. The collection also includes adult books for teens, magazines, and in-house board games and computer games. Shelf-top racks and a free-standing display unit showcase new materials. Circulation for 2005 is 18,190 items, a 19.5 percent increase over 2004. Audiobooks, DVDs, and CDs are housed in a separate audio-visual section of the library.

Young Adult Population and Community: In a centrally located transportation hub that is Wyoming's meeting place, the main library in downtown Casper serves the city's population of 49,644, as well as Natrona County's population of 66,533. Its teen population comes from six junior high schools and three high schools enrolling a total of 5,457 students. The county library has two branches in more rural areas as well as a bookmobile. Approximately

51 percent of county residents are NCPL patrons. In terms of ethnicity, Natrona County is 94.6 percent white, 4.9 percent Hispanic, .8 percent African American, 1 percent Native American, and .4 percent Asian American. Natrona County's per capita income is consistent with statewide patterns, but less than national figures. Most employment is in service, retail, and construction.

Hours, Staffing, and Teen Traffic: The Teen Zone is open during all operating hours of the library: Monday to Thursday from 10:00 a.m. to 7:00 p.m., Friday and Saturday from 10:00 a.m. to 5:00 p.m., and Sundays from 1:00 to 5:00 p.m. during the academic year. The service desk in the Teen Zone is staffed by the YA specialist during after-school hours with assistance from two part-time paraprofessionals who work on weekends and evenings. Approximately 35 students in grades six through twelve frequent the area per day during those service hours. Parents may accompany their children in the Teen Zone or browse its collection during school hours. Other adults are discouraged from using the Teen Zone.

Planning Process: Prompted by a 2001 visit to Teen Central at Phoenix Public Library in Arizona ("YA Spaces," *VOYA*, December 2003), plans to add the Teen Zone to Casper's 1910 library began with a brainstorming session among teens, librarians, and architects in the summer of 2002. Soon fundraising began (a combination of private and public funds made Teen Zone construction possible), and teens and librarians continued to provide input as design plans progressed. Construction began in fall 2004. The space opened to the public on November 22, 2004, but was not finished until mid-January 2005. On February 1, 2005, a grand opening/ribbon-cutting ceremony welcomed the community. An open house, complete with pizza and cake, door prizes, crafts, and a visit from the architects was held for teens on February 10, 2005.

Youth Participation and Programming: A core group of approximately ten teen volunteers offer their time by reading to young children during Saturday Storytimes, participating in "adopt-a-shelf" to maintain order in their favorite library sections, helping with teen programs and other library events, creating bulletin boards and displays, and other tasks. Teen programs include two book clubs, one for sixth to eighth graders and one for ninth to twelfth graders; a summer reading program in which teens earn prizes for reading and participate in many library and community programs from craft projects to movies, from card tournaments to minor league baseball games; and library teen events offered year-round from one to three times a month. These well-attended activities include Murder Mystery Nights, Scrapbooking Workshops, Dinner and a Movie @ Your Library, Poetry Slams, and a monthly Anime Club. The library also collaborated with Casper's art museum and a group of teens interested in local government and volunteer efforts to create "Somethin' to Do," a series of programs for teens, by teens. Such events have included workshops on hemp weaving and beading as well as henna tattoos, and an afternoon of mural painting.

True Confessions From Young Adult Specialist Emily Daly

This is the YA space of my dreams because . . .

It was designed for and by the teens who use it. Its décor is highly appealing to teenagers, and the unique components of the space (movie lounge, vending machines, funky furniture and shelving) make it a fun and interesting after-school and weekend hangout spot. The atmosphere of the space is warm and inviting and truly teen-centered, and I love that I have a public service desk in the Teen Zone so that I can be a part of the energy and excitement of the teens who use it every day.

I still dream of these improvements:

I hope one day to increase the number of computers in the Teen Zone and perhaps add a small audio-visual collection. I also hope to increase staffing so that we may reach more kids inside and outside the library. Overall, however, I feel that the facility itself meets the needs of the teens who use the space.

Teen Patron Comments

"I love the new Teen Zone because it's so comfortable and relaxing. I like the coffeehouse feel of it and that kids who never used to come to the library come now just to hang and look at books."—Bethaney, 15

"I like to come to the Teen Zone to do homework and spend time after school, and I love the cool chairs—they're so comfortable!"—Sara, 13

"The Teen Zone is a cool place to hang out with friends because you can talk and be kinda loud. And I really like the movie area."—Jana, 15

"I like the machines with food and the movies and how you can come here and do homework—they have pencils and everything all ready for you."—Josh, 13

Natrona County Public Library, 307 East Second Street, Casper, WY 82601, (307) 237-4935
http://www.natronacountylibrary.org/

Teen Section

Middleton Public Library
Middleton, Wisconsin

Rebecca Van Dan

Description: When teens pass through an elegant wood and glass-block gateway with a curved copper roof, beneath a copper-trimmed sign proclaiming "TEENS" in blue neon, it's obvious that they have entered their own Teen Section. In the back of the upper level, their space is separated from the rest of Middleton Public Library by extensions on each side of the teen gate. As one enters, to the gate's left is a striped sofa that faces both outward and inward, set at an angle beside tall shelves of teen fiction that border the section. To the gate's right is a shelf of popular teen nonfiction, flanked by a terrarium containing Smaug, a live bearded dragon in miniature—he is normal size for a teenaged dragon from Australia, in the lizard family. The Dragon's Lair is visible from within the Teen Section as well as outside it, for children on their way to their Storytime Room. Teens take turns feeding live crickets to Smaug.

Just inside the gate is a display easel promoting teen programs, and a round wooden table with three plum-colored butterfly puff chairs. Six spinners surround the table with new YA books, new magazines, and paperbacks. Past the spinners and along the back wall are two popular destinations: a booth with two benches at a table with a listening station, and two back-to-back gaming computers in the corner. These stations devoted to gaming contain the only computers within the Teen Section; online catalogs are nearby and Internet access is on the lower level. Two additional comfy butterfly chairs back one of the booth's benches. On the wall behind the booth and computer station are colorful READ posters; between them is a teen bulletin board with notices and photos of teen programs.

The 900-square-foot Teen Section manages to be integrated with the rest of the library while maintaining its cozy—and sometimes noisy—autonomy. It shares the library's beige walls and multi-colored plum/beige/blue carpet. On the curving pathway to the Teen Section, teens pass by two other imposing structures. To the right, beside the Children's Section, is the Youth Services Desk for both children and teens, decorated for the summer reading program with a medieval castle look—grey "stone" paper and knights' shields. To the left is an impressive elevator tower that looks like a tall house, alongside a stairway going down where teens will find another space planned with their needs in mind. This quiet area on the lower level contains nonfiction and other materials for research, individual study rooms, and a computer lab where word processing and unfiltered Internet access are available. Upstairs, along the path between the tower and the gate to the Teen Section, are paperback spinners with classics, romance, nonfiction, and adult science fiction and fantasy to the left, and a four-shelf wooden unit with graphic novels, humor, and Newbery/Caldecott Award books along the edge of the Children's Section. In another upper level corner is a reading room with a fireplace, a favorite spot used by all ages for book discussions—and the only quiet space upstairs.

Collection: Mostly for recreational reading, the 5,680 books in the Teen Section include YA fiction, picture books and adult books for teens, popular nonfiction, comics and graphic novels, and magazines. Media includes audiobooks, 650 music CDs, more than 500 videos and DVDs, board games, and 70 computer games—some loaded on the game computers, and all available for checkout. Rotating racks contain paperbacks (9 square feet) and new books (5 square feet). Metal shelving holds fiction (24 linear feet) and wood shelving holds media (10 linear feet). New magazines near the display table are shelved separately from older issues, which are on the wall beside the bulletin board. A special display features books written by teens, and local high school newspapers are also collected. In 2004, circulation for all YA materials was 27,573.

Young Adult Population and Community: Middleton is an affluent suburban community of 16,000 residents. Very close to the major Wisconsin city of Madison, Middleton boasts a quaint downtown area and a new outdoor shopping mall. It was ranked #7 in *Money* magazine's "Best Places to Live 2005." Among its majority of white residents, a large Hispanic community enjoys their own section of the library, with many materials in Spanish. Another significant population is Asian Indian; the African American community is smaller. The library serves 3,050 students in two middle schools and one high school. Middleton Public Library is a member of South Central Library System (SCLS), a consortium of public libraries in south central Wisconsin. In Hennen's American Public Library Ratings for 2004, the library was ranked with the second highest score in Wisconsin, and eleventh in its service population category (10,000–25,000) nationwide.

Hours, Staffing, and Teen Traffic: As part of the upper level, the Teen Section is open during all library hours: Monday to Thursday from 9:00 a.m. to 9:00 p.m., Friday from 9:00 a.m. to 6:00 p.m., Saturday from 9:00 a.m. until 5:00 p.m., and Sunday (September to May) from 1:00 to 5:00 p.m. It is staffed from the Youth Services Desk shared with the Children's Section; all three staff members take turns answering questions from teens and children. One of them, the full-time professional Young Adult Librarian, has primary responsibility for the teen collection and programming. Another, a paraprofessional Library Assistant, specializes in programs for "tweens" (ages eight to twelve). After-school hours are crowded with teens aged twelve to nineteen, six or more depending on the time of day. Weekends bring at least thirty teens. During school hours, older patrons are attracted to the comfortable butterfly chairs.

Planning Process: Founded in 1926, the library moved in 1990 to its current location. The entire library staff (including the YA librarian), board, and administration devoted a year to planning a renovation. The old Teen Section was squeezed between the adult and children's areas in the middle front part of the library, where it couldn't easily be reserved as a space for teens, and had little space for decorating with posters or other inviting teen displays. The YA librarian planned a more defined space with room for wall decorations in a lively area where noise was allowed, balanced by a separate quiet space for study. Excavation began in September 2003; the library closed only briefly. For the entire weekend of April 23 to 27, 2004, the library celebrated its reopening. Two teen rock bands from the local high school played in library meeting rooms.

Youth Participation and Programming: Teen volunteers assist with shelving, make posters, cut and staple display items, and do program setup and cleanup. The Teen Advisory Committee (TAC) suggests displays and other features for the Teen Section as well as new materials for purchase and programming ideas. Each year's Teen Summer Reading Program offers a chance at a grand prize drawing for everyone who reads for a hundred minutes, as well as smaller prizes for reading ten to thirty books. Books & Bagels is a monthly book discussion that sometimes compares books to their movie versions. A varied menu of teen programs has included belly dancing, salsa dancing, mehndi, tie-dying, fencing, an anti-Valentine's Day event, culture nights such as an India Night, movies, an art contest, and a yearly writing contest. One repeating program, "Sick and Twisted," shows student videos from the local high school in a unique school/library partnership. When a student reported in a TAC meeting that a video he created in a school computer art class would not be shown to students because school officials objected to its content, the YA librarian contacted the teacher to offer the public library as a showcase for such videos. With a stated mission to foster a better understanding of intellectual freedom, the resulting library program attracts a huge audience of older teens and parents.

The library's teen Web page (*http://www. midlibrary.org/library/teen*) features pictures of teen programs and the Teen Section, a Teen Reading Blog, and a teen e-newsletter (by free subscription) that covers upcoming programs and new items in the teen collection.

True Confessions from Young Adult Librarian Rebecca Van Dan

This is the YA space of my dreams because . . .

"I finally have wall space to hang posters, a neon sign that can be seen upon entering the library, and a terrarium (the dragon!). The defined space makes it very cozy."

I still dream of these improvements:

"I'd love to see some teen Internet computers upstairs."

Teen Patron Comments

"I like the neon light."—Ray, 17

"The dragon is awesome! I like that there are two games computers now, so there are less kids around one computer. I also like all the teen programs and how they have developed."—Nora, 17

Middleton Public Library, 7425 Hubbard Avenue, Middleton, WI 53562, (608) 831-5564
http://www.midlibrary.org/library/default.asp

Dreams Become Reality

Harris County Public Library
Houston, Texas

Sarah Booth

It's a young adult librarian's dream—walking into the library after school and seeing teens. Lots of teens, all busy. Busy playing games at the computer. Busy talking to friends. Busy doing homework. Busy looking at books. We all have this dream about the public library engaging that hard-to-fit teen population.

At Harris County Public Library, a system serving the suburban areas surrounding Houston, Texas, that dream is a reality. In the last five years, many of our branches have been rebuilt or renovated. Five of our 26 branches now have dedicated areas designed to fit the needs of teens. Our reward is to see teens using the library.

Committed to implementing innovative and cutting-edge policies and technology to serve the community, HCPL has also instituted in-house laptop use. Throughout the system, 134 wireless laptops are available to be checked out and used in the library when our 1,205 public-access computers are in use. Since 2002, customers aged twelve and above have swarmed to use the laptops for homework, surfing the Internet, or playing games.

Library Director Cathy Park says, "Providing teen spaces, programs, and YA librarians sends the message that we want teens at the library." Although each branch is unique and serves a different community, all five teen spaces possess common elements. They contain the YA collection of fiction, nonfiction, magazines, and graphic novels as well as test guides and career and college prep books. Comfortable seating is a priority, from beanbag chairs to diner-style booths. Each teen space has its own flavor.

High Meadows Branch

After closing for six months, the High Meadows Branch Library reopened in November 2005 with extensive renovations. Located in a lower socio-economic area of Houston, the branch serves mostly Hispanic residents. Sandwiched between a high school and a middle school, High Meadows desperately needed a space dedicated to teens. The new teen space is a 560-square-foot rectangle between the adult and children's areas. One recent Friday afternoon, the entire library was filled with teens of all ages. Every one of the 26 computers was in use. Teens sat together in the YA space looking at magazines. Some commented that they love the look of the library: "It looks modern," said one. "I come every day."

All sections of the library were designed to flow together. The Gates Computer Lab has glass pocket doors that allow for movement to other areas. In the teen space, a diner-style table with long benches welcomes get-togethers. All tables for teens have electronic access ports on top. Assistant Branch Librarian Melanie Atkinson likes the way the tables are arranged "for group interaction. The orange and rust and green color scheme is cool." Upholstery is complemented by the colored geometric shapes in the carpet and the hanging light fixtures. High above, a green "Teens" sign is also translated into the Spanish "adolescencias."

High Meadows has a full-time YA librarian, but everyone helps with programs and displays. Daily teen programs range from Movies and Games to an Anime Club and "Teens N Da House"—an open house where teens use computers, listen to music, or just talk. A Teen Activity Board meets monthly.

Aldine Branch

If the High Meadows Branch gets too busy, teens can go to the Aldine Branch about fifteen minutes away, which was renovated and enlarged in 2001. It serves many of the same residents. Next door to a high school, Aldine also attracts many teens; Branch Librarian Jim Pearson realized their need for their own space. In a far corner where beanbag chairs are the only furniture, the teen area is 225 square feet. Teens manage to lounge and use the library's laptop computers simultaneously, playing games or doing homework. "We like to chill on the beanbags," say Lucy and Angel, pictured doing exactly that. Although there is no YA librarian, all branch staff help with YA programs, including a Teen Time twice a week and monthly book discussions. A Teen Advisory Group meets monthly.

Barbara Bush Branch

In the affluent suburb of Spring, the Barbara Bush Branch Library, named for the former First Lady, is one of the system's largest branches at 32,000 square feet. Harris County's first YA librarian was assigned to this branch. Its teen area is in the back corner of the second floor, near adult fiction. The 500-square-foot rectangle contains generous shelving, dedicated YA computers, and comfortable seating that offers privacy for group work and hanging out. The recent neon paint and updated furniture in rounded contemporary shapes was donated by the Friends of the Library. Sloping, colored strips of lime green, peach, and gray on one wall, and blue stars on another, set off the space in its own landscape. Mobiles with blue and green dangling circles mark it from above. The branch has a full-time YA librarian who is working on establishing a Teen Advisory Board.

Tomball College and Community Library

Tomball is a small, rural suburb almost an hour outside the city of Houston. Its library is a joint-use facility for the public and the Community College. The rebuilt 72,000 square-foot library, which opened in January 2005, was designed to accommodate teens. Their own glass-walled room is 1,440 square feet, shaped like a harp. Ten flat-screen computers overlook the campus, with orange and blue chairs in funky shapes nearby. A curved area contains a viewing station for watching television or DVDs from a semicircular gold and orange couch. Weekly teen programs are held in the room.

Teens love the area, leaving many written comments. One anonymous comment: Diana wrote, "I like this place. I will start coming to the programs. You guys are awesome. Changed my concept about libraries! Thanks!!!" Full-time YA librarian Catherine Pells says that this is the YA Space of her dreams because "it's a comfortable, inviting area for teens to read, use the computers, or just hang out—and they know it." She is working with the Tomball Area Chamber of Commerce and the Tomball Youth Initiative to form a Teen Advisory Council.

Clear Lake City County Freeman Branch

Located near NASA, the Clear Lake City County Freeman Branch reopened in a new 42,000 square-foot facility in 2004. The city of Clear Lake serves a diverse, multicultural community. The library was named for astronaut Captain Theodore C. Freeman; a "space" theme dominates the building's design. The Teen Zone is no exception—on deep blue walls around its entrance are fanciful planets. On the second floor with the adult collection, the trapezoid-shaped 2,176 square-foot Teen Zone is a glass-enclosed area where teens read, work together, or watch movies. Inside the entrance, two space-age diner-style booths feature prominently, with ports for laptaps on the tables. At the back of the room is a large-screen TV and more seating.

Teens notice and appreciate the retro design. One said, "The decorations are cool. The chairs are comfortable, and it's a good place to study." Other comments: "I like the movie room because you can hang out and play board games" and "I like that this area is separate from the children's area." The Freeman Branch has one full-time YA Librarian, one full-time YA assistant, and one part-time YA assistant who provide weekly programs for teens.

At HCPL, the staff recognizes the need for separate, teen-friendly spaces as the bridge that connects the gap between childhood story time and adult usage.

Harris County Public Library, 8080 El Rio Street, Houston, Texas 77054, (713) 749-9000
http://www.hcpl.net/

The Got Art? Gallery

William K. Sanford Town Library
Town of Colonie, New York

Maureen DeLaughter

Recently a thief in Paris nearly managed to steal several paintings from the Louvre. After carefully planning the crime and getting in and out past security, he was captured only two blocks from the museum when his van ran out of gas. When asked how he could mastermind such a crime and then make such an obvious error, he replied, "I had no Monet to buy Degas to make de Van Gogh."

Teens Love Jokes, but They Love Art More

In the new Teen Room at the William K. Sanford Town Library in Loudonville, New York, a hamlet of the suburban Town of Colonie near Albany, the state capital, members of the newly formed Teen Advisory Group were discussing decorating ideas. Behind a front wall of glass and a door that closes on their own space, several thought that teen art would be nice. Someone suggested a gallery dedicated to art by teens. Although I was excited about the idea, the Teen Room had little wall space. When I approached the administration about transforming a small study area just outside the Teen Room into a gallery, they were enthusiastic. Opening in November 2005, the Got Art? Gallery has been a tremendous success that other libraries might emulate.

A Grant, a Committee, and a Gallery Begins

Each year, our Upper Hudson Library System offers the opportunity for member libraries to apply for small outreach grants. When I received a grant in April 2005 for just over $1,000, our town library matched the funds so we could create a unique gallery to showcase artwork by local teens and college students. The gallery's components included several tall metal grids that allow for a flexible configuration, two display cases, a system for hanging pictures on the one available wall, a viewing bench, and a café table and chairs. I also bought twenty-five art books for our YA collection with the grant money.

After the components were ordered, I posted flyers and wrote an article about the gallery for our town newsletter to encourage interested high school students to attend a meeting. Ten teens came to the first meeting. Twenty participants over the summer became a core group of eight teens, just the right size group to get the work done.

During July and August the group met often to flesh out a logo contest, a gallery Web page, and a brochure. Members made T-shirts to distinguish themselves as gallery "staff." Using puffy, day-glow paint on black shirts, they placed the words "Got Art?" on the front, and recreated their favorite pieces of famous art on the back, from Munch's *The Scream* to the Linux mascot Tux the Penguin.

To communicate between meetings, I created a blog for the group. It worked wonderfully for about a month. Then a combination of my naiveté about blogs (I didn't realize I could make the blog private to prevent outsiders from posting comments) and my naiveté in choosing the name TArtGallery (for Teen Art Gallery) created a situation which I'm sure *VOYA* readers have already guessed. Needless to say, we got some unwanted postings. The original blog was abandoned and a new one was created, but it never really took off.

In September when school began, we asked local art teachers to encourage their students to participate in the logo contest. Because the prize was an MP3 player, I expected entries to pour in. Two days before the contest deadline, I had only five submissions and began to panic. Teen librarians with more experience than mine are probably nodding because they know that teens always wait until the last minute. Forty-five more entries arrived on the last possible day.

After I explained the basic rules of a good logo, the gallery committee spent several hours helping to choose the winning logo. Narrowing the choices to ten, we debated the pros and cons of each until the group finally picked five, from which I chose the winner. We asked the winning artist to modify the design slightly when members thought that some red coloring looked too much like blood.

The grant required us to work with community partners; I had commitments from both local school districts to work with us on the exhibits. Our first show included artwork from their students. To announce the opening, I created postcards for those students to send to friends and family members. Our library has another space that shows artwork by adults. By coincidence, our first opening occurred simultaneously with one of theirs. Many visitors to that show also visited ours; now I purposely plan coinciding openings.

Our second show featured designs by a local college student who had studied fashion in New York City. Her exhibit included design boards, sketchbooks, and mannequins sporting her creations. That show was followed by a photography exhibit depicting one college student's year in Japan. We just finished a new exhibit called "Graffiti: Art or Vandalism?," which created itself throughout the month as the public was invited to use the paint markers provided.

Each show features an educational component. For instance, the graffiti exhibit included a history of graffiti, several biographies of famous graffiti artists, and a place for the public to vote on whether they felt graffiti is art or vandalism. Books on each exhibit topic are also integrated into the shows. Another show will allow a group of students to share their experiences of traveling to Mexico to learn about global commerce by hanging photos of their trip and presenting a lecture about their experience.

Cultural Excursions

Because the No Child Left Behind Act places schools under pressure to ensure that students pass standardized tests, many schools have little time for out-of-classroom learning. Yet field trips offer students—some who might not otherwise have the opportunity—the chance to visit a museum, see a play, or hear a concert. In February 2006, our library offered the first of what we hope will be many cultural excursions for teens. I took a group of high school students to MassMoCA (http://www.massmoca.org), the Williams College Museum of Art (http://www.wcma.org), and the Clark Museum (http://www.clarkart.edu). The Town Youth Bureau allowed me to use one of their twelve-passenger vans, and the library paid for gas. Participants paid only the entry fees, amounting to a mere four dollars per person since two of the museums were free. For our April excursion, we visited Dia:Beacon (http://www.diabeacon.org) and the Storm King Art Center (http://www.stormking.org).

Thinking Outside the Box

These trips are an example of getting away from the usual library mindset that counts books borrowed and people who come through the door. Having begun my library career in our Children's Room with enormous summer reading program attendance, I saw circulation and minutes of reading as barometers of success. When we began to offer programs for teens, I knew in my heart that what worked for young children would not work for this age group. A lackluster turnout for teen book-related programming during our first summer proved my intuition true.

Teens are busy with jobs, sports, clubs, and schoolwork. In their free time, they just want to hang out with friends. Rather than making books and reading the focus of teen programming, I decided to make the library a place where teens want to be. If they notice the new Guinness Book of World Records or a Stitch 'N Bitch book winking at them from the Teen Room's face-out display, wonderful. If they don't check out a single book, that's okay. When you offer programs on their terms, they will remember that libraries are cool places when they leave their teen years, returning as tax-paying adults.

The Got Art? Gallery and related cultural excursions are ways to offer service to teens on their terms. We also have after-hours teen-only coffeehouse programs (attended by as many as 150 teens), movie nights, sleepovers, and Ultimate Frisbee contests. Our Teen Advisory Group represents the library at the annual American Cancer Society Relay for Life, and works at the Town's KidsFest each year. During after-school hours with tutors from the school system, our Teen Room has become a wonderful, alternative-school space for teens unable to function in regular school.

The figures tell us that our philosophy is working. Program participation for teens is up dramatically, with an additional 400 attending various teen programs in 2005. Circulation for the YA collection also increased significantly: YA fiction was up from 9,612 in 2004 to 14,611 in 2005, and YA nonfiction went from 2,450 to 4,647.

It took a little money, several months, and hard work by a dedicated group of teens to create Got Art? as a permanent public place for young people to display their talent. The process gave me the opportunity to partner with local community resources and to bring more teens into the library. It gave the gallery committee members a chance to learn about curating art shows, handling public relations, and guiding a project from inception to completion. Lots of bang for the buck!

William K. Sanford Town Library, 629 Albany Shaker Road, Loudonville, NY 12211,
(518) 458-9274
http://www.colonie.org/LIBRARY/

Teen Central

Delray Beach Public Library
Delray Beach, Florida

Lisa Kreutter

Description: Through a glass door in the southeast corner of the second floor of Delray Beach Public Library, teens enter their own unique and sunny room, Teen Central. Dominating the center of the 600-square-foot space are two rectangular white pedestal tables containing laptop outlets, placed side by side. Aligned with the tables and facing each other—reminiscent of café booths—are four sofa-like seats upholstered in black with a white geometric dot pattern. Three matching chairs line the wall to the left as one enters; the windows above them look into a hallway. On the wall opposite the doorway, alongside two heavy, black cast-iron end tables, four comfy and curvy wood-framed chairs feature seats and backs made of black seatbelt material. Along the wall to the right of the door, four study carrels with bright yellow and black rolling chairs double as book display areas with laminated booklists such as "If you like the Gossip Girls, you might like . . ."

Study/computer carrels are in temporary use as book display areas.

Catching the eye in the far corner past the carrels are four clocks displaying the time in Tokyo, London, Los Angeles, and Delray Beach. Below the clocks, a bulletin board headlined "What's going on @ teen central?" holds information on everything from authors and higher education to writing contests and other library events. Made of squares, the carpet is brown, tan, and black. Three framed American Library Association (ALA) "Read" posters (Orlando Bloom, Serena Williams, and Enrique Iglesias) adorn the painted taupe walls. Four frames contain artwork from an anime club Halloween contest, and winning pieces from the Teen Tech Week Digital Art Contest in March 2007 have joined them. Like the rest of the library, Teen Central has Wi-Fi access.

Collection: Young adult fiction shelves holding 3,000 titles fill the entire left wall beneath a neon sign that says "plugged in @ teen central." These shelves wrap around the left corner until they meet a magazine rack displaying *Mad, Word Up!, Teen Ink, Shonen Jump, Thrasher, Realms of Fantasy, Cosmo Girl!, Teen People, Vibe*, and *Wizard* as well as a growing zine collection. Smaller shelving units contain books that are required reading at local middle and high schools. A collection of two dozen audiobooks, primarily CDs, is growing.

Sofa-like seating at tables in the center of the floor; seatbelt lounge chairs are against the wall.

81

Plugged-in blue and white neon lights up the YA fiction shelves.

The glass teen central doorway looks out to a hallway, from which an inviting teen space beckons, with palm trees peeking through the sun-filled south windows.

In the four-month period from October 2006 through January 2007, YA fiction circulation was 2,069. Young adult nonfiction, shelved within the adult collection, circulated 1,719 times during the same period. Space constraints prevent the graphic novels, housed in the adult section under the 741.5 call number, from fitting into Teen Central. Videos, DVDs, and music CDs are located on the library's first floor.

Young Adult Population and Community: Located in the southern half of Palm Beach County, the city of Delray Beach—the only Florida city to earn an All-American city designation twice (in 1993 and 2001)—has a population of approximately 64,000 people but maintains a small-town atmosphere. The library's clientele swells in the winter as "snowbirds" migrate south. All year, the library is host to a variety of young professionals, families, seniors, immigrants, and international travelers. The ethnic mix includes Haitian and Latino populations, for whom the library purchases books in Spanish, French, and Creole. Within the county's entire urban area of 1,268,548 residents, the cost of living is above the national average, with 2006 median home prices at $384,700.

The library serves approximately 9,100 students from eight middle and three high schools—two public, including a vocational charter school, and one independent. Toussaint L'Ouverture High School for Arts and Social Justice serves the growing Haitian community.

Hours, Staffing, and Teen Traffic: Teen Central is open during regular library hours: Monday to Wednesday from 9:00 a.m. to 8:00 p.m., Thursday to Saturday from 9:00 a.m. to 5:00 p.m., and Sunday (September through May) from 1:00 to 5:00 p.m. Teen Central is used by 25 to 30 teens on weekdays and evenings after school, and on weekends by 20 to 25 teens. A sign on its door announces that the room is intended for patrons aged 13 to 17. Adults are gently urged to use other parts of the library so that teens can have a space of their own. Only one staff member, a professional Reference and Young Adult Librarian, is assigned to Teen Central.

Planning Process: After seven years of planning, the new 47,000-square-foot Delray Beach Public Library, including Teen Central, opened to the public on Sunday, January 8, 2006. The Grand Opening festivities included a brigade of more than 700 volunteers who symbolically passed books from the old library to the new, a distance of three-tenths of a mile. The $12.5 million-dollar building was funded through a combination of private donors, a $500,000 state

Anime artwork by teens overlooks the magazine

Global timekeeping @ teen central.

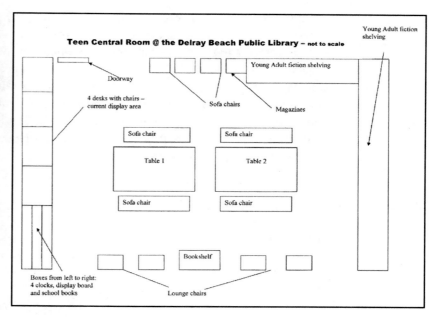

grant, and $4.2 million from the City of Delray Beach. Its airy quarters offer state-of-the-art technology, including wi-fi, a waterfall and bamboo garden, plenty of meeting space, and a café serving coffee, pastries, and sandwiches. The library's Teen Council worked with the previous director to give input on the name of the new teen room as well as its furniture and features. The old 1958 building had no young adult space. Melissa, a member of the Teen Council planning committee, noted that the new room "provides a place just for teens."

Youth Participation and Programming: The Teen Council that helped to design the new space is not currently active. Students can fulfill school requirements for volunteer hours by shelving, shelf-reading, or attending Teen Central's biweekly teen book discussion group that focuses on award-winning young adult novels about topics relevant to teens' lives. A weekly anime/manga interest group is facilitated by a local anime/manga enthusiast. An anime Halloween event with a costume contest attracted more than forty participants. Three programs marked the first Teen Tech Week this March: a 2-D Digital Art contest, a duct tape iPod cover-making class, and a podcasting workshop. Teens' podcasts of their own thirty-second to three-minute book reviews, now produced regularly by the book discussion group, are posted on the library's *MySpace* page at *http://www.myspace.com/delraybeachpl*.

Summer 2007 program plans include yoga, pilates, and tae kwon do or jujitsu classes and regular movie afternoons. Coinciding with the release of *Harry Potter and the Deathly Hollows* on Saturday, July 21, will be a showing of the movie, *Harry Potter and the Goblet of Fire*, along with a trivia contest with bookstore gift certificate prizes.

True Confessions from Young Adult Librarian Lisa Kreutter

This is the YA space of my dreams because . . .

"The space is inviting, open, and bright, with plenty of comfortable and unique furniture, including our lounge chairs constructed from seatbelt material and the neon sign. The room is a cozy, quiet oasis filled with relevant young adult books, magazines, and zines."

I still dream of these improvements:

- More magazines.
- The purchase of Playstation 2 with *Dance Dance Revolution*, *Guitar Hero*, and additional games for regular game nights.

• A solution to one of our recent challenges, the temporary removal of computers because of security concerns. Taking advantage of the fact that Teen Central is not directly staffed during library hours, patrons tore off the wireless antenna component on three of the four computers. While we figure out how to make the computers more secure and tamper-proof, teens are able to bring laptops to use with the library's wi-fi connection, or use library computers in the adult and children's areas. The reintroduction of two Internet computers into Teen Central is in the works, and staff is looking into purchasing computers without an exposed antenna. Having relevant technology available in the room is of utmost importance, both for staff and for this generation of wired teens who don't remember a world without computer technology.

Teen Patron Comments

"It's a space where you can be away from the adults. You can do your homework; you can hang out. It's a multi-purpose room."—Melissa, 18

"I like the chairs."—George, 18

"It's quiet and isolated."—Suhas, 18

"It's full of possibilities."—Rumen, 17

Delray Beach Public Library, 100 West Atlantic Avenue, Delray Beach, Florida 33444, (561) 266-0194
http://www.delraylibrary.org/

Tech Annex

Blue Island Public Library
Blue Island, Illinois

Darren Thompson

Description: Beneath the main level of the Blue Island Public Library, both the future and the past come to life. In the back of the Youth Services department, beside the history museum, far away from the library's hushed voices and serene atmosphere, teens enjoy their own unique and creative room, Tech Annex. In this space, youth are encouraged to see, hear, think, and do all things technological. As one can imagine, it gets noisy when twenty teens are playing *Wii Sports* or making voice-overs for their machinimas, but the quiet studier can move outside the room to the study table area. The 569-square-foot Annex doubles as a lounge/program area and has a staff workstation. Nine computer stations line the perimeter; each has a specific function. If a teen wants to create a Web page, she can go to station C5 (see floorplan on page 87). Another teen might want to edit a video so he would go to station C8. Each station hosts a black, wheeled office chair, and twelve wooden chairs sit around the collaborative worktable in the center of the room. The walls are sprinkled with donated movie posters and artwork, including paintings, charcoal sketches, lithographs, black-and-white photographs, and a mural. The Audio Production station is on the far wall and contains an advanced sound card, sound editing software, a Yamaha keyboard, a mixer, and microphones. The white wall on this side of the Annex serves as the projection area. Immediately outside the exit to the museum is a section used for podcasting. Microphones and headphones are set up in this acoustical area.

Lena's classmates were able to listen to the podcast of a children's book that she created for the library.

The Tech Annex provides resources for teens to work on technological creation, production, development, and animation. The workstations offer Microsoft Office, the library catalog, filtered Internet access, and various databases, including FirstSearch, ArticlesFirst, Eric, WilsonSelectPlus, EbscoHost, and NewsBank. Console games, such as *PlayStation 2* and *Xbox*, are played on the VCR/DVD-combo television that sits next to the magazine rack. The computers have DVD players and can also be used as video stations.

Collection: YA-specific items are located around the entire library. Most materials, including CDs, DVDs, reference, and nonfiction are interfiled with adult material on the first floor. Because the YA and adult collections are purchased from the same account, the library cannot keep track of its YA circulation figures separately. One large shelving unit next to the entrance outside of the Tech Annex holds

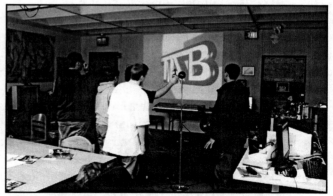

These teens are using radios to add voice-overs to their Halo machinima.

After the Passport to Chile event, youth branch off to their preferred stations.

After teens create a video, it is displayed on the wall for easy dialogue synchronization.

all 1,320 YA fiction titles. Across from it, a four-sided metal rack with wheels contains graphic novels. Teen specific magazines have a separate shelving unit inside the Annex next to the fire exit. Board games and video games are also stored in the Annex. The library uses a Sears Catalog arrangement consisting of Marc records with Dewey numbers and Sears subject headings. The 2007–2008 calendar year will be the first in which YA circulation figures are separated from the adult circulation figures. The books are projected to circulate 11,200 times.

Young Adult Population and Community: Located within the Chicago metropolitan area but keeping its quaint-town feel with only 23,473 citizens, Blue Island is so named because early pioneers thought the ridge of land looked like an island in the prairie from a distance. The city hosts a diverse population, with fairly equal numbers of Hispanic (37.9 percent), white (36.2 percent), and African American (24.1 percent) residents. More than 13 percent are below the poverty line; many have no computer access at home. The library serves 2,740 students from one middle and one high school—of these students, 71 percent are classified as low income. The high school did not meet its Adequate Yearly Progress (AYP) in the 2006–2007 school year.

Hours, Staffing, and Teen Traffic: Blue Island Public Library is open Monday to Thursday from 9:00 a.m. to 9:00 p.m., Friday and Saturday from 9:00 a.m. to 5:00 p.m., and Sunday from 1:00 p.m. to 5:00 p.m. Tech Annex is open special hours in conjunction with the library: Monday to Thursday from 3:45 p.m. to 8:45 p.m., and Saturday and Sunday from 1:00 p.m. to 5:00 p.m. Because the room is out of sight from the staff workstations, it needs to be covered when teens are present. The Annex draws approximately 65 youth daily during afterschool hours and 25 teens on weekends. Adults and children may use the room during special programs or outside of the teen hours, but the 13 to 18 age limit is enforced. In addition to covering IT issues within the library, the IT Department manages the Tech Annex. This staff consists of one full-time professional IT, Technical, and Young Adult Programming Manager; a part-time professional IT Assistant; and two part-time paraprofessional IT Clerks. There is also a full-time professional Youth Services Manager who oversees the YA collection.

Planning Process: The Blue Island Public Library has renovated only once since its construction in 1971—the 2006 addition of a YA space. The planning started in September 2005 when Darren Thompson, Manager of IT, Technology, and YA Programming, wanted to bring a technology center to the library. He was inspired by the Wired for Youth (WFY) Centers in the Austin Public Library, Austin, Texas, and used his background in virtual reality, medical imaging, computer vision, the motion capture industry, and the gaming industry to design and create the Tech Annex. After receiving approval from Library Director Patty Wanninger, they jointly presented the idea to the Library Board. With the Board's okay, Thompson approached the Blue Island Public Library Foundation and the Friends of the Blue Island Public Library for donations, who contributed $3000 and $500, respectively.

Renovations started in December 2005 and took only four months to complete. A fifth month was reserved for selected students to use the resources and provide feedback. Any necessary changes in the software and hardware configurations were then made. New electrical work, an Ethernet drop, and a video patch panel were installed; the room was painted; a projector was mounted; and new carpet and furniture were added. To allow for maximum flexibility in content creation, ten computers were built with video and audio production, graphic arts, 3D modeling and animation,

Web development, and game design capabilities. To keep costs low, computers were built in-house and Thompson secured donations and loans for the artwork. On April 6, 2006, the mayor of Blue Island officially opened the room to the public with a ribbon-cutting ceremony. The library's teens created a 3D animation opening video to demonstrate the potential uses of the Annex's resources.

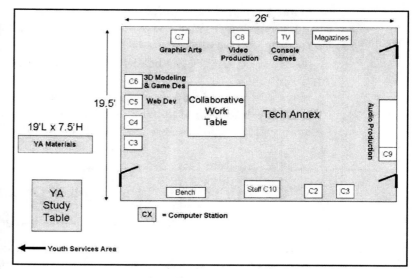

Youth Participation and Programming: The library's Teen Advisory Board (TAB) meets monthly to give a voice to teen patrons and also to serve as volunteer coordinators and staff members for the Tech Annex in the following areas: Video Production, Audio Production, Graphic Arts, 3D Modeling and Animation, Web Development, and Interior Design. These teens work on individual tasks and projects for the library and the community. For example, they created a mural in the Annex and helped with the digitization of the museum to make it accessible from the Web. An anime interest group, facilitated by a local volunteer, meets monthly. Some teens participate in the Reading Buddies program that gives young children a head start in reading by having the teens read to them. Other activities include OpenMic Night and Passport To . . ., which involves traveling to a different country each month using *Google Earth*, listening to the country's music using *Winamp*, and sampling some of the country's recipes. In the past, they have "visited" places such as Turkey, Chile, and Japan, and in January 2008, the teens journeyed to India. *Youth's Corner* (*http://www.blueislandlibrary.org/library/5d.htm*) is the teen page on the library's Web site where youth can listen to podcasts and watch videos of their own recordings; find links to school resources, sports and fitness Web sites, and books of interest; and read reviews of the latest YA books.

True Confessions from IT, Technical, and YA Programming Manager Darren Thompson

This is the YA space of my dreams because . . .

"It stimulates creativity and higher-level thinking skills, has great artwork, and it is very functional and flexible. [Creating] the Tech Annex has been a great experience, and it's been both fun and exciting to watch the teens grow and watch them learn while they're having fun."

I still dream of these improvements:

"A larger space, a designated audio recording studio, a designated video production studio with blue screen capabilities, [different] furniture, video conferencing, virtual reality, and more advanced software and hardware."

Teen Patron Comments

What do you think about the Tech Annex? "The Tech Annex's friendly environment is what attracted me to it in the first place. Not only is it fun and full of many diverse people, but it also gives great opportunities to those who wish to work in the video game industry and the movie industry. You learn and you grow here, and I like how everyone is accepted."—Tiffany Cole, 15

What have you been doing in the Tech Annex? "I have been . . . making a machinima using *Halo* and two *Xboxes*. A machinima is video produced from the recording of game play. Dialogue and sound effects are added after the video has been produced. At times it can be difficult to make."—Brian Moreno, age 15

Have you learned any new skills? If so, what? "I've learned how to manage time to meet a deadline and to think on a more professional level in order to improve the quality of my work."—Brit L. Castañeda, age 17

Darren's Tips for Designing and Operating a Similar Space.

- Involve the teens in the design process and allow them to add artwork and content to their space.

- Hire the right staff to supervise the space. Look for someone who is mature, is not intimidated by and likes to work with teens, is a mentor and not their "best friend," is not afraid of technology and has a good technical skill-set, is creative and self-motivated, can tolerate higher noise levels, and is a team player.

- Try to design and locate the space so that the louder noise levels are not an issue to the rest of the library. Work closely with local schools so that when school resources are unavailable, students can work on their projects at your library. For students not enrolled in music, art, or production classes, the library becomes the outlet in which teens can learn and use those resources.

- Record events at the local schools and post the content on the library's Web site for the entire community to enjoy.

- Have the teens work on community projects, such as documenting the history of the library's city.

- Ensure that the teens feel they have ownership of the space.

Blue Island Public Library, 2433 York Street, Blue Island, IL 60406, (708) 388-1078
http://www.blueislandlibrary.org/

Young Adult Center in the Port Jefferson Library

Port Jefferson Free Library
Port Jefferson , New York

Erin Schaarschmidt

Description: The 583-square-foot Young Adult Center is located directly across the street from the main library in a quaint, old, green-and-white building that was once a bookstore. The Friends of Port Jefferson Free Library occupy the front room of the building, and the Young Adult Center is located in the back room. The teen area has its own door to separate it from the Friends area, although the door is usually kept open because the Teen Services Librarians' desks are in the front room. The small space between the front and back rooms serves as the teen art gallery, complete with a café-style table and high stools. Painted crimson and displaying artwork mounted by strings, the gallery transitions a pretty, reception-looking area into a cozy, creative hangout for teens . A multicolored Young Adult Center sign is painted above the entrance to the teen area. Bright, primary-colored couches and chairs and vibrantly painted fluorescent lights welcome teens to this innovative space, while maple wood floors and beige ceilings and walls give the room a touch of class. On the far wall, the sun shines through three large panel windows and entices readers to relax on the padded window seats equipped with storage space. Books encompass the walls on nine-foot shelving units, which are illuminated by curvy track lighting. The two couches and three comfy chairs are arranged around a small coffee table for group study. There are four black, wooden tables with wheels around the room so the teens can conveniently join them together to form one large table or move them around freely. Three matching chairs accompany the tables. Even the bathroom is visionary with a funky décor and inspirational and funny quotes written on the walls.

A large, plasma television hangs over the doorway; a Nintendo Wii, DVDs, and Playstation 2 are nearby

Comfortable window seats and ample lighting make this relaxing area the perfect place to read.

The young adult center is an oasis of books and color— both of which brighten the lives of Port Jefferson teens every day.

89

Only one door serves as the entrance and exit to the teen area.

The teen librarian's desk sits in the front room but is still very accessible to the teens because the door is always open.

for teens' use. Two areas of the front wall are covered with black chalkboard paint on which the teens can express themselves. Behind the librarian's desk are ten accessible laptops (seven PCs and three MacBooks), complete with an online catalog, databases, word processing, and unfiltered Internet access. The newest additions to the area are its mascots, Napoleon and Pedro, who reside in the Guinea Pig Hilton at the front of the room. Young adults love that their area was designed so that they don't have to be quiet. If students want a quieter space, there is a study area in the main library that is available for their use.

Collection: The walls around the Young Adult Center are home to 3,447 young adult titles, including fiction, picture books, and adult books for teens. There is a shelf of new nonfiction in the Young Adult Center with titles suitable for recreational reading. All other YA nonfiction is located in the main library and considered part of the adult collection; however, the YA librarian orders these books. If a teen is interested in a nonfiction title, the YA librarian will accompany the teen to the main library to locate the book. The teen titles are arranged in alphabetical order, although the main library uses the Dewey system. September 2007 YA circulation was 4,485, but this figure included audiovisuals that may go out to adult patrons. The teen center subscribes to a dozen magazines and has a vastly expanding media collection of 100 CD titles, 34 audiobooks, 65 DVDs, and 17 in-house video games for the two gaming consoles. There are also 20 board games dispersed on shelving units around the TV, including multiple versions of everybody's favorite interactive DVD game, *Scene It?*

Young Adult Population and Community: A historic ship-building village, Port Jefferson is a seaport situated near the heart of Long Island's north shore. Only 56 miles from New York City, this town is popular among day-trip tourists, but there is also a small-town feel to the 3.05 square-mile area where historic buildings house specialty shops and restaurants. The library serves 13,515 patrons, some of whom are contract patrons from the surrounding areas of Mount Sinai, Miller Place, and Sound Beach. The rural village boasts a very high-income level with the surrounding areas tapering off to a more modest middle-income level, making $50,046 the median income of library patrons. There are 1,584 teens in Port Jefferson; the library serves 921 of these teens from three middle and three high schools.

Hours, Staffing, and Teen Traffic: Port Jefferson Free Library is open Monday, Wednesday, Thursday, and Friday from 9:30 a.m. to 9:00 p.m., Tuesday from 10:00 a.m. to 9:00 p.m., Saturday from 9:30 a.m. to 5:00 p.m., and Sunday from 1:00 p.m. to 5:00 p.m. During the summer months, the library closes at 5:00 p.m. on Fridays and is closed on Sundays. Port Jeff. Library @goodtimes is open special hours in conjunction with the library: Monday to Friday from 10:00 a.m. to 8:00 p.m., Saturday from 10:00 a.m. to 4:00 p.m., and Sunday from 1:00 p.m. to 4:30 p.m. Opening a half hour later gives the YA librarian a chance to process books in the morning, and closing an hour earlier gives the cleaning crew time to tidy up the building before heading over to the main library. Between 20 and 35 teens use the Young Adult Center daily; on weekends, the figure grows to 45 teen users. Although everyone is welcome in the front part of the building, the 13 to 18 age limit is enforced in the teen area. The YA area staffs one full-time librarian, two part-time librarians, one substitute on-call librarian, and three circulations clerks.

Planning Process: In October 2006, the library director approached YA librarian Erin Schaarschmidt with the idea of renting the first floor of the building across the street from the library. The plan was to rent the retail space to serve two purposes: as the headquarters for Friends of Port Jefferson Free Library and as the home to YA services, equipped with the PJFL young adult collection and a hangout space for teens. Schaarschmidt excited that the Board of Trustees felt that the teens needed their own space and was eager to begin the renovation. Her excitement dwindled when she entered the front door of the former bookstore they would be taking over. The building was a disaster.

The largest obstacle was getting the Village of Port Jefferson to approve the work that would need to be done to the building. Once this endorsement was obtained, the head of Building Operations and his crew had to tear down the walls and the front door and figure out a way to make the area handicap accessible. The library employed Lightly Salted Woodworks to do the carpentry, including build the Librarian's desk and create shelving for the walls. An electrician installed more outlets and lighting. This rebuilding process occurred between May 2007 and July 2007.

During the annual budget vote, patrons selected the name of the new building. Goodtimes was the name of the used bookstore that previously occupied the space. In July 2007, only nine months from the idea's conception, renovations were complete and Port Jeff. Library @goodtimes was almost ready for its doors to open. In the next month, the staff worked on moving the YA books to the new facility and waited patiently for the air conditioning to be turned on in the 90-degree heat and high humidity. August 18, 2007, marked opening day and plenty of good times to come.

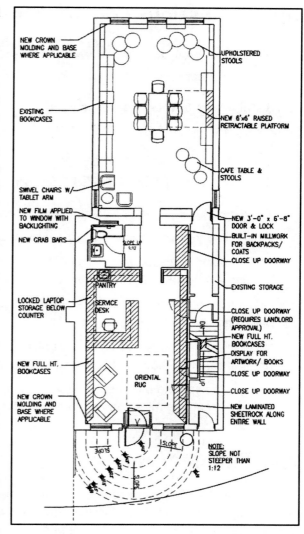

Youth Participation and Programming: The library's eight-member teen advisory council, called TAG, met every month to discuss the project of creating this space. The group no longer meets, but there are plans to continue with a TAG in the future. The teen volunteer program thrives because there are many tasks for which teens can receive community service hours. These opportunities include assisting the children's librarian and participating in Tales 4 Tots, a program in which teens read to youngsters.

Discussion groups, summer reading programs, and lock-ins are ongoing programs at the YA center that teens can read about in the library's teen activities brochure created by Schaarschmidt and library clerk Nicole Greenhalgh. The brochure is posted online every two months and can be accessed at *http://pjfl.suffolk. lib.ny.us/docs/yabroc.pdf*; the programs are also listed on the YAC's *MySpace* site (*myspace.com/pjya*). The brochure highlights activities for young adults age thirteen and up; sometimes there are as many as four programs per week. Also in the brochure are occasional programs such as Open Mic Night every last Friday of the month and Literary Magazine meetings every Wednesday. Any teen with a PJFL library card can attend Lit. Mag. meetings and submit work. Supervised by Librarian Trainee Lauren Bernat, the Lit. Mag. is composed of teens' artwork, photos, poems, short stories, and other written word. A fused glass class was held in late April in which teens learned to make glass pendants using dichroic and other types of glass. The class is held frequently because fused glass is one of Schaarschmidt's hobbies and she's a great teacher. The teens love it!

True Confessions from YA Librarian Erin Schaarschmidt

This is the YA space of my dreams because . . .

"The teens really enjoy it. They love that it is like a living room."

I still dream of these improvements:

"An overhead projector for movies [and] additional staffing would improve the [teen space]."

ERIN'S TIPS FOR OPERATING A SEPARATE YA BUILDING

- Try to have enough staff so that there are at least two people scheduled to work, even during the day.

- Have a security plan in place. Walkie-talkies located behind the desk can bring help from the main building.

- Weekly communication with the other building is important to keep staff up to date on what is happening in my building and to keep myself current on the main building's policies/procedure changes.

- Gchat (part of Gmail) is a lifesaver. I keep it open when I am working and can type instant messages to other departments in the main building.

- Make sure that the seclusion doesn't alienate the staff. My librarians collaborate with other departments on programs so that they don't feel like they are alone.

- Being in a separate building has HUGE advantages. The teens don't have to be quiet, they have a space of their own, and the rules can be more lenient, e.g. allowed to use cell phones, eat, and drink.

Teen Patron Comments

"A library just for teens, that's what we need! We designed a Web site survey so students could make suggestions on what it should look like and what book collections and activities or events they wanted there."—Katharina Ross, 9th grade

"I'm glad it turned out to be what we (the PJYA Board) planned!" —Christa Ghosio, 10th grade

---

Port Jefferson Free Library, 100 Thompson Street, Port Jefferson, NY 11777, (631) 473-0022
http://portjefflibrary.org/

A Carnegie Library for Twenty-First Century Teens

Franklin Library, Hennepin County Public Libraries
Minneapolis, Minnesota

Angela Fiero and Johannah Genett

How does a tiny Carnegie library in a community over-flowing with library customers meet the needs of energetic and creative teen users? Staff at Franklin Library, part of the Hennepin County Library system in Minneapolis, Minnesota, rose to the challenge, and after months of brainstorming and innovative teamwork, a new Teen Center opened in April 2008. We wish to pass on a few tips to other libraries hoping to do the same.

Background

Franklin Library is located in the heart of Minneapolis's Phillips neighborhood. This colorful neighborhood is composed of a variety of cultures, including Native Americans; African Americans; recent East African, West African, and Latino immigrants; as well as residents with Western European roots. Although still an economically challenged neighborhood, recent business and community developments have greatly improved the morale and safety of the area.

Our youth program specialist gathers teens to brainstorm ways to make playing video games fair. Teens are involved in the writing of policies for the teen center.

The library itself was built in 1914 and renovated in 2005. This renovation provided some much-needed repairs, beautified the building, and allowed us to expand the children's section. After our grand reopening, the library was brimming with customers, especially teenagers who appreciated our homework help program, extensive teen collection, and friendly gathering places. The teen section simply wasn't big enough to house all of the teens visiting our library. Because of the library's commitment to providing rich out-of-school programming opportunities for youth, we knew we had to do something. After hearing input from more than one hundred teens and youth-serving organization representatives during a library-sponsored, youth listening session, we decided it was time to secure funding to create a Teen Center.

We were unable to locate our Teen Center on the main floor of the library, given the small size of our historic

Teens use the living room area for relaxing, browsing magazines, hosting book clubs, and working on writing projects.

building. Instead we decided to turn our community meeting room into the Teen Center by redesigning and adding teen elements. The room also serves as a multipurpose space to successfully meet our diverse programming needs, but only during times when the teens are not using their space (i.e. when they are in school). The teens have a real sense of ownership and do not mind sharing their space during non-designated open hours. They are aware of the library's advocacy on their behalf for a dedicated teen center and of our staff's commitment to provide a teen-friendly environment.

The Space

Our 835-square-foot Teen Center is located below the main library in the southeast corner of the garden level. It has four

The southeast corner of the sunny teen room is home to a study table and adjacent to a wall of computers.

main areas: the living room area, the gaming area, the computer bank, and the table area. The twenty feet of shelving by the fireplace houses materials like board games, uncataloged paperbacks, magazines ordered specifically for the Teen Center, and our book club books. Our cataloged teen collection—which includes magazines, fiction, nonfiction, and graphic novels in English and Spanish, as well as audiobooks on both CD and cassette—is found upstairs with the rest of the library's collections.

Our primary Teen Center colors—maroon, mustard, and sage—were chosen to match the rest of our classic library, but bright greens and reds were added to make the room "pop." Marker and magnetic boards decorate the walls, and unique lighting fixtures such as floor lamps and bubbly tabletop lights make the room shine. Black leather couches, comfy maroon and sage chairs, bright red computer chairs, yellow novelty chairs, and black and orange stools create a variety of seating options. Teens can use our coffee and end tables, half-moon granite colored tables, and movable folding tables for a multitude of activities.

Five computer stations are in high demand for homework needs and leisure surfing. Although we have headphones available, we also allow teens to play music for the benefit of everyone as long as our Teen Center Respect Policy is observed. From our computers, teens can access the Internet and our online catalog and databases. Each computer has CD-Rom, Microsoft Word, PowerPoint, Excel, and Access capabilities. We have three digital cameras available for checkout and Microsoft Photo Editor on the computers. Electronic gaming options include Nintendo Wii and Play Station 2.

Teens love playing both board games and video games during O.P.E.N. time.

How We Started

Plans for the renovation started in the fall of 2007. The library staff received guidance and support from our External Relations and Partnerships and Capital Projects departments, and also consulted with our teen customers—a critically important part of the process. We met nine teens aged twelve to fifteen from three different schools in the area. We discussed furnishings, activities, and policies for the teen space. This discussion helped guide our choices and ideas for the Teen Center. We also polled the teens for their preferences constantly throughout the process to ensure a positive outcome.

We ran into a number of setbacks when choosing our furniture. At the time, we were limited to a select number of companies from which to order. Our first furniture selection was discontinued before we could even order it. Our sofa order was lost. The planning of the Teen Center was complicated by the fact that our city library system (Minneapolis Public Library) merged with the Hennepin County Library system in January 2008. From this experience, we learned to monitor progress on all facets of development and completion of the project

The Teen Center celebrated its grand opening on April 29, 2008. Sambusas, fresh veggies, and bottled water were served. Sound Art performance duo Beatrix* JAR helped the teens create and play musical instruments made from recycled battery-powered toys.

The Stats

Our Teen Center is open Tuesday and Thursday from 3:30 p.m. to 8 p.m.; Wednesday and Friday from 3:30 p.m. to 6 p.m.; and Saturday from 11 p.m. to 5 p.m., with expanded summer hours. The Teen Center is open fewer hours than the library to reflect the visiting patterns of our teens and so that the room can serve as a gathering space for our community. When the Teen Center is open, only young adults are allowed to access the space.

The number of teens using the Teen Center has skyrocketed since our grand opening from 170 attendees during our first six weeks to more than 400 in the last three weeks of August! Teens using the center are twelve to eighteen years old, or sixth grade and higher; some programming is geared to specific age groups.

"The Franklin Teen Center is a great example of what can be accomplished when an innovative library staff is willing to explore new options to meet a customer service need," said Lois Thompson, Hennepin County Library Interim Director. "The result is a win-win for the library and our teen customers."

The Center is grant funded by the Library Foundation of Hennepin County, now united with the Friends of the Minneapolis Public Library. Additional funding from the City of Minneapolis Youth Coordinating Board permitted extended hours during the summer of 2008 and the purchasing of additional equipment and materials.

Special events are booked by the youth program specialist, the Youth Services Librarian, and the Senior Librarian. When there are no special events, our youth program specialist, a paraprofessional position, supervises the use of the space. During these O.P.E.N (Options for Play and Enrichment Now) times, teens may use gaming equipment, play board or card games, use the computers, read magazines and books, quietly study, or converse.

Youth Participation and Programming

Our Teen Center supports varied special events and ongoing program opportunities, including a Teen Advisory Group, a Teen Leadership Camp, workshops on cartooning, financial literacy, college and careers, literary and visual arts, and a variety of clubs, including book discussion, design, writing, fundraising, and service clubs. In summer 2008, our first two teen assistants mentored youth and helped monitor our center's activities, gaining valuable leadership experience through this internship opportunity. Teen Center participation levels continue to grow as word spreads of our friendly and creative space for youth at Franklin Library.

Teen Center's Impact on the Rest of the Library

As mentioned, our library might be small, but it is filled with activity. We are home to three other major programs: the Phillips Technology Center, the Franklin Learning Center, and Homework Hub. The latter two programs were directly affected by the creation of our Teen Center.

The Franklin Learning Center provides one-on-one tutoring to adult customers in citizenship and GED testing, reading, writing, and math. The center was gracious enough to change its operating hours to accommodate moving our Homework Hub into its space during afterschool hours so that we could use the Homework Hub's previous location for our Teen Center. This move required major staff scheduling changes as well as new opening procedures. The Learning Center now opens earlier than the library with a volunteer monitoring student access to the facility.

Homework Hub is one of our most successful programs here at Franklin. In the 2006–2007 school year, we had 4,336 homework help transactions. The Teen Center greatly complements our Homework Hub program because students who have finished their homework are able to move to our Teen Center, rather than linger and possibly distract others in the Hub space.

True Confessions of the Librarians

This is our dream YA space because it allows for flexibility. The room can still be used to host our preschool storytimes, adult book clubs, and reservations by the public. It is also a closed space, allowing the teens to get a little rowdy without disturbing other customers. Whether they are choosing programming, working as assistants, or simply hanging out, our teen customers have evolved into engaged members of our library by using and contributing to our Teen Center.

Teen Patron Comments

"What is the best part of the Franklin Teen Center? You get a flow of enthusiastic love from the people here at the Franklin Teen Center. Who can hate that? Cheers and laughter everywhere. Who can hate that? Smiles [that] shine as bright as the lights. Who can hate that? And the best part is the atmosphere. Who can hate that?"—Ifrah, tenth grade

"I think the teen center is a safe . . . cool place where teens can hang out and have fun. It is a great place for me to hang out. There is no racism of any kind."—Mohamed, eighth grade

Franklin Library, Hennepin County Library, 1314 E. Franklin Ave., Minneapolis, MN 55404
(612) 543-6925,
http://www.hclib.org/AgenciesAction.cfm?agency=Fr

Teen Department

Hampton Bays Public Library
Hampton Bays, New York

Theresa Owens

Description: The Hampton Bays Public Library is located just one-quarter mile from the local middle school and one mile from the high school. This prime location means the teen department located on the lower level of the library is a very busy place after school every day.

The department is eighteen hundred square feet, arranged in two adjacent rectangles. A stairwell and an elevator provide ADA-compliant access to the teen area. Collections are in both rooms and one room has a quiet study room and a teen services office for storage and for employees to work during off-desk time. The two rooms connect through a maze of doors into a large community room for programs, a lounge with a kitchen (which makes program prep and clean up easier), and restrooms dedicated to the teen services room. The color scheme is taupe and ivory and the walls are decorated with many decorations, including teen art work, art work created by the pages, photos of programs and more, depending on the season. There are no windows, since the space is located below ground.

Ten or more signs with the teen services logo market the teen department throughout the library. The display area is in the downstairs lobby, located between the teen department and the stairwell. Each month current program fliers are posted.

The teen department has seven tables, thirty-five chairs, and metal single- and double-faced shelving. There are nine computer work stations, including

Room 2 is where most of the books are located. The poles were painted by page Brittany Youmans.

Polka dots in bright colors liven up the area above the fiction collection.

The popular graphic novel collection has over one thousand volumes.

Magazines are displayed on the left and new books (less than two months old) on the right.

The fantasy mural was painted by librarian Thomas Casper.

an online catalog, links to databases, links to popular sites, word processing capabilities, and filtered Internet access using a regional filter service, BASCOM, to comply with Children's Internet Protection Act. A television is provided for teens to play Wii, Xbox, and *DJ Hero.*

Collection: In teen reference, there are eighty-four items including a variety of encyclopedias, dictionaries, atlases, and readers advisory books. Over eleven hundred nonfiction titles include science books about forensics, entertainment books, baking books, art books, and poetry. In the college/careers section, there are SAT, ACT, GRE, GED, AP, and PSAT books, and more. Most of the college and career books include a CD Rom so students can take practice tests. We have about one hundred seventy-five biographies that cover a wide variety of subjects. About one thousand graphic novels and over fifty manga series make our collection known as one of the best in Suffolk County.

The YA fiction collection has over twenty seven hundred titles, and all of the books have genre labels on the spine, which helps teens select titles and helps make readers advisory easier for the librarians. The collection has a few picture books for teens, with plans to add more. The teen department has PC games, plus over one hundred video games for circulation for Wii, Xbox 360, Nintendo DS, Playstation 2, and Playstation 3. The games circulate for five days. We have over forty popular audio book titles, over one hundred videos, over one hundred DVDs rated G, PG, or PG-13. DVDs circulate for three days. The music CD collection includes rock, rap, pop, R&B, 70s, 80s, boxed sets, and a Spanish CD collection. The teens' tastes in music vary tremendously, some like Queen and Pink Floyd, while others love Eminem and Notorious BIG. All of our CDs are edited, which parents appreciate.

Recreational books, like *Guinness Book of World Records* and *A Really Short Book of Nearly Everything* are usually placed on tables so teens can look through them after school while hanging with friends. We also place books directly related to computers and video games on the computer towers.

The teen department offers sixteen different magazines including *Alternative Press, Filter, Gamepro, J-14, Latina, Lucky, Nintendo Power, Seventeen, Skateboarding, Spin, Sporting News, Surf, Teen Vogue, Thrasher, Upfront,* and *Wizard.*

Our teens love board games. We own about sixty games including Apples to Apples, Boggle, Chess, Scrabble, Stratego, The Twilight Game, Uno, and many more. In 2008, the library circulated 6,634 items in the teen department and in 2009 that number increased by 33 percent to 8,872 items.

Young Adult Population and Community: According to the **2000 Census**, the total population of Hampton Bays is 12,802. Of the total, 12.3 percent are African American, 75 percent are Caucasian, and 12.3 percent are Hispanic. The teen population is comprised of 444 students in grades six through eight, and 563 students in grades nine through twelve. The local schools report that 39 percent of the teens are Hispanic/Latino, 17.9 percent speak a language other than English at home, 9.2 percent of families are below poverty level, and 12.4 percent of individuals are below poverty level.

Hours, Staffing, and Teen Traffic: The teen space is open Monday through Thursday, 2:30 p.m. to 9 p.m. during the school year, and 10 a.m. to 9 p.m. during the summer and school vacations. Friday hours are 2:30 p.m. to 7 p.m. during the school year and 10 a.m. to 7 p.m. in the summer. Saturday hours are 10 a.m. to 5 p.m. year-round and Sunday hours are 1 p.m. to 5 p.m. year-round.

Since we have such a huge area dedicated to teens, we usually get forty to fifty teens, ages ten to seventeen, after school each day. They do homework, log onto the computers, and attend programs. On the weekends, fifteen to twenty teens regularly occupy the space. Two full-time and two part-time teen services librarians are on staff.

Planning Process: The Hampton Bays Public Library opened in 1963 and was last renovated in December of 2002. The planning process for the teen department started in the summer of 2005. It took approximately one year for fundraising, design, construction, processing, and implementation. The library director, Mike Firestone, the YA staff, and the board of directors planned the space. Fundraising secured about $40,000 between local donations and private and state grants. The new teen department opened on September 5, 2006. The grand opening festivities included a ribbon-cutting ceremony, an open house tour, a birthday cake that was cut by local teens, and some speeches by local supporters of the project.

Youth Participation and Programming: The Hampton Bays Library teen department works with the community to provide opportunities for teens to contribute. Each month, the teens make something special for the animals at the Southampton Animal Shelter: bedazzling dog collars, decorated bowls, and no-sew blankets. The library has drives three times a year to collect treats, food, and blankets for the animals. Teens love to help out, and they also get some of their fines forgiven for donating. In the summer, we built and painted a goat house for the Double D Ranch in Manorville, NY. This ranch rescues farm animals that have been neglected and or abused. We will be taking a trip there so the teens can see the completed work the have done for the animals.

We partner with Debra Layman of the Hampton Bays United Artists Theater four to five times per year. When an exciting new movie comes out, teens can enter related writing contests at the library. Recently, we held The Lightning Thief Contest: Create Your Own Fantasy Story about Long Island, NY. The teens had to write a short story about where they live—Long Island. The top three winners received a pair of movie tickets to the *Lightning Thief* premiere, a behind-the-scenes tour of the movie theater, tickets to a future movie, and a certificate of appreciation.

When teens were creating dog collars for the Southampton Animal Shelter dogs, shelter dog Lucky stopped by for the program.

Sixty teens attended the teen party celebrating our 50th anniversary to watch an illusionist perform tricks, enjoy a DJ, and eat pizza.

We often utilize the talents of other teen librarians who work at libraries on Long Island. Andrew Bollerman, a talented artist and YA librarian who works at Sachem Public Library, facilitates the Artist Café program twice a month. The program varies in materials and genre, and encompasses the fine arts, crafts, and mixed media. Tom Casper, of the Mastics-Moriches Library, runs the Camera Club twice a month. A prize is given for the Photo of the Month, which is chosen by the group of teens who attend.

Full time Teen Librarian Jacqueline Dunn is a creative jewelry designer. Once a month she facilitates Jackie's Jewelry Club in which teens can learn the basics of jewelry design as well as make a variety of projects. Some recent projects include bangle bracelets with memory wire, beaded key chains, and polymer clay beads which the teens sculpted themselves.

We have extremely talented pages on hand—Brittany Youmans and Lucy Tzitzimititla—who create displays for the department each month. They created a display highlighting our 50th anniversary with pictures of the 50th Anniversary Party (sixty teens attended), Earth Day Project, Pokemon Club, Artist Café, and more. Brittany painted all of the poles in the department with dragons, unicorns, and anime characters. Brittany will be attending an art school in New York City next year. In September, we were lucky enough to have a double author visit: Erik P. Kraft, author of *Miracle Wimp*, and Charles R. Smith, author of *Chameleon* and 2010 winner of the Coretta Scott King Award for Illustration. In December, teen art and photography will be on display for everyone to see.

The Teen Advisory Group (TAG) meets once a month and discusses current and future programs. In a past TAG meeting, the teens decided that they wanted live animals at the library so we hired the Quogue Wildlife Refuge to come to the library. They brought owls, falcons, chinchillas, reptiles, and more. This is now an ongoing program throughout the year.

High school students volunteer and receive community service credit by helping out at programs, helping with the St. Patrick's Day float for a parade, or working in the bookstore on Saturdays. Teens also review CDs, DVDs, and books for the library newsletter.

Share a Book, Share a Bite, a book discussion group, meets a few times a year. The teens discuss their favorite books while eating pizza and socializing. It is a way for the teens to find out about new and exciting books while sharing ideas with each other.

Each year we participate in the New York Summer Reading Program. Teens fill out a reading log, which is kept in the teen department. Teens add titles to their logs after they complete a book. For every book and every program they attend, they receive a raffle ticket. The teens attend a party at the end of the summer program where they put their raffle tickets in a box for whichever prize they would like to win. Prizes may include gift cards, tickets to a local amusement park, movie tickets, and books. Local companies are asked to sponsor the program.

Gaming programs are offered three to four times a month. Since we own the *Beatles Rock Band*, the Nintendo Wii, Xbox 360, *DJ Hero*, and *Guitar Hero*, we utilize all of the systems on a weekly basis. Since they were all purchased in 2008 and 2009, it costs nothing to run these fun programs this year.

The Hampton Bays Library Web site is located at *http://hbay.suffolk.lib.ny.us,* which is linked to the Teen Blog at *http://hbayya.blogspot.com.* Online homework help and tutoring is provided by Suffolk Homework Help at *http://www.suffolkhomeworkhelp.org.* Suffolk Homework Help is available seven days a week from 2 p.m. to 11 p.m. A live tutor answers questions for students in grades K to 12. We have a link to the Hampton Bays School on our blog in case students want to log on. A DVD was created for this Web site and is featured on Youtube at *http://www.youtube.com/ watch?v=qd92lKx18ls.*

Each month we create a slideshow of new books, DVDs, CDs, video games, and board games for the blog. We also promote all monthly programs to publicize the date and time of each event. We have links to the popular music group Fall Out Boy, The Hampton Bays Schools, Southampton Animal Shelter, **Runescape, YouTube,** and more. Anytime we have a contest, such as the Funniest Pet Photo, we add it to the blog. Our teens love to win contests. When a teen logs on to the computer, he or she is automatically directed to our blog. The teens love to see what is new in teen services.

True Confessions from the Head of Teen Services Theresa Owens

This is the YA space of my dreams because . . .

"We are extremely lucky to have the entire lower level dedicated just to the teens."

I still dream of these improvements:

"We would love more computers. Since we normally have forty to fifty teens after school and only nine computers, there is always a long waiting list. We would also love to provide our teens with a different program every day if we could! However, this would require an unlimited budget. We try to provide the best programs with the money that we do have. We would also love to provide snacks to teens after school, since many don't eat until late at night."

Teen Patron Comments

"The teen department wasn't always this much fun. We used to have a very small space upstairs, but now we have a large space that is all our own!" —Savannah Medina, 13

"I love all of the programs, CDs, DVDs and video games, especially the Wii games."—Robert Scott, 11

"The selection of books, games, and other entertainment is perfect and extensive. The library truly has become a sanctuary for teens all around Hampton Bays . . . including me!"—Annika Kennedy, 12

Hampton Bays Public Library, 52 Ponquogue Ave., Hampton Bays, NY 11946, (631) 728-6241
http://hbay.suffolk.lib.ny.us/

All statistics were compiled by Hampton Bays Public Library Reference Librarian Wendy Bennett.

Part 3

Large Teen Spaces More Than 1001 Square Feet

A Place of Our Own

Garfield Park Branch, Santa Cruz Public Libraries
Santa Cruz, California

Sandi Imperio

Description: This small 1915 stucco Carnegie library was redesigned eighty years later as a young adult branch that includes the whole building. Only 1,450 square feet, the rectangular floor area is divided into smaller spaces. Its décor is forest green with off-white walls to show off the green-tiled fireplace, allowing signs and artwork to be easily seen. Walls are earthquake-reinforced.

Furniture: One round table and one conference table with 9 chairs and 5 extra folding chairs share space with 840 running feet of free-standing shelves. The is one PAC computer and an electronic homework center containing four ADA/ergonomic computer station with PCs, all with headphones, educational databases and CD-ROMs, word processing, computer games, and unfiltered Internet access with personal user accounts.

Collection: Approximately 40,000 volumes are organized in Dewey classifications with genre sections for fiction, science fiction, and Web design. The collection includes hardcover and paperback YA and adult fiction, picture books for teens, nonfiction, comics, audio books, videos, and magazines. Recreational, school-related, college/career, and reference materials are provided.

Young Adult Population: The Santa Cruz Westside contains three thousand youth aged ten to sixteen, with about two-thirds in junior high and one-third in high school. Most of their families are wage-earners without computers at home. Two elementary schools, three junior highs, and two high schools serve the area with a mix of traditional, alternative, and accelerated programs. The library attracts primarily junior high students, in after-school numbers from five upward; in such a small space, a group of fifteen is a crowd that spreads out by sitting on the floor. In the first two years after the library was transformed, the number of YA patrons tripled. About two-thirds of branch users are youth; the rest are adults who also enjoy the computers. In a 1997 user survey, an adult commented, "It's fun to be around the kids who come here," reflecting a generally cordial relationship between the two groups. However, only the staff's determined youth advocacy keeps some adults from undermining the branch mission to youth.

Hours of Operation: Monday/Friday 1 p.m. to 6 p.m.; Wednesday 1 p.m. to 8 p.m.; Saturday 1 p.m. to 5 p.m., for a total of thirty-three hours a week.

Staffing: One full-time Branch Manager/Senior Library Assistant; one full-time and one half-time clerk; two pages from school/work programs.

Youth Participation: Ever since A Place of Our Own was merely a dream, the YP philosophy prevailed: "involving the young people themselves is the key to providing effective services to young adults." After helping with the heavy work of painting and renovating the branch—and choosing the colors and décor—volunteer Young Friends aged thirteen to fifteen still remain displays, design bulletins boards, and do routine clerical jobs. "Fueled by pizza," a Teen Advisory Committee (the TAC) of about ten members aged ten to fourteen meets once a month to recommend materials and subjects that need expansion in the collection, advise staff on branch problems and regulations, and plan a monthly Teen Movie Night. The TAC also launched and continues to produce an electronic newsletter available on the library's Web site.

Planning Process: Open only fourteen hours a week in 1993, the Garfield Park Branch rearranged those limited hours to serve the neighborhood's neediest group, teenagers, after school and Saturdays. A 1995 user survey identified technology and longer hours as major desires. A Library Services and Construction Act (LSCA) Title I grant was obtained for the computers, while local funds covered renovation, rewiring, and increased staff for more open hours.

After the grant commenced in September 1995, the branch closed for about six weeks of renovation and installation of electric homework centers. The name A Place of Our Own was suggested by library staff and approved by the TAC. For more details on how this project was planned, see the grant manual on the branch Web site. The library system has already opened a separate room as a YA area in another branch, modeled after this one, with plans for another.

Librarian's True Confessions from Branch Manager Sandi Imperio

This is the YA space of my dreams because...

"...young adults actually feel comfortable here and have a sense of ownership. It's not a forced place of study or just a place to go when you *have* to research, but a fun place to come to."

These are the only nightmare elements of my dream:

"Acoustics are terrible in this old building and the noise level builds to a very loud pitch with fifteen teens or more are just talking normally. We're filled to capacity already with no room to grow."

Teen Patron Comment

"I've been coming here for about two years and I spend a lot of time because many of my friends work or hang out here. It's the only place I can get Internet access. I love the great selection of books and hardly ever have any trouble finding just what I want."—boy, eighth grade

---

Garfield Park Branch Library, Santa Cruz Public Libraries, 705 Woodrow Avenue, Santa Cruz, CA 95060-5950, (831) 427-7709
http://www.santacruzpl.org/branches/9/

Submitted by: Janis O'Driscoll, Coordinator of Youth Services, Santa Cruz Public Libraries, e-mail odriscollj@ santacruzpl.org.

Young Adults, Libraries, and Ritual Space

Echo Park Branch, Los Angeles Public Library
Los Angeles, California

Anthony Bernier

Jerry, Bill, and I were fourteen when we punctured our right thumbs and rubbed our blood together. In that smelly, old, abandoned garage-*cum*-clubhouse, we became larger than our individual selves. We became immortal brothers. But we were also mixing with a long legacy of youth rituals. From not stepping on the cracks ("to save our mothers' backs") through the more problematic fraternity and sorority hazings, young people have continually invented rituals to order their universe and to make it more their own. Libraries could learn something here.

At the end of the school year, my branch of the Los Angeles Public Library staged their own ritual: we embedded Central High School's time capsule project in the building itself, vowing to return ten years hence to recover the treasure and to see how we had weathered.

For many youth in this neighborhood, and perhaps for other youth as well, thinking ten years into the future is a bizarre abstraction. These kids of America's abandoned urban agenda, the "cutback kids" under constant police helicopter surveillance, the kids of our post-after-school playground inner-cities with few other legal enrichment activities. This experiment in ritual forced a future vision of themselves, a future even with spouses and children.

Central High exists as a Los Angeles Unified Public School District "Options" school. Established to accommodate the soaring aspirations of returning World War I veterans, Options programs now provide school-aged parents, together with working and at-risk teens, innovative, comprehensive, and individualized study curriculums leading to high school diplomas. For these Options students, however, the diploma comes with a tradeoff; a diploma in exchange for access to a school library, a football team, a prom, a school newspaper, a senior class photo, a speech club, a yearbook. In other words, Central High students earn their diplomas at the sacrifice of common rites of passage.

Working closely with Central High students and their talented teacher, Patricia Butler, we developed the "time capsule" concept. The heuristic process of making all the associated choices proved most fruitful: what to keep in, what to leave out, how to identify meaningful items for ten years into the future, how would the students' future children understand (they are to be part of the final "reunion" as well). When these debates subside and the final selections were made, students wrote brief essays exploring each item's respective cultural or anthropological significance. The essays were then excerpted, reduced by photocopier, and attached to the appropriate items: fashion designer tags from pants, shirts, and jackets; US currency reduced to the size of a credit card; somebody's pager; photographs of family cars; poetry samples; a special brand of sunglasses; an issue of *T.V. Guide* with highlighted favorite programs; an inscribed belt buckle; the cover of Gary Soto's *Chato's Kitchen* (Putnan's, 1995)—the picture book illustrated by Susan Guevara that I read to them to demonstrate the importance of reading to children—and a library card. Many items were students' personal property, reflecting how they came to care about the idea of a time capsule and its embodiment of community.

Beyond the prioritizing of significant material culture, beyond the challenging critical thinking and writing and rhetorical skills required of this time capsule project, the ceremony and ritual still looms large. On the final day, after everything was labeled and stowed, we tied the capsule up with nylon yarn as students said goodbye to a defining moment in their lives. Together with our library's clerk, Lupe Lainez, who offered to stand and watch over the capsule (or pass the guardian role on to her successor), we sealed up the treasure in a false wall compartment of the library. Two students have promised to maintain a class address list to ensure everyone gets invited back that spring in the decade of 2000, when we will unearth the capsule and revisit who we were ten years ago.

I have been fortunate to attend many new library building openings in my career. I have listened to the politicians, the clergy, the teachers, and the library administrators talk over the heads of the children assembled there for a photo opportunity—and to symbolize the light that libraries hold. The young people must sit and listen to lectures on how to respect and cherish. But rarely does any part of the ceremony—the ritual—actually include youth culture.

In completing the time capsule ritual, and for at least the next ten years, the students of Central High will connect to this library in ways that our overdue notices have not managed to accomplish. They will see themselves, their pasts, and their futures tied to this space by something thicker than a taxpayer's burden—something closer to blood.

Echo Park Branch, Los Angeles Public Library, 1410 W. Temple Street, Los Angeles, CA 90026, (213) 250-7808
http://www.lapl.org/branches/Branch.php?bID=8

Teen Center

Shaker Heights Public Library
Shaker Heights, Ohio

Jennifer M. Asher

Description: On the renovated second floor of the Main Library, the new Teen Center has 1,650 square feet of space where teens can read, study, use homework resources, listen to music on headphones, converge in small or large groups, and enjoy light snacks in a relaxed atmosphere where socializing is permitted. While the general young adult collection is located on the main floor next to the adult fiction collection, this upstairs space is a place apart, dedicated to teens aged twelve to seventeen. The Center is open four days a week during after-school hours on a membership basis. Young adults must complete an application, have it signed by a parent or guardian, and return it along with a photo to the Teen Center. Membership is considered a privilege; currently 326 members are registered.

Entered through a door off a carpeted hallway by the elevator, the Teen Center is visible through windows cut in the inner wall. With eight large windows on the outside and eggshell-colored walls, its décor generates a pleasant, bright atmosphere. Dark blue carpeting with tan specks framed by a wavy blue border gives the room a new age look. The space formerly housed two school classrooms; the original 1912 chalkboard now serves as an interactive board where teens can write poetry or other expressions. Atop the bookshelves on the south wall is mounted "The Three Seasons of Lisa's Life," an artistic memorial to a former library teen page who died in 1990. Three tri-fold screens hold forty-five pieces of delicate paper art and the lighting behind the screens evokes an ethereal quality.

Furniture: A large, crescent-shaped reference desk faces members as they enter the Center. There are two couches, four clover-shaped tables with four chairs each, eight study carrels, three computers with Internet access, and a word processor (there is also a computer lab next door). Bookshelf tops serve as a display space, and paperback-sized shelving holds a popular collection of books for recreational reading and music CDs. On the side of the room away from the couches and computers, most of the study carrels and bookshelves are grouped as a "study area." If it is too loud, the teens can also use the Quiet Study Room down the hall. To create program space for small groups, the couches and other furniture on the "non-study" side of the room are easily moveable into a variety of configurations.

Collection: The Teen Center houses more than 700 books, magazines, and resources. They range from recreational reading to the Shaker city schools' core curriculum textbooks for grades seven through twelve, from music CDs, comics, and board games to calculators and a small reference collection for homework help. Nearly every item is duplicated in the larger YA collection downstairs, which contains 9,500 volumes of young adult fiction, series, comic books, graphic novels, science fiction, fantasy, nonfiction, biographies, books on tape, magazines, pamphlets, the high school paper, and Cliff Notes. The Bertram Woods Branch Library has a smaller but similar YA collection of 5,400 items.

Shaker Library has 3,099 registered YA library card users. In 1999, this group checked out over 25,000 titles, including adult, YA, and children's items. Circulation has increased approximately 7% since 1997 and the library anticipates a continued increase.

Young Adult Population and Community: Shaker Heights Public Library was founded in 1937 as a school-district library. Bordering Cleveland, it serves a diverse population of 31,000 people in a city cited nationally for its pro-integrative housing initiatives and exceptional public schools. The main library occupies 60,800 square feet in the city's commercial district, including eight community meeting rooms, a Quiet Study Room, Computer Center, Coffee Bar, and Teen Center. Circulation figures are well over twice the national average for libraries in communities of comparable size. In 1960, a branch library was built on property bequeathed to the library.

The Main Library is four blocks from Shaker Heights High School, attended by 1,669 students in grades nine to twelve. In Shaker Middle School there are 850 students in grades seven and eight. The diverse student body is

51% African American, 42% White, 3% Asian/Pacific/Islander, 2.7% Multiracial and .8% Hispanic. Census figures project a 10% increase in the YA population between 1990 and 2000.

Hours of Operation and Teen Traffic: The Teen Center is open Monday through Thursday from 3:30 p.m. to 7:30 p.m. Most of the teens who use the Center range from twelve to fifteen. A month-long Visitor Use Survey determined that 917 young adults used the Teen Center during that time, approximately 30 per day. Peak hours are between 4:30 p.m. and 5:30 p.m., and Monday is the heaviest-use day. Teen Center use plummets dramatically during school breaks and on weekends: its hours cover the after-school demands of a large "latchkey" population.

Staffing: The Young Adult Librarian, with direction from the Adult Services Supervisor, oversees the Teen Center, as well as the YA department at both libraries. She orders materials for the YA collection, schedules programs of interest to young adults, and manages a volunteer Teen Council. Other staff includes a Teen Center Library Aide, who is in the Center during operating hours.

Planning Process: After a partial renovation of an old school building, Shaker Heights Main Library opened in 1993. Peak hours from 4 p.m. to 8 p.m. found the library filled with children, adults, and teens. Before the Teen Center was built, boisterous teens crowded the library steps, blocked the entrance, and took over many of the study tables and chairs, prompting older library users to complain. Like many libraries nationwide, Shaker Library is a magnet for "latchkey kids" who use the library as an after-school haven until parents come home from work.

A 1996 bond issue dedicated one million dollars to library renovations that would include a Teen Center and a Computer Center. The Teen Center was envisioned as an appealing space exclusively for teens, where hanging out could blossom into actual library use. Since the Teen Center opened up on the second floor on December 6, 1998, the library's first floor is noticeably more quiet and controlled. Young adult materials can be moved and used on either floor; when the Teen Center is closed, staff retrieve any items needed.

Membership: The use of membership cards evolved from the original idea of placing stickers on teens' library cards to allow entry into the Teen Center. Many teens who migrated from downstairs or the front steps, however, had no library cards, nor were they interested in obtaining them. They offered reasons such as "My parents won't let me get one," or "I had one but my fines were to big." Picture membership cards better served the purpose. Because parent signatures are required, applications become parent awareness forms; parents know were their teens are and what the Teen Center offers. Holding members' cards when they arrive, the YA librarian learns names easily and responds to parents who ask if their son or daughter is there. Teen Center membership grows through word of mouth in a domino effect; friends bringing friends who bring friends. The YA librarian promotes membership when visiting schools, especially at the Orientation Night for incoming freshmen. Programs held in the Teen Center such as Open Mic Poetry Night, bring in new young adult faces. The Teen Center is advertised in local publications and the Recreation and Counseling Centers.

Youth Participation and Programming: The Teen Council has existed since 1997, before the Teen Center opened. Its role is to foster an interest in library leadership, help plan programs with YA appeal, and set direction for the Center. With applications increasing since the Teen Center opened, Council memberships total twenty-five. A dependable core group of fifteen meets one Saturday afternoon a month in the Teen Center. Council members recommend materials for purchase and suggest program topics. They volunteer at library functions, including Friends of the Library book sales. They maintain the bulletin board in the teen area, represent the library in the Memorial Day parade; and help staff the library's ice cream social to kick off the summer reading program.

Since last winter, a new Teen Volunteer program has attracted eleven teens in two branches, who assists with programs, clean books and shelves, and help in the local history area with light archival tasks and other jobs.

Foremost among young adult programs for the past five years has been a very successful Teen Job Fair, a library collaboration with the city recreation department that matches teens with local employers. Both the Teen Job Fair and the Teen Center were chosen by the Young Adult Library Services Association (YALSA) as exemplary programs to be featured in the forthcoming third edition of *Excellence in Library Services to Young Adults*. One of thirty libraries in the nation to be so honored, Shaker Library was the only library to have two programs selected. Two awards of $200 each will be used for further YA programming.

True Confessions from YA Librarian Jennifer Asher

This is the YA space of my dreams because...

"I love the fact that the Teen Center is such a revolutionary concept, finally implemented. The spacious room is located away from the children's department, and because members must be twelve to seventeen years old, it gives the true meaning of 'young adult' to the space."

I still dream of these improvements:

"To make the space more colorful, I anticipate working with an artist in residence and young adults to create another memorial, this one to a former Teen Center member. I also dream of helping young adults become active library volunteers, instilling in them the importance of giving back to the community that so generously provided the resources for the Teen Center."

Teen Patron Comments

"The Teen Center is a place where teens can be teens. We can eat and talk to friends. It's an extension of the library."—I.T., 14

"Who would have thought there would be something this cool in a place so boring?" —Shatira Jackson, 16

"It's the spot...the place to be."—Paraphrased from a group of male teens, 15 to 16

"The Teen Center is a very interesting place with new laughing faces every day."— Ericka Foy, 17

Shaker Heights Public Library, 16500 Van Aken Boulevard, Shaker Heights, OH 44120, (216) 991-2030
http://www.shakerlibrary.org/

TeenS'cape Takes on the "New Callousness"

Los Angeles Public Library
Los Angeles, California

Anthony Bernier

During the past year, two of the largest and most famous public scandals ever to rock a city have rocked Los Angeles. The police department's notorious Rampart Division threatens to bankrupt the city treasury from lawsuits. Recently unraveled corruption and misconduct has the Department of Justice threatening to take over. Then there is a United School District's Belmont High School catastrophe. Planned as the most costly high school in the nation, the half-built project must be scrapped entirely due to mismanagement. The doubled-barreled ricochets of both scandals fit a far larger pattern. And in California it's looking like an old story.

In the 1980s, former Governor Pete Wilson gained national reputation by incarcerating more youth than in any other state and by raising fees and repealing Affirmative Action at the University of California. Despite the city's burgeoning numbers of young people (100,000 more today than in 1980) and population densities that rival Manhattan's, Los Angeles has failed to build a single high school since passage of the legendary Proposition 13 sparked a national anti-tax revolt in the mid-1970s. Meanwhile, the District Attorney has inspired a region-wide flood of dubiously legal "zero tolerance" crackdowns against youth; new injunctions, curfews, and youth-targeted "nuisance" ordinances control what teens wear, who they can be seen with, where they can and cannot be. L.A. arrests 12,000 youths every year for curfew violations alone. In addition to these anti-youth acts, in March of this year, voters passed into law the jailing of fourteen-year-olds with hard-core career criminal adults.

Considering this anti-youth legacy, it is not difficult to see how L.A. regards its young people. National conservative columnist Arianna Huffington calls it part of "the New Callousness," where even with our own youth, retribution is the only answer. California State Senator, Democrat Tom Hayden, calls it "an emerging garrison state for the poor and the young." I call it a "Geography of No." No place for youth to grow. No place to learn. No place to hide. And no room for mistakes.

This all-punishment-all-the-time-age-profiling public policy flies in the face of facts gathered from every major category of youth behavior. As sociologist Mike A. Males tells us, teenage felony and murder rates are lower today among all the races/ethnicities in L.A. than they have been in a quarter century, despite a doubling in youth poverty rates. Youths, Males rightly claims, are being "framed" and "scapegoated."

On the other hand, there is the Los Angeles Public Library, the unsung civic hero, standing up against their bitter wind for the young people it serves. As of March 14, the Library launched its spectacular TeenS'cape enlargement, which it sits smack-dab in the middle of the city's cherished 1926 Central Library. At 3,780 square feet, TeenS'cape is arguably the biggest, the best, and most technically sophisticated library space for teens anywhere in the country. Set against the city's anti-youth "Geography of No," this elegant and affirming gesture might find another name: reparations.

Local youth named TeenS'cape when it was opened in two years after the 1992 L.A. riots. They wanted the name not only to reflect a territory of escape but also to suggest a measure of ownership and community. In its small, experimental, cramped, leftover space, the original TeenS'cape received no redesign, no furniture, no permanent status, no directional signage, or even a place on the building directory. Still, during its incubation stage, the facility was popular with teens. Recent reports document a 26% jump in computer usage between 1997 and 1998, and an even higher rise in reading material circulation.

However, modest its beginnings, TeenS'cape served as a biblio-bleachhead, seeking to correct the previous total "erasure" of young adults from their own library. Far more significantly, it initiated new criteria by which to assess library space programming. In Los Angeles, at least teens no longer get leftover library space. Triple the size of the original, the enlarged and renovated TeenS'cape embraces visitors with exciting post-modernist architecture – juxtaposed against, yet respectfully nested within the building's historic walls and ceilings.

TeenS'cape is executed in six separate "zones." In Cyber Zone, the department's signature element, one enters under a metal mesh awning – sleek, scalloped, teal-colored, and decoratively lit from beneath. No slapdash acoustic-tile drop ceiling and institutional fluorescent lighting here! The awning creates a room-within-a-room. Together with colorful patterns of wall-to-wall carpet, it raises conversation comfort while suppressing ambient background noise. Design here evokes the emerging new wave of Silicon Valley's ultra-hip "dot-com" start-up spaces. Cyber Zone also playfully anticipates tomorrow's techno-savvy collaborative works spaces. Four circular blond wood café tables support nineteen flat screen Virtual Library computer terminals connecting teens to the Internet, as well as to over five hundred electronic databases, LAPL's online book and magazine catalog, and a state-of-the-art array of electronic resources. Peripheral wall alcoves cuddle eleven multimedia computers for private music listening and computer gaming, as well as accessible message boards and glass-enclosed display cases.

The Living Room is another TeenS'cape zone, well-appointed with a fifty-inch plasma-screen television; DVD, CD, and video equipment, a Dolby surround-sound system; and un-library seating options such as plush sofas and movable cushy lounge furniture. The Living Room encourages solitary recreational reading, complete with adjacent magazine display shelving. It is also a versatile space capable of hosting small performances and class visits. During a bevy of re-opening activities for instance, TeenS'cape hosted a dramatic performance by New York's American Place Theater. Local high school classes comfortably enjoyed the production of Claude Brown's 1965 classic, *Manchild in the Promised Land*. Undisturbed by activity in other zones, the Living Room's great sound system ably accompanied the performance with the beats and pulse of period jazz.

The Lounge zone provides space for out-of-the-way activity. Here TeenS'cape meets history. Appointed with the same custom furnishings that appear in the Living Room, the Lounge perches just behind a low-slung curved wall, adjacent to the Library's historic dome rotunda with its stunning 1930s Federal Artist Project murals of California history.

For all its size, however, TeenS'cape surprises at every turn and in every corner. Life-sized blowups of Spiderman, Buffy the Vampire Slayer, and *Star Wars'* Yoda entreat the city's youth to use the library to "get the bad guys and to stay in touch with *The Force*. On the way from the Cyber Zone and into the Lounge, young adults pause at the automated "Self-Check" bay to borrow library materials without waiting in lines with all those—well—*adults* downstairs. As one young man, quoted in the *Los Angeles Times*, characterized it, "This is way off the scale. It's like landing on Mars!" In TeenS'cape, the hip, the mod, and the magnificent come together in a monumental civic structure.

But TeenS'cape is not all fun, games and kicking back. The Study Lounge zone provides eight dedicated word-processing computers adjacent to shelves of ready reference volumes. Another zone offers three canvas-roofed small group Study Rooms that face a reference desk staffed by professional young adult specialists librarians and devoted paraprofessionals. The TeenS'cape collection includes nearly 30,000 books, a fantastic magazine collection of 150 different titles, graphic novels, videos, and CDs. That collection only serves as a springboard, however, to the Central Library's massive holdings and to the almost six million items housed in LAPL's expansive sixty-seven branches.

Los Angeles City Librarian Susan Kent says that "TeenS'cape demonstrates the Los Angeles Public Library's commitment to meeting the education and recreational needs of our city's teenagers." But Kent does not go far enough. The energy propelling TeenS'cape also rejuvenates the way in which new branches design space. Voters recently approved a bond measure to rebuild many of the huge library system's older facilities. Blueprints now inscribe young people into the plans rather than erase them.

With TeenS'cape, LAPL shows a kind of courage. The Library assumes a more fitting role within the community and in the lives of young people it serves. Envisioning teens on this higher and more optimistic ground—more true to *evidence* about youth culture—rejects prevailing anti-youth hysteria. Furthermore, beyond serving as response for damage done to teens elsewhere, TeenS'cape also nails young adult spaces to the public library design agenda. Isn't it about time?

Central Library, Los Angeles Public Library, 630 W. 5th Street, Los Angeles, CA 90071, (213) 228-7272
http://www.lapl.org/index.php

Young Adults Services

Allen County Public Library
Fort Wayne, Indiana

Sheila B. Anderson

Description: On the ground floor of the Main Library is the Young Adults' Services Department (YAS)—within a huge library, it is a small library devoted exclusively to serving teens. The department's 4,500 square feet contains a YA reference desk staffed during all the library's open hours, and a complete collection of print and electronic resources for teens. Materials from this main YA collection are often sent to the other thirteen branches in the county system.

The rectangular young adult space is adjacent to Readers' Services, the auditorium, three television stations, and a computer lab. Two walls are all windows, and several skylights provide lots of natural light. The accent is a neutral color, with off-white walls, earthly heather-toned carpet, live plants, and dark wood. The upholstered chairs are blue and green. The spare wall decorations pictured here have been recently enhanced with new READ posters and six huge felt banners, eight feet by five feet, designed and made by local teens on the themes of mystery, sports, fantasy, science, the arts, and education. A "Teen Talk" board features a different topic each month. A staff workroom has a desk for each YA staff member, three computers, and a manager's office. (See the floor plan on page 115.)

Furniture: Six larger study tables seat sixty people, very useful during school visits. Three round tables seat four people apiece, and ten cushy chairs encourage hanging out, with low tables designed for feet. There are fourteen paperback spinners. Hardcover nonfiction is housed on several banks of tall five-shelf units. A mixture of high and low units holds fiction and special collections. Five various-sized shelves contain face-out magazines, comics, graphic novels, and displays of high-interest, easy-reading non-fiction; new books; and topical sections such as "Problems" Here's Help!" Books are also displayed on the tops and sides of shelving units. Eight computer workstations are for teen use: two word processing terminals, one chat/e-mail/surfing terminal, three Internet/database research/catalog terminals (one of which supports the Homework Help program), and two terminals with CD-ROM educational games that also support the Homework Help Program. Internet access is unfiltered, and adults may use YAS terminals only when school is in session; teens have first priority. Three staff terminals are at the reference desk, two are in the workroom, and one is in the manager's office.

Collection: The 45,000 volumes in the YAS collection include YA fiction, picture books for teens, adult books for teens, nonfiction, comics and graphic novels, audio books, music CDs, homework help, reference, and magazines. Some CD-ROMs/software/computer games are for in-house use, and some can be checked out. General arrangement is by Dewey classification, with sections for horror, careers, education, study notes (Cliff and Monarch), mysteries, short stories, romance, adventure, comics, graphic novels, science fiction, controversial issues, sports, Christian fiction, and classics. There are special collection youth services workers, homeschooling, and books in Spanish. Although teens use additional resources from subject-oriented departments such as Business & Technology, YAS has a thorough collection of materials for young adults.

Young Adult Population and Community: The library serves a population of 300,836 with an ethnic/racial composition of 87.8% white, 10.1% African American, and the remaining 2.1% a mix of Native American, Asian, Hispanic, and other groups. More than half the residents live in Fort Wayne; the rest are in several surrounding rural towns, including large Amish and Old Order Mennonite Communities. The median household income is $31,835. Within the service area are 36,000 students in eighteen middle/junior high schools and sixteen high schools; many school groups visit the library. There are several homeschooling associations.

Hours of Operation and Teen Traffic: As part of the Main Library, the YAS Department is open the same hours as the rest of the building; Monday through Thursday from 9 a.m. to 9 p.m., Friday and Saturday from 9 a.m. to 6 p.m., and Sunday from 1 p.m. to 6 p.m. (except summers). During after-school hours, twenty to seventy teens from eleven to nineteen years old use YAS each day. The age range expands on weekends from ages ten to twenty-one, largely due to the huge career/college section, with 100 to 250 young patrons using YAS on Saturdays and Sundays.

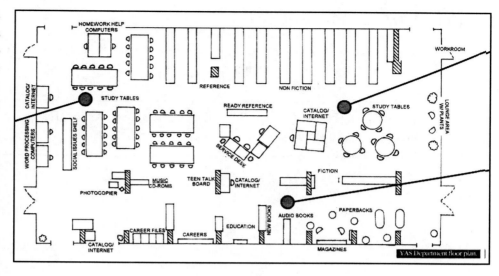

Staffing: Eight staff members are assigned to YAS; one full-time and one part-time Librarian II, one full-time and one part-time Librarian I, and one part-time Clerk.

Planning Process: The main library building opened in 1968; the original YAS department had been established in 1952 in another building. In 1981, YAS moved to a new wing, which is the current department. The first Manager of YAS ran the department from 1952 to 1992, having the most input in planning.

Youth Participation and Programming: The Teen Advisory Board meets once per month at YAS and various branches, helping to plan the summer reading program and other activities. The popular Young Adult Summer Reading Program, with a budget of $55,000, provides books and free trips to swimming pools, bowling alleys, laser tag, golf, and other entertainments. The Homework Help program operates six hours per school week on three different nights, when adults in the community volunteer to assist students with homework. Three YAS computer workstations are devoted to Homework Help; its extensive listings can be viewed in the Teen section of Allen County Public Library's Web site (*http://www.acpl.lib.in.uc*). Other YA programs include science fair preparation, Teen Read Week activities, video judging for the Selected Videos Committee of the Young Adult Library Services Association (YALSA), and the Teen Agency Program (TAP). This library was a test site for *Output Measures! And More; Planning and Evaluating Public Library Services for Young Adults* by Virginia A. Walter (American Library Association, 1995/VOYA February 1996). Two Allen County programs, the Young Adult Summer Reading Program and the Teen Agency Program, are featured in *Excellence in Library Services to Young Adults: The Nation's Top Programs.* 2nd edition (ALA Editions, 1997 *VOYA* February 1998).

True Confessions from YAS Manager Sheila Anderson

This is the YA space of my dreams because...

"It is similar to the children's department in that is has a huge collection devoted to teens with eight staff members and a very generous budget. This situation is unique in the U.S. We are not a space, but an entire department. Our fiction collection is awesome and students love our nonfiction areas."

I still dream of these improvements:

"Having recently fulfilled my dream of teen artwork with the mounting of the new banners made by participants in the 2000 summer reading program, I hope to continue creating a more aesthetically pleasing environment with matching furniture, computers clustered in one area instead of spread throughout the department, and the expansion of our crowded, well-used space."

Teen Patron Comment

"I was so impressed with how helpful and friendly the staff in Young Adults' Services was."—Karen Phelps

Allen County Public Library, 900 Library Plaza, Fort Wayne, IN 46802, (260) 421-1200 *http://www.acpl.lib.in.us/*

Dragons and Dreaming in a Sensuous School Library

Base Line Middle School Library
Boulder, Colorado

Nancy Jane Moore

The first school library to apply to become *VOYA* "YA Space of Your Dreams" is described by its librarian, Nancy Jane Moore, as "a dreamed-up place for teenagers by teenagers." Base Line Middle School Library underwent a major facelift from 1995 to 1997 that happened only because Moore listened to her students, working with them and the wider community. Even before its renovation, dressed in drab institutional clothes, this small middle school library, about 50 by 70 square feet, was remarkable for its 25,000—volumes almost as many fiction as nonfiction—and 6,000 books a year in circulation. Unusual for a middle school library, the collection contains graphic novels and picture books and adult books for teens, as well as young adult fiction and curriculum-related materials.

Books circulate at Base Line because Moore booktalks from her superb collection enthusiastically and often, and because she creates an atmosphere in which her students feel welcome—along with their parents, community members, and students from the nearby University of Colorado, who also wander in to check out books from this almost-public library, open on school days from 7 a.m. until 4 p.m. Students who move onto high school often return to use Base Line Library, claiming that its collection is better than the high school's. The library houses a computer lab; Internet access is not filtered, and computers also contain an online library catalog, databases, and CD-ROMs.

Moore works closely with both teachers and parents to integrate the library into the school community (see her article, "We Were Reading Geography Books! I Thought We Were Just Reading for Fun': Parents and a Librarian Take on Seventh Grade Book Groups," *VOYA*, December 1999, page 310). There is always something going on in the library, from Science Club to Yearbook, from Socratic Seminars to History Day, from book groups to Internet cruising. In the well-heeled city of Boulder, whose 100,000 citizens often are considered as mostly "whitebread," this school library hosts a Native American student group, a Latino boys group, and a Latina girls group. Among Base Line's nearly five hundred students in sixth through eighth grades are sixty students from around the world, enrolled in the English as a Second Language Program (ESL). During days of dwindling resources for drama, visual arts, and instrumental music, Base Line is also Boulder's Arts Focus School. It is one of ten middle schools in a city with five high schools and a new trend toward K-8 schools, two of which were built recently.

How did Base Line Library, a dull 1977 addition to a 1950s building, become a sensuous den for dragons and dreaming? Following is Moore's account of its transformation.

Teens Dream Up Their Own Sensuous Library

The good news was that windows were everywhere. The bad news was that the original "interior designer" was into dark brown. The bookcases were dark brown Formica, complemented with scarred mustard-colored pressed-board shelves. The walls were covered in dark brown indoor/outdoor carpeting. The chairs were black plastic, now split and sporting abstract hunks chewed out at interesting angles. Graffiti had been carved into the Formica tabletops.

The DeWitt Wallace Foundation gave us a $5,000 Library Power Grant to fix the place up—more than we had received in almost thirty years of school funding. To visualize a new library design, a group of twelve students accompanied me to our favorite places in Boulder. We sat, trying to figure out why they were our favorite places. We listened. We looked. We sniffed. We touched. Our forays took a couple of weeks. Then we did the same thing in the library. At last we came up with a cool list and a yucky list—which nearly gave the principal a heart attack! What we wanted was a sensuous library. We wanted interesting things to see, hear, touch, and smell. Taste was the only sense left out—not by the students, but by the librarian. Any youth advocate knows that a coffee shop or juice cookie bar is what teens want, but school rules do not allow food in the library.

The students asked me if we movers and shakers in education had taken courses in ugly just to remind them that they were in school. Down came the brown wall carpet. Up went wallboard, which a local artist turned into a giant fantasy "window" with a dragon peering in. A big natural granite foundation went into the center of the library with plants and benches around it. We searched used furniture dealers for comfy couches and chairs.

The money was gone, but we were on a roll. We passed out flyers in the neighborhood to remind people over sixty that they could work off taxes by volunteering in nonprofit places, such as painting the Base Line Library. We were told that paint would not stick to Formica and metal. We chose electric turquoise and hot pink and started sanding, priming, and painting anyway. It looks great. I learned how to operate a can of spray paint. (The teens were very good at spray-painting already.) We painted clouds on blue-sky walls. Parents brought yards of cranberry cloth to make curtains to cover the cement black walls. We bought navy window shades. We hung Chinese kites and twirly kites with long rainbow tails from the heating vents, hoping to cover the stained acoustic tile ceiling. The assistant superintendent of schools was so impressed with what we had done with love, sweat, and nerve, that he bought us brand new chairs and tables—real oak ones. That was expensive, bless him!

After two years and countless hours of work from many volunteers, we have our sensuous library. Students love this outrageous space. It has a place for everybody, and an eighth grader explains, pointing to the stuffed furniture: "That's my place to hang out with my friends, but Nick can go over there and do his Internet thing alone. The studious people can go to the reference room while the ethnic groups can chat in a conference room. Everywhere you look there are corners of individuals." Yes, sensuous corners of individuals.

Another eighth grade student says that she loves the library because it is full of books. She can find Pulitzer Prize-winners right along with picture books. She sees other school libraries as computer labs with hardly any fiction—or other books for that matter. They are either way too dark or way too proper.

Still another student reports that when the district History Day was held here, other teenagers were saying, "Wow you guys are so lucky! How did you get a library like this?"

Another says, "It's just like my room, only more interesting."

And another enthuses, "There's something to look at everywhere and it's so bright and so soft and the fountains is so wonderful. I don't want to grab a book and run. All of us want to stay and snuggle! I like to focus on the dragon kites and dream."

Still Dreaming

As the librarian, I still dream of clerical help. The school cut all aside positions, so I have no parapro—and no parent volunteers, who are time-consuming to train. Although last year twenty student aides fought for the honor of working in the library, this year there are none; the district has a new edict keeping students in academic classes all day. I need time to be with the kids teaching, leading groups, discussing, exploring the Net, and storytelling. The practical part of being a librarian—cataloging, shelving, weeding, and processing—could be done by someone else. Keeping the computers up and running is almost a full time job in itself, unfortunately coming with library territory. Extra staffing would also make it possible to stay open later every day and perhaps Saturday afternoon, now that we have a security system.

We would love a glassed-in wall for art displays in general. We'd like to be a gallery of sorts. We'd like to form a partnership with a local bookstore to share author talks. We'd like to mute or turn off fluorescent lighting and have lamps instead. The students want sliding doors leading onto a deck with hammocks and deck chairs—not a bad idea in sunny Colorado. They also want a music or listening center—unlikely without more library staff. The library is a work in progress; our used furniture never lasts more than a year, kites need replacement, new paintings are added. Maybe someday when pigs fly and libraries are funded as they deserve…oh well, I can dream, can't I?

Base Line Middle School, 700 20th Street, Boulder, CO 80302
This school no longer exists.

The Reading Room

Lindbergh Middle School
North Long Beach, California

Helen Cox

Like a yellow brick road, colorful and exuberant works of art point the way to the school library. Parading along the hallway toward the library door are enormous meticulously drawn posters featuring scenes from Harry Potter and other popular books. The route from outdoors is through a patio at the front of the school, its walls decorated with a mural of a fantasy garden designed by students, full of dragons and storybook characters. The double front doors hold twelve stained glass paintings copied from book illustrations. Above these doors is a proud painted sign showing an open book, letters marching across pages that proclaim "The Reading Room: Where Scholars Are Born." This bright fanfare opens onto a key-shaped den of books and nooks. Running above the bookshelves on every wall is art of an earlier period: a green-tinted 1940 mural painted by an artist during President Roosevelt's Work Progress Administra-

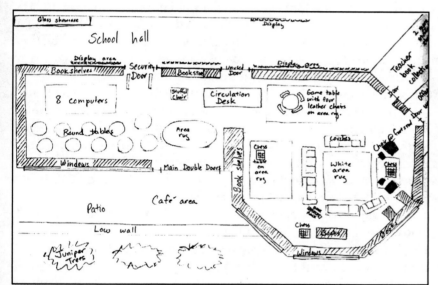

tion (WPA), depicting the history of flight to fit this 1929 building named after aviator Charles Lindbergh. The only wall without the mural is filled with tall windows.

It's no surprise that before she took over the library, Helen Cox was the art teacher in this crowded urban school. Ravaged by Proposition 13's destruction of library funding, the dingy school library was the last place students wanted to go. Its dusty old tomes went as far back as 1913; nothing new had been added for years. When the librarian retired in 1994, Cox emerged from her art classroom with a radical proposal for the school principal: complete library transformation. She wrote a Statement of Need: "In the absence of scholarly experience and learning incentives, children from poverty are deprived of realistic choices and clear directions." That led to her Statement of Vision for a library "dedicated to providing at-risk students a scholarly environment to prepare them for a higher education and meaningful employment. Our commitment is to provide our children the highest quality programming and materials available anywhere."

North Long Beach is an insular urban community ranging from low income to working class. Lindbergh's 1,400 students in grades six through eight come from uneducated, mostly poor families of a rich multicultural mix: 50% Latino, 25% African American, 12% Asian, 5% Pacific Islander, 5% Anglo, 1.5% Filipino, and 1.5% other groups. Many have single-parent families or homes in which parents work long hours; 80% are on free or reduced-price school lunches. Some students have never been to a bookstore or public library. More than two-thirds are several years below grade level. Students who are winning the reading battle are termed "emerging readers," while those behind them are "struggling readers."

Given the green light by her principal, Cox began her struggle toward library transformation in 1995. An army of parent volunteers painted the library. Cox scrounged and scrubbed furniture from foreclosed properties. She weeded extensively, discarding books that hadn't circulated since the 60s. The remaining books were so dirty that their edges had to be scraped with sandpaper. Partially restored state library funding and grants have allowed Cox to upgrade the collection gradually. Her initial focus was on adding works of cultural diversity, fiction and biographies that would identify the newly christened Reading Room as a place that affirmed the students' identities with material relevant to them. A collection evaluation in October 2000 revealed that 56% of the nonfiction and reference books need replacement—Cox's next goal.

The amazing transformation of Lindbergh's library began with Cox's vision and her administration's support. It continues through the determination and generosity of many helping hands. "Although there was no formal input in the way of a planning committee of teachers, parents, or students," says Cox, "their constant input and ideas, their volunteerism, and their donations have helped shape the changes and direction in The Reading Room."

Layout, furniture, and decor: Modeled after a bookstore, the circular end of the key-shaped floor plan contains mostly fiction and high-interest topics on shelves around the walls. Its center floor space is an inviting, comfortable lounge area with five couches, two velvet armchairs, and four imitation leather armchairs. Over the dark green carpet is an additional creamy rug in the middle of the ring of lounge seating, with floor cushions and more space for relaxing. A mini-bookstore in glass cases labeled "Once Upon a Story" sells books, bookmarks, and school supplies. Also in the circular section are game spaces set off with area rugs: two marble and one wood chess table, and a game table with four leather-look chairs. Stuffed animals are handy for cuddling with kids and books.

The long rectangular area contains nonfiction and eight computer workstations with word processing and CD-ROMs; four have filtered Internet access. Mission-style oak chairs with green-checked upholstered seats are ranged around ten round oak tables to seat forty. The circulation desk, containing the only online catalog, sits in the middle of the room. (The catalog will become available on a second computer.) Off the circle is a teacher library with classroom sets; beside it is an office/work room. Office space consumes 682 square feet; the rest of the library measures 2,550 square feet.

Collection: On 1,200 linear feet of dark oak shelving are 11,000 volumes; the collection is growing. Nonfiction is arranged in Dewey order, with curriculum support, reference materials, and a careers section. A "Writer's Corner" contains how-to-write books, anthologies of poems and essays by young writers, and author information. The recreational reading area is organized in these categories: mystery/horror, science fiction, fables, classics, humor, historical fiction, general fiction, holidays, animal stories, poetry, art, self-help, sports and recreation, and picture books for teens (labeled "Reading for Pleasure"). There are also magazines and paperbacks, classic comics, and adult books with teen appeal. Circulation has doubled since 1997-98; last year 6,068 items circulated.

Hours of Operation and Teen Traffic: The Reading Room opens at least three and a half hours each week outside school time. School is open from 8 a.m. to 3 p.m. weekdays. The Reading Room is closed Fridays due to limited staffing. On the other four days it opens at 7:30 a.m., usually staying open until 3:30 or 4 p.m., except Thursdays when it matches the school closing time. On the patio, Les Literati Café is open Monday to Thursday before school from 7:15 to 7:55 a.m., with free magazines and muffins and juice at fifty cents each. Each day thirty to forty students choose to visit the library before and after school; daily classes in the library total 180 students.

Staffing: One full-time professional library media teacher is on a 182-day contract. Two college aides each work sixteen hours a week. One hourly employee coordinates two grant-funded projects. There are countless parent, student, and community volunteers. Last year volunteers donated 448 hours tutoring students and processing books, the equivalent of hiring one full-time employee for eleven weeks.

Programming: The Reading Room hosts an ambitious array of programs for students, parents, and families. In order to qualify as a Distinguished Scholar, students must read in the library for three thirty-minute periods a week, and also write a one- to two-page research paper. Their rewards are visits to colleges, universities, and businesses to explore career opportunities. A related project was the development of a brochure, "How to Raise a Scholar," through discussion forums with parents, teachers, and students.

"Stories Alive" is a grant-funded program that gives students the opportunity to learn about story structure and storytelling from professional storytellers, a Shakespeare performance, a book cover contest, and family literacy events such as holiday read-alouds. Other literacy projects include Rolling Readers, in which a dozen volunteers from the Toyota company tutor struggling readers for an hour each week; and Read-to-Me, which pairs Lindbergh's emerging readers with children from a local preschool for two one-hour read-alouds.

In a district-wide authors festival, a published author works intensively with students for half a day. There's a Career Day, a Poetry Group, and a Chess Club with several tournaments.

True Confessions from Librarian Helen Cox

This is the YA space of my dreams because . . .

". . . anything is possible. In five years we have transformed a dusty, mildewed room filled with discarded furniture and rotting books into a vibrant and dynamic place, with students lined up at the door to come inside as early as 7:15 a.m.! We recruited parent volunteers when everyone said it wouldn't happen, and we plowed ahead with change even before there was money to back our dreams. The Reading Room has promoted a love for reading and books, and provided our at-risk students with a scholarly environment to prepare them for higher education, meaningful employment, and exposure to the culture of literacy."

I still dream:

"Our commitment is to provide our students with the highest quality programming and materials available *anywhere*. Our goal is to develop a book collection that meets or exceeds *national* standards. We still have a long way to go. One of our current difficulties is trying to serve 1,435 students in a space designed for 900. Our staff was allotted for a single-track school on a traditional calendar and now serves a four-track, year-round school. We simply cannot meet the demands from our enthusiastic patrons! A new vision is emerging of a stronger collaboration with our nearby public library to provide services for our students on evenings and weekends. There should be at least two full-time librarians and one full-time clerk. Just think of the things we could do! We cannot eliminate the poverty in the homes of our students, but we *can* provide them with the richest experiences imaginable."

Teen Patron Comments

"Why couldn't the library have been like this when I went to school here?"

"Your Reading Room is the best I've ever seen in my whole twelve years!"

"Are these books really exciting or do you just make them sound that way?"

Lindbergh Middle School, 1022 E. Market Street, Long Beach, CA 90805, (562) 422-2845
http://www.lbusd.k12.ca.us/Schools/school_finder_results.cfm?schoolID=58

[Editor's Note: See also "Resurrecting a Dead School Library" by Jim Trelease, well-known creator of *The Read-Aloud Handbook* (4th ed., Penguin, 1995), on the author's Web site at http://www.trelease-on-reading.com/whats_nu_lindbergh.html.]

Teen Lounge

L. E. Phillips Memorial Public Library
Eau Claire, Wisconsin

Kati Tvaruzka

Description: The new Teen Lounge is an open area on the library's second floor that fills the entire space to the left of the stairwell. The glow of its lights—from colored sheaths covering the lightbulbs—creates a special atmosphere that draws people to the 1,125 square-foot space. Within a rectangle 25 feet wide and 45 feet long are a lounge area, a computer counter, and low, golden oak shelving, accented with purple and green hues in the carpet and upholstery. The center of the space is dominated by a large, custom-designed piece containing two restaurant booths on one side (each seating four) and an arced computer counter (with three chairs) on the other side. Funky pendant-shaped lights hang over the booths. Along a bank of windows are four comfortable chairs with two coffee tables. On the back wall are two study tables, two paperback spinners, and magazine shelving. The Teen Lounge is near the library's art gallery, administrative offices, and adult nonfiction.

Collection: On four ranges of low wooden shelving (120 square feet) are young adult fiction, nonfiction, and audiobooks. The entire YA collection of 5,850 items—reference, recreational, and curriculum support—is shelved in the area, including comics, graphic novels, and magazines. Because teens often use the adult video/DVD and CD areas, popular items from those sections are displayed in the Teen Lounge. The three computers offer word processing, Internet access, and an online catalog.

This largest public library in west central Wisconsin serves a metropolitan area of 150,000 people. Eau Claire itself has a population around 62,000, mostly white with a significant Hmong minority of about three percent. The city is a major center for technology, health and professional services, education, retail, trade, and industry. Public schools contain 6,000 students in three middle schools and two high schools.

Hours and Teen Traffic: The Teen Lounge is open during all library hours, Monday to Thursday from 10 a.m. to 9 p.m., Friday from 10 a.m. to 6 p.m., Saturday from 10 a.m. to 5 p.m., and winter Sundays from 1 p.m. to 5 p.m. Its teen inhabitants—numbering six to fifteen after school and ten to twenty on weekends—range in age from middle to high school. Many adults enjoy the space during the day; the rest of the building lacks comfortable reading areas.

Staffing: Youth Services staff works with both children and teens; no one works solely with young adults. One full-time professional librarian is responsible for the YA collection, oversight of the Teen Lounge, and all teen programming. One part-time paraprofessional associate coordinates the Young Adult Advisory Board (YAAB) and does some YA programming. A part-time assistant helps to run the teen summer reading program. The Young Adult Advisory Board (YAAB) of thirteen members meets monthly to plan programs and events, suggest purchases for the YA collection, and make reading/ listening/watching picks. Book groups, one for middle schoolers and one for high school students, meet each summer. In the annual summer reading program that draws more than three hundred teens, participants collect Book Bucks for reading time, attending programs, and writing reviews; they "buy" small prizes throughout the summer or bid on large prizes during the Silent Prize Auction at the end. Summer also offers teen volunteer opportunities in the Children's Room. The library is rich in teen programming year-round, from a writers group to game nights and large annual events such as a talent show. Find the library's teen Web site at *http://www.eauclaire.lib.wi.us/ youth/teens/default.htm.*

122

How We Get Them Here and Keep Them Comfortable

A whirlwind of teen activity over the past few years at the L. E. Phillips Memorial Public Library has been fueled by a strong interest in creating an environment that teens will want to visit. To get to know the teen population, we began with programming and outreach that equipped us to create a space to their liking—and one beyond my wildest dreams.

Teen services and programs were minimal until the fall of 1999, when I began my then unofficial position as young adult specialist by founding a Young Adult Advisory Board (YAAB). At our first meeting, the YAAB unanimously decided that the library must have a much cooler area for teens. Behind the adult reference stacks, the area designated as young adult contained nothing but a few "READ" posters and books with yellow YA stickers. The YAAB and I hoped to wrangle at least $500 to raid thrift stores and yard sales for "new" furnishings. We never dreamed that three years later, we'd be sitting in our own $25,000 Teen Lounge.

Our mission was to provide what YAAB members thought was lacking in our community: a common place for teens to get together and have fun. It was my agenda to convince teens to use the library and its services as well. We wanted the library to become the "it" place for big events, doing away with its image as a boring, uncool place. Our first attempt was an outdoor street dance during Teen Read Week 1999. This trial-by-fire drew more than 500 middle and high schoolers to the library for the evening. Subsequent events, such as our annual Back to School Bash concerts and extreme sports demonstrations, have attracted at least 250 teens. We had made a name for ourselves in the community; now our library needed a better space for teens.

When Children's Services became Youth Services in 2000, YA services found an official home. Capital improvement money was designated for renovation of the Children's Room. In the fall of 2001, we contacted Uihlein-Wilson, a Milwaukee architectural firm which had worked on several Wisconsin libraries and schools. Its architects visited our library for a three-day workshop to discuss plans for the children's and young adult areas. Two architects and one interior designer listened to our ideas, our needs, and our dreams, noting everything about our staff, our customers, and our space needs. It was a wonderful experience, for they were able to look at our space with fresh eyes, seeing things that we had never noticed, and coming up with ideas that never would have entered our minds. The next day, they presented us with several possible plans for both areas. Their plan for the Young Adult area took into account all our needs: comfortable leisure space; quiet, individual study space; space for groups; computers; and most important, the necessity for the area to be eye-catching and easy to find, so that teens would know it was theirs.

A few weeks later, we visited Uihlein-Wilson's office in Milwaukee for a tour of libraries that they had designed. I strongly suggest such a tour for anyone working with architects. We got to know their staff, developed a good feel for their style, and talked to librarians who had worked with them on renovation projects. This visit solidified our desire to work with these architects. We asked the Library Board to approve a full renovation of the young adult area with funds allocated for the Children's Room. We hoped that it would spark public interest in renovating other areas of the library as well. With Board support, work began in July 2002.

We didn't expect to be the general contractors for this project, but the architects were hired only to give us their drawings and specifications. Shelly Collins-Fuerbringer and I, who were not at all versed in purchasing or construction, became responsible for contracting out to all vendors. After five long months of purchasing, arranging for installation, and dictating where things should go, the renovation was completed in November 2002.

We have yet to see the Teen Lounge's full potential, as it's still new—we're having a hard time keeping adults from using its comfortable, open space. Our new teen area is a great community asset and we're proud of the accomplishment of our Youth Services staff and YAAB members in giving teens their own home at the library.

True Confessions from Youth Services Librarian Kati Tvaruzka

This is the YA space of my dreams because . . .

". . . there is no question that this area is for teenagers. It's large, easy to find, and accommodates those who want to study, or use the computer, or lounge in comfy chairs to read, or hang in groups."

I still dream of these improvements:

"One day I would like to have music listening stations—or more accurately, the YAAB would like that! I hope that other areas of the library can continue to be updated so that adults don't hang out in the YA space as much."

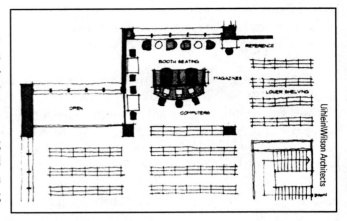

Teen Patron Comments

"The Teen Lounge is a great place for young adults to study and read all on their own, where they can interact with others their age. The Lounge brings a whole new attitude to the library."—Matthew, eighth grade

"The tables are awesome! They look like real booths from Borders, and they're just as comfy. The new computers are too cool!"—James, sixth grade

"The Teen Lounge is a great place to go just to study, read, or hang out with friends. It's comfortable and cozy."—Amanda, eighth grade

L. E. Phillips Memorial Public Library, 400 Eau Claire Street, Eau Claire, WI 54701
(715) 839-5004
http://www.ecpubliclibrary.info/

Teen Central: Safe, Structured, and Teen-Friendly

Phoenix Public Library
Phoenix, Arizona

Karl Kendall

It's 3 p.m. Like clockwork, the after-school rush begins at Teen Central, Phoenix Public Library's 5,000-square-foot teen space. Hundreds of teens from public, private, and charter schools pour through the door. Some check in with the staff at the desk, while others head to the living room to see what movie is playing today. Still others just want to unwind and play RuneScape® on the Internet with their friends. What keeps these teens—more than 10,000 each month—coming back to Teen Central? It's not just the twenty Internet PCs, the large-screen TV, the surround-sound stereo music, and the loaded vending machines. Those bells and whistles are great, but I'll let you in on a secret: They're not the main reason that Teen Central is so busy. The real reason for its enduring popularity is that it offers a safe, structured environment with friendly staff.

A Sanctuary

How many places in your community can teens call their own? School, where they are constantly one misstep away from falling down a rung on the social ladder, where they are tested and re-tested? What about the mall, where adults watch their every move with suspicious glares? It's rough being a teen, always judged or challenged. Many teens face additional challenges: poverty, domestic strife, homes in areas of high crime. A space like Teen Central offers teens a chance to get away from the constant grind, a place where, as one teen described to me, "we're not in shackles."

That's a powerful statement. It's the kind of sentiment shared by many teens who visit Teen Central. They view it as a sanctuary from the outside world, a place where they can be themselves. Teens feel safe and secure in Teen Central, both physically and psychologically.

The teens who frequent our space appreciate that Teen Central is a structured environment not only with things for them to do, but also with rules to be followed. They appreciate the fact that, in the words of one teen, "If something happens, it's going to be handled by a mature adult." One girl talked to me about the time two girls started harassing her in Teen Central and following her around the rest of the library; she was really scared. She was so glad when Teen Central staff asked our security guard to step in and make the girls leave her alone. Another teen told me about the time that some teens stole his prized possession: his portable CD player. Security was on it, and within a day, his CD player was returned to him and the thieves were ejected from the library. This sort of structure and physical safety is a huge reason for Teen Central's success with teens.

Inside Teen Central

- A café with vending machines is restricted to teens only.

- The music collection contains more than 5,000 CDs.

- The living room has a dance floor.

- Staff includes one full-time librarian, two full-time library assistants, and three part-time library assistants.

- The Teen Council meets twice a month and acts as an advisory board for the room, also planning and funding programming.

- *Create! Zine* is published biannually; its material is selected and formatted by our Zine group called Coffee Asylum.

125

Since teens know that Teen Central is a safe place to hang out, they begin to let their guard down around the staff and other teens alike; they feel psychologically safe. This neutral environment is free of many constraints that teens find elsewhere in their lives. In the words of one teen, "There's no 'social standing' or cliques here." This neutrality is amazing to watch, as teens from different schools and various social and academic backgrounds mix and become friends. One girl proclaimed proudly, "I met my first lesbian here." A shy boy gradually came out of his shell and developed a huge circle of friends. He explained to me how happy he was that when he started high school next year, he'd have lots of friends, most of whom he had made at Teen Central. Teens also appreciate the extra leeway they are given in Teen

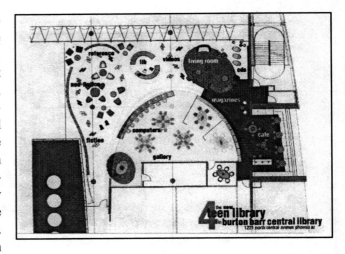

Central that they can't find in the rest of the library. "You can be more yourself without being kicked out," says one teen, while another adds, "You can actually talk without the librarians busting you."

The openness created by this psychological safety extends to the staff. Teens new to Teen Central often approach our staff warily at first, but once they see that these adults care and take the time to listen, many of them begin forming relationships with us. In fact, many teens feel so relaxed that they open up about difficult situations in their lives. Pregnancy, issues of sexual identity, homelessness, abuse by parents and boyfriends—these topics and more have come up at Teen Central. Our staff has been able to guide teens toward resources that will help them cope with these problems. For a time, Teen Central piloted a partnership with the City of Phoenix Human Services Department. A caseworker was dedicated to Teen Central, here to take our service to teens to the next level when needed. In addition, the caseworker held focus groups with teens on topics of importance to them, such as relationships and teen rights. Phoenix Public Library continues to see the importance of this partnership, and is seeking funding to sustain the caseworker position.

Teen Central's collections also foster psychological safety. As one teen said to me, "There are teen resources here. Adults don't like this stuff, so it's like our own little world." Teens know that whether they need information on pregnancy, books for a report on the Holocaust, the latest *Gossip Girl* paperback [Little, Brown], or if they just want to check out a cool CD or graphic novel, they need look no further. In addition, they can hop on the Internet and watch music videos with their friends, or interact in online communities such as chat rooms and game Web sites. Teens know that when it comes to meeting their educational, recreational, and social needs, they can count on Teen Central. That's a secure feeling.

A Community Asset

Teen Central has been widely supported by the larger community. The citizens of Phoenix recognize the need for safe spaces for teens and value the fact that Phoenix Public Library had the courage and foresight to develop Teen Central. From the very beginning the community was on board, with donations flying in to support its construction. In addition, the Library ensured the buy-in of its teen users by involving them from the start. Teens were invited to five different focus groups during Teen Central's planning process, where they interacted with the architect and librarians to help plan every aspect of the room, including the floor plan, collection, and services. The opening of the space in April 2001 was a huge event, with local newspaper reporters on hand and a TV news station reporting live.

The attention has not faded. Articles continue to be written about Teen Central and its great programs and services. Teachers bring their students in for tours, encouraging them to use our space after school. Group homes bring their residents here to use our resources. Many other community organizations also want to be part of Teen Central, approaching us to form partnerships. We partnered with the Phoenix Art Museum when some of our teens produced a print piece for one of their exhibits. Our teens worked with the staff of KNOW 99, the Phoenix Educational Channel, to produce a short commercial advertising all that Teen Central has to offer. These examples are just two of our many community partnerships.

But perhaps our most important feedback comes from the day-to-day comments we receive from adults in our community. They are ecstatic that their teens have a safe place to go. They thank us repeatedly, saying "Why couldn't they have had something like this when I was a teen?" Just like their teens, they know how vital it is to have Teen Central in the community.

The Challenge

I can't think of a single reason why every library's priority should not be to provide a safe space for teens, where their educational, recreational, and social needs are met. If Teen Central has taught me nothing else, it's that such a space is not only critical for teens themselves, but is also craved and valued by the community as a whole. Teens need spaces where they feel both safe and cherished. Such needs are not going to go away. Libraries must make a choice: Do we take the path of least resistance and continue to ignore or marginalize these needs, or do we accept the challenge and work toward providing teens with the best and safest space that libraries can offer?

Burton Barr Central Library, Phoenix Public Library, 1221 N. Central Avenue, Phoenix, AZ 85004, (602) 495-5114
http://www.phoenixpubliclibrary.org/branchinfo.jsp?bid=BBB

Teen Realm

City of Mesa Library
Mesa, Arizona

Diane Tuccillo

Description: On the north central side of the Main Library's first floor is a roomy, 2,300 square-foot space that belongs to teens alone. Perched atop a column, a blue neon sign proclaims the Teen Realm name in old English lettering. Divided from the Adult area by a long shelf that contains the combined YA/Adult science fiction/fantasy collection, the Teen Realm feels like a separate space. The other two sides of the triangle are white walls covered with shelves, displays, posters, and bulletin boards, such as Mesa Youth Placement Service's board with weekly notices and applications from this teen employment service co-sponsored by public schools and local businesses. Displays are always changing: a "Post-a-Poem" board celebrated Teen Read Week, and teens can sign up for bulletin boards to display their own artwork or other items. A striking wall display features enlarged jackets of books nominated for Teens' Top Ten.

Blending with the blue-gray carpet are dark blue-green upholstered chairs: 8 lounge chairs around two low wooden tables, and 32 desk chairs around 5 study/work tables. Signs on the tables declare: "Tables reserved especially for Teens." Through a door is a large Youth Activity Room for programs, shared with the Children's Room; dividers allow more than one group to use it simultaneously. A Youth Services desk serves both the children's and teen areas; beside it is a volunteer desk where teen volunteers assist teen patrons.

Collection: The Main Library's entire Young Adult collection of 23,045 volumes is housed on 332 shelves in the Teen Realm, including YA fiction and nonfiction, picture books for teens, adult books for teens (Alex Awards and classics), teen series paperbacks, YA Reference, YA College/Career Collection, comics and graphic novels, audiobooks, videos, music CDs, magazines, and board games for use in the Teen Realm. Shared with Adult is science fiction/fantasy on 119 additional shelves that border the area. In the 2002–2003 fiscal year, 115,191 YA items circulated at the Main Library. (Two branches have YA collections, not counted here.) The two computers in the Teen Realm contain only word processing; a computer area nearby has 8 computers for use by teens and children, with the online catalog, various databases, and filtered Internet access. Computers in the Adult areas are not filtered.

Population and Community: Located in the Phoenix metro area, Mesa is the third largest city in Arizona and the fortieth largest in the U.S. Teens and preteens comprise about 15 percent of a growing, diverse population of 440,000 which is 73 percent white, 20 percent Latino, 3 percent African American, 2 percent Native American, 1.5 percent Asian, and .25 percent Pacific Islander and "other." The library serves 26,257 students in 13 junior high schools and 6 senior high schools. The system's Red Mountain branch has its own Teen Realm, and the Dobson Ranch branch has a YA collection with no special space. Both branches have YA specialists.

Hours and Teen Traffic: The Teen Realm is open during all library hours: Monday to Thursday from 9:30 a.m. to 9:00 p.m., Friday and Saturday from 9:30 a.m. to 5:30 p.m., and Sunday from 1:30 p.m. to 5:30 p.m. Teen traffic, ages twelve to eighteen, varies according to the time of day or day of the week. Charter schools bring in weekday classes, and in after-school hours or on weekends, five to twenty teens are usually using the Teen Realm.

Staffing: Young adult services are part of Youth Services, with a staff of nine also working with children. The Youth Services Supervisory Librarian oversees the whole department. The YA Coordinator is in charge of the Teen Realm. The remaining four full-time librarians and three part-time librarians all help with YA programming, and three have special YA duties: one is in charge of the YA/Adult SF/Fantasy collection; another is in charge of the series paperbacks, college/career collection, and bulletin boards; and a third helps with displays and the teen Web team. With the YA Coordinator, they are instrumental in running teen events and booktalking for school visits.

Planning Process: The original library building had a "very '70s" YA area. The new 1981 building had a YA Room much smaller than the Teen Realm. In February 2003 when the first floor was remodeled, a bigger space was

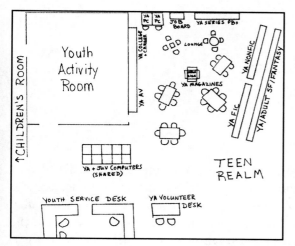

planned for teens, closer to Adult and further from the Children's Room. The long-standing Young Adult Advisory Council (Y.A.A.C.) was asked for input, choosing the Teen Realm name and the neon sign. They also specified cool new furniture, but budget cuts forced the use of the old tables and chairs from the YA Room—fortunately still in good condition—as well as lounge furniture hand-me-downs. Y.A.A.C. hosted the Teen Realm's Grand Opening on November 1, 2003, from 2:00 to 4:00 p.m., with two bands playing and freshly made cookies donated by a restaurant. In the open-house atmosphere, the 60 teens attending explored the Teen Realm or listened to the music in the Activity Room.

YA Programming: Founded in the late '70s, Y.A.A.C. is one of the oldest teen library councils in the U.S. Their main mission is to promote books, reading, and the library to their peers, producing the "Open Shelf" book review. (See Y.A.A.C.'s profile on the Young Adult Library Services Association's TAGs Web site at *http://www.ala.org/tags*.) They also plan programming such as teen poetry slams each fall and spring. Separate teen groups include Teen Takes, who design and write for the library's teen Web page (*http://mesalibrary.org/teens*), and the editorial staff who publish the annual teen literary magazine, *FRANK*. Teen volunteers work at the YA volunteer service desk, helping patrons, setting up the Activity Room for programs, and doing various other tasks. Last year's annual teen summer reading program, "Great Books Make Great Movies," was run as a Maricopa County cooperative with local sponsors offering prizes such as movie and concert tickets.

True Confessions from Young Adult Coordinator Diane Tuccillo

This is the YA space of my dreams because . . .

"Our teens have a generous amount of space and a large, well-maintained materials collection that covers all genres and topics of interest. It is a comfortable area for browsing or just hanging out, and also for doing school work."

I still dream of these improvements:

- More and better equipped computers in the Teen Realm.
- More funding to keep the collection fresh and current.
- New furniture that the teens help to select.
- More library branches with teen spaces.

Teen Patron Comments

"I like the wide selection of books—there is everything from historical fiction and fantasy to nonfiction and books on current social issues. Plus, the Teen Realm is a place where teens can be themselves."—Danielle, 16

"The new Teen Realm is awesome! We have so much space now, and a place that's not also for little kids. Plus, there are all the activities available to us. It's really great!"—Alyssa, 14

City of Mesa Library, 64 E. First Street Mesa, AZ 85201, (480) 644-3100
http://www.mesalibrary.org/Home.aspx

The YA Stop

Avon Lake Public Library
Avon Lake, Ohio

Karen Scott and Jill Ralston

Description: A main "avenue" runs the length of this open-plan library, with alcoves on either side. The YA Stop is centrally located off the avenue in an alcove just beyond the adult audio-visual area and across from Adult Reference. An open space of 1,226 square feet with a high, vaulted ceiling, the YA Stop's large alcove has three large rectangular windows and one large round window, letting in lots of natural light. Two round study tables have four chairs each, two upholstered booths with tables also seat four each, and a lounge area has a seven-piece sectional sofa beside a gas fireplace, which is extremely popular during long, cold winters. After school when the fireplace is roaring, teens plop down on the hearth and sofas to warm up and visit with their friends. On order is a customized neon sign to designate the area as The YA Stop. It will hang over the fireplace on a brick wall.

A patterned carpet with large geometric shapes in vivid colors of navy blue, green, purple, and burgundy is echoed in the upholstery, a combination of prints and solids in the same colors. Movie, music, and reading posters adorn the cream-colored walls. One wall features a hanging display system for student art work from local schools. There are two other special walls: a small magnetic poetry wall and a slat wall for displaying graphic novels. Most of the YA materials are spread around the perimeter. Just outside the alcove is the YA staff desk; adjacent are six YA computer work stations with unfiltered Internet access, databases, word processing, and the online catalog.

Collection: A collection of 5,200 items includes recreational reading, homework and curriculum support, and reference. Oak bookcases hold 239 square feet of metal shelves with magazines, comics and graphic novels, audiobooks, young adult fiction and nonfiction, and adult books for teens. Black wire racks hold 89 square feet of paperbacks, videos and DVDs, and music CDs, each in their own section. Even board games have a special section. All library teen materials are housed in the YA Stop, which circulates 3,050 items per month.

Population and Community: Avon Lake is a suburban community of 19,000 on the shores of Lake Erie, covering eleven square miles approximately twenty miles west of Cleveland. With a median income of $66,000, the population is 96.4 percent white, 1.2% Hispanic, and .8% of two or more races. Local employment is split between education, health and social services; manufacturing; and professional, scientific, management, administrative, and waste management services. The teen population includes 2,200 students in two middle schools and an elementary/middle private school, as well as a high school adjacent to the library parking lot.

Hours & Teen Traffic: The YA Stop is open during all library hours: Monday to Thursday from 9:00 a.m. to 9:00 p.m., Friday and Saturday from 9:00 a.m. to 5:00 p.m., and Sunday from 1:00 p.m. to 5:00 p.m. from September to May. The high school next door is dismissed at 2:52 p.m., making 3:05 p.m. the busiest time of day when the students arrive. At any time after school, twenty to twenty-five teens ranging in age from eleven to eighteen occupy the YA Stop. Adult patrons use its computers during the morning and early afternoon, but all six YA computers are in use most evenings by teens. On weekends, the space attracts fifteen to twenty teens at a time. In quieter moments, they curl up with comic books and graphic novels. Occasionally even an adult reads in the area.

Staffing: Although the YA space has existed for ten years, it has had its own staff for only four years. Previously staffed from the Adult Reference desk, the YA Stop currently employs one full-time professional young adult librarian and one part-time paraprofessional youth services associate. The two cover all the hours that the library is open.

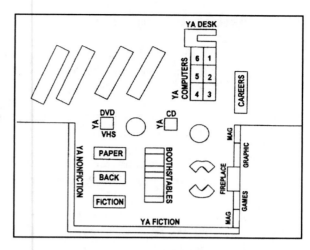

Planning Process: To the original 1958 library building, a 1983 addition of 18,000 square feet was made. The second renovation in 1994 added 35,000 square feet, which included the YA space. The library staff was encouraged to offer their input during the planning process, visiting other libraries with YA spaces to generate ideas. Their goal was to create a space that encouraged safe, constructive interaction and study. In August 1994, the whole library hosted a huge grand opening for the community with much fanfare, attended by local dignitaries. Remarkably, the library's 1994 designers had such vision that their YA creations have needed little updating. Four years ago when the current YA staff came on board, they replaced old wooden paperback shelving with wire racks, and added the AV collection. The poetry and graphic novel walls were added two years ago. When the new neon sign was recently approved, the current teen users of the space renamed the old YA Department as the YA Stop, recalling the historic cable car line that once had "stops" along Electric Boulevard, the street that runs by the library. And they also prefer the name "YA" to "teen"!

YA Programming: Although there is no teen advisory council, teen volunteers work with the children's department and DiscoveryWorks (our unique hands-on science center), assisting with programs, story times, crafts, and other tasks. The library offers an annual summer reading theme with teen appeal. Teens fill out forms for each book read to submit for weekly prize drawings such as gift bags from Target, Old Navy, and Claire's. Our grand prize last summer was a DVD player. Three times a year, winter, summer, and fall, the library produces a program booklet for all ages, each featuring a few ongoing YA programs, one or two new YA programs, and a craft. Ongoing programs have included a babysitting clinic sponsored by the Red Cross, ACT-SAT test preparation workshops, and Yu-Gi-Oh Card Jams. Other programs are mystery lunches, bake-offs, a teen spa, chess bonanza, anime and cartoon drawing, and wet-n-wild trivia (with water guns or water balloons). Craft projects have produced duct tape wallets and purses, hacky sacks, garden stones, birdbaths, homemade gift boxes, CD picture frames, and more.

A new YA Stop page is currently being designed for the library's Web site at *http:// www.alpl.org.*

True Confessions from Young Adult Staff

This is the YA space of my dreams because . . .

"We have our own space and staff. The YA Stop has a very welcoming atmosphere and allows for a lot of interaction with the teens. Making those connections is really important. Being responsible for our own collection development is also a plus."—Jill Ralston

"It's great to see the teens enjoying an area that is truly their own. We are very fortunate to have an administration that supports our efforts."—Karen Scott

I still dream of these improvements:

"I would like to see some color added to this high-ceilinged, open area with all cream colored walls—possibly painting the soffits by the ceiling. The teens would tell you, 'More computers!' I don't know if we could ever have enough of them!"—Jill Ralston

"Some additional soft seating around the fireplace would be nice. Our teens like to get comfortable when reading or meeting their friends."—Karen Scott

Teen Patron Comments

"It's a good place to stay and hang out with friends while waiting for your parents because we can play on the Internet and listen to music on the computers, and the librarians are really nice."—Kati Titus, 15

"They offer many programs and graphic novels to keep us busy, and I enjoy that."—Amanda Olson, 15

"The computers are always available and it's probably the best connection to the Internet I have."—Paul Henry, 18

Avon Lake Public Library, 32649 Electric Boulevard, Avon Lake, OH 44012, (440) 933-8128 *http://www.alpl.org/*

YA Book Nook

Hays Public Library
Hays, Kansas

Erin Downey Howerton

Description: Teens in Hays, Kansas, enjoy a large section of the Marianna & Ross Beach Wing of the new Hays Public Library that is devoted just to them. From the library's main lobby, teens climb the stairs to their own 3,000-square-foot space on the second floor, the YA Book Nook. As they enter, a round skylight in the New Materials Lounge makes the floor glitter with sun, highlighting the rich colors of the blue velvet couch and green suede easy chairs and chaise. Rolling ottoman cubes covered in a vivid modern print with stripes of purple, orange, yellow, and green match the throw pillows on the chairs. Beanbag chairs are everywhere. New YA fiction and nonfiction books sit face-out on a long row of shelves. Beside the graphic novels are displays of YA award books. A wheeled glass case features monthly displays created by teen groups such as Drama Club, introducing their activities. Near the stairs are slant-shelved magazines. The neon YA Book Nook sign, designed by a Teen Advisory Board (TAB) member, hovers above the magazines. The wall around the neon is covered with padded fabric panels, on which posters, notices of current events, and signs—in a barcode font—are pinned. On other lounge walls, original art pieces share space with READ posters. The lounge is a transition point between the Young Adult Department and the Children's Department, which shares the second floor. But it is only the start of the teen space.

A short hallway leads to restrooms, drinking fountains, and built-in cubbies for storing backpacks. Past the cubbies, the main floor holds the bulk of the YA collection as well as the YA HQ—the service desk. Across from the desk are four dark blue cafeteria booths. Two have brushed aluminum desk lights and two have accent lamps: one pink neon flamingo and one blue glitter lava lamp. Over two booth tables, sound domes dangle.

Radiating from this open area are three more rooms for teens: a round study room with space for eight; a computer lab (also serving as a tech classroom) with nine stations containing unfiltered Internet access, word processing, online catalog access, and any games teens bring; and the Trish Davies Young Adult Performance Center with a sound system for CD and radio. Its wood laminate flooring makes teens feel onstage as soon as they enter the room. Across from the modular stage are four high café tables beside a popular snack vending machine. Additional modular tables and chairs seat twenty-four people. All three rooms overlook downtown Hays through floor-to-ceiling windows.

Collection: The entire young adult collection of 6,500 items is housed on 930 square feet of shelving in various units throughout the YA Department. The main floor contains YA fiction and nonfiction in Dewey order, with a face-out biography section, large print fiction, and audiobooks. The lounge houses new materials plus comics, graphic novels, and magazines. The reference collection lives in built-in shelves in the Study Room, and the music CD collection perches above board games and card games in a built-in unit in the Trish Davies room. Since the YA Book Nook opened in February 2004, between 350 and 400 items a month have circulated.

Young Adult Population and Community: Hays Public Library is part of the multi-county Central Kansas Library System, serving a larger rural area beyond Hays. Hays itself has a population of around 20,000 people, is the seat of Ellis County, and provides resources to surrounding smaller communities. Fort Hays State University is a real presence in the town, bringing in a different mix of patrons. The dominant minority group is Hispanic. Because the library serves teens from the two middle schools and two high schools (one public, one parochial) in Hays as well as teens from surrounding areas, the library's teen population is difficult to estimate. It is probably between 2,400 and 3,000 teens.

Hours & Teen Traffic: The YA Book Nook concentrates its staff's services on after-school hours and weekends; hours differ from the rest of the library. It is open from 2:00 p.m. to 9:00 p.m. Monday through Thursday, 2:00 p.m. to 6:00 p.m. Friday, and 1:00 p.m. to 5:00 p.m. Saturday and Sunday. After school, between twenty and forty teens fill the department; on weekends traffic varies with activities. Ages range between eleven and nineteen. During off-hours when the teen population drops, patrons of all ages from college students onward have adopted the space to study and hang out.

Staffing: One full-time professional librarian is YA Department Head, and two YA assistants work part-time.

Planning Process: The original Carnegie library opened in 1911, and was bulldozed in 1968 in favor of a new building. YA materials and programming were offered through the adult department beginning in the early 1980s. Various YA materials spaces grew over the years, from 180 square feet in 1986 to 567 square feet in the 1990s. After 1992, when a new library was anticipated, teen focus groups provided continuous input. Teen advisory boards drew sketches, poured over color samples, and dreamed up all the main elements in the finished department today. The end result was decades in the planning, and reflects continuous care and attention to detail for a dedicated teen space.

During the entire library's grand opening, a community open house on February 14, 2004, patrons enjoyed free pizza while a local radio station broadcasted live from the YA area. Teens called in to the deejays with answers to book trivia questions for gift certificate prizes. People tried out the board games and enjoyed tours of the new space.

Youth Participation and Programming: The Teen Advisory Board (TAB) holds semimonthly meetings when they hang out in the new space, make wish lists of new materials, and plan events. TAB members often clean up the space, create displays, and place genre labels on books, among other projects. They always decorate the library's "Frost Fest" float for the winter holiday parade.

In 2004, the library incorporated the Get Lost @ your library state YA summer reading theme with regional history and a performance by an actor playing Amelia Earhart. Throughout the year, murder mysteries happen at least twice, and Fridays after school involve

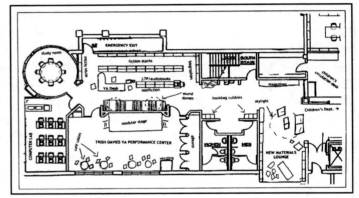

some sort of game tournament, free popcorn or snacks, music, and a relaxing atmosphere. Most YA Book Nook programs are informal and free-flowing. Homework Helpers meet formally on Wednesdays between 3:30 p.m. and 5:00 p.m., but it is understood that anybody can meet in the study room any afternoon, when middle and high schoolers help each other with schoolwork in a "get help, give help" system that teens conceived for themselves.

True Confessions from Young Adult Department Head Erin Downey Howerton

This is the YA space of my dreams because . . .

There is a space for every teen who comes here! Whether they're interested in computers, books, a quiet place to study, to dream (that SKYLIGHT!), or to get together with friends after school, teens can do it in our new space. They have a ton of ownership, and we take all requests and suggestions seriously, emphasizing freedom of speech and the responsibility to make their own choices.

I still dream of these improvements:

Storage is at capacity already, so we are looking into ways to maximize our closet space. Many teens have asked for a sharper definition between the children's and YA departments, and that's a project that we are considering from different angles. A warning to YA librarians planning more space: You will have more traffic, so staff accordingly! Our popularity has dramatically increased the need for both volunteer and paid help in order to maintain the department.

Teen Patron Comments

"The other [space] was boring and now it's more fun. I like the new computer lab and the café tables."—Brendon McCampbell, 14

"I love this place! How old do you have to be to work in the library? I'm coming here first thing when I turn 16 and I'm going to be a librarian."—Tyler Fross, 14

"Well, now it doesn't suck! It's nice to have a place to go that's not in the middle of the adult area where we can have music and food, too."—Emma Detrixhe, 16

Hays Public Library, 1205 Main Street, Hays, KS 67601, (785) 625-5916
http://www.hayspublib.org/

Teen Center

Newport Beach Public Library, Central Branch
Newport Beach, California

Genesis Hansen

Description: The Teen Center at the Newport Beach Public Library has found a new home and a new look, and the reaction from local teens is glowing. A bright orange neon sign above the Young Adult Librarian's desk announces the Teen Center, newly located on the second floor of the Central Library in a rectangular space of 1,058 square feet. A wall of floor-to-ceiling windows frames a view of the Pacific Ocean, palm trees, and sunshine. A funky sofa, three lounge chairs, and two ottomans—each in a blue, turquoise, or purple hue—face this great view. Five wood tables have seating for fourteen.

A wall of display space is painted forest green with a faux granite look, on which is mounted a classic round wall clock labeled "TEEN TIME" underneath. Along this wall are teen magazines, graphic novels, new YA fiction, and new nonfiction for teens. Paperbacks are shelved along the back wall on three tall banks of shelving (about nine square feet). Two ranges of low shelving (about eighty square feet) in the center of the area hold the main collection of YA fiction, audiobooks, and YA reference. The blue-green shelving complements the colors of the display wall and the lounge furniture. The beige walls and patterned light and dark green carpet blend in neutral tones. Three bulletin boards display local teen art. The Teen Center is its own room, opening onto an adjacent area

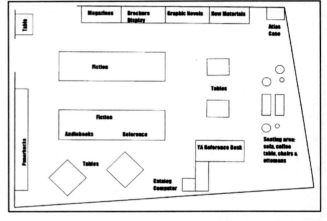

with many study tables and 29 public computer terminals, which have Internet access, Microsoft Word, PowerPoint, Excel, the library catalog, and a variety of research databases. A library catalog computer is dedicated to teens during Teen Center hours. The library also offers wireless Internet access, allowing teens to bring their personal laptop computers into the Teen Center to connect to the Internet.

Collection: The Young Adult collection includes approximately 7,500 books, 500 audiobooks, 9 teen magazines, and a variety of graphic novels. Displayed face-out, graphic novels and magazines have seen a marked increase in circulation since the Teen Center relocated in December 2003; overall YA circulation increased 16 percent in that time. New nonfiction for teens is housed in the Teen Center in Dewey order; after a year it is interfiled in the adult nonfiction collection. Videos, DVDs, and CDs are shelved in the Popular Library for all library patrons.

Young Adult Population and Community: Newport Beach is an oceanside community in Orange County, California, with a stable population of 72,500 residents. About 5,800 young adults are enrolled in one middle school and three high schools. According to the 2002 Census, 8.4 percent of the population is between the ages of ten and nineteen. Newport Beach is a mostly white, affluent community. The city-run library also serves much of southern Orange County, with a more diverse but still middle- to upper-class population.

Hours and Teen Traffic: The Teen Center is open during all library hours, beginning at 9:00 a.m. Monday through Saturday, but is reserved exclusively for teens Monday to Thursday from 4:00 p.m. to 9:00 p.m., Friday from 4:00 p.m. to 6:00 p.m., Saturday from 1:00 p.m. to 6:00 p.m., and Sunday from noon to 5:00 p.m. Because the Teen Center is so near the large study area and the computers, teens are often in and out; the number of visitors can range from three to twenty at any given time. Most teens use the area to study and catch up on homework, but many can be found taking a break and browsing through the graphic novels and magazines.

Staffing: During special teen hours, the Teen Center is staffed by one of two Young Adult Librarians, Melissa Hartson and Genesis Hansen, who also work at the Adult Reference Desk. The librarian on duty is always available for reading suggestions and assistance in locating the next resource for a teen's research project.

Youth Participation and Programming: An active Young Adult Advisory Council (YAAC) meets monthly. The 25-member YAAC plans programs and gives input into library issues, such as voicing their opinions on the styles and fabrics for the new Teen Center furniture and suggesting new CDs for library purchase. They also host and help coordinate library scavenger hunts for younger library customers several times a year. A new endeavor for the YAAC is "The Read World," a program that discusses books and promotes reading on the local public access television channel.

In the Teen Summer Reading Program, teens are eligible to win prizes ranging from paperback books to major league baseball tickets for reading a book and entering weekly drawings. Each week's entries are eligible for the grand prize drawing at the end of the program. This year's grand prize was a mini-iPod. A strong crew of teen volunteers assists with the Summer Reading Program and Read-to-me Program registrations in the Children's Library, as well as other tasks.

Finding the Right Home: The Central Library, built in 1994, officially opened the Teen Center in October 1999. The Newport Beach Public Library, the NBPL Board, and the YAAC were all strongly committed to enhancing teen services at the library. The library had just hired its first Young Adult Librarian, Terri Wiest, who carved out a corner for the Teen Center on the main floor of the library not too far from the Children's Room and the Popular Library, where new books and magazines are housed. The Teen Center had comfy chairs and sofas, two large tables, and four dedicated teen computers. Teens often came to browse the collection, but quickly left. Circulation statistics showed that teens were checking out books; they just weren't making the most of the area as hoped.

After four years, the Teen Center was seeing a small but steady stream of usage. The circulation statistics were up 100 percent, but the teens still weren't really hanging around in the space. When the opportunity arose to move the Teen Center upstairs to the Business Room, the YA librarians jumped at the chance. The whole library closed for a week during December 2003 for a number of repairs and renovations, and the Teen Center moved to its new home. The following weeks proved that this move was successful; some afternoons and evenings, no seating was available—a rare occurrence in the old Teen Center. The proximity to the adult collection, the large picture windows with a view, the comfy seating, and the abundant display area endowed this room with an entirely new teen-friendly feel. Local teens are responding by their presence day after day.

True Confessions from Young Adult Librarian Genesis Hansen

This is the YA space of my dreams because . . .

"It's great to have a really functional and inviting space—with an ocean view, no less! Our teen patrons seem to agree and are using the room and materials much more than they did in the old space—I think that they feel more at home here. Most of all, I think it demonstrates that the teens at NBPL get our best instead of our leftovers."

I still dream of these improvements:

"I'd love to make this room a place for more recreational use, adding a teen CD collection and listening station, and possibly a gaming station. We're also hoping to get some laptops that can be checked out by teens to use in the Teen Center."

Teen Patron Comments

"I like it better because the old Teen Center was too close to the Children's Room and you could kind of hear them. Plus this one is bigger and way nicer."—Ashley, 14

"It looks so cool!"—Bridget, 15

"I just like it and it has a nice view."—Alex, 13

Newport Beach Public Library, 1000 Avocado Avenue, Newport Beach, CA 92660, (949) 717-3800
http://www.newportbeachlibrary.org/

Club Q & A

Southfield Public Library
Southfield, Michigan

Shari Fesko

Description: From Southfield Public Library's lobby, teens go "through the looking glass" of swirly rainbow window panels below a multicolored sign shaped like a sideways question mark that might belong to a hip night club—Club Q & A (Question and Answer). Inside the entrance, a semicircular bank of seven flat-screen computers, each in its own niche of gold or lime green or royal blue, supports the impression of a private, alternate world for teens only. Wrapped around the other side of a wall that surrounds a circular staircase, the swirl of computers echoes the large golden swirls in the dark blue carpet and complements the room's quirky shapes and colors. Rounded "bambo" chairs perch on pedestals at each terminal. A huge, lime-green pole supports the ceiling.

Opposite the computers are three café-style booths of blue and white, each with its own TV/DVD/ video player recessed in the wall. In the center of the floor are three round study tables, each with four blue mesh chairs. A second entrance in the glass wall from the Youth Room opens into a lounge area where teens congregate on shiny, metallic blob chairs with low, kidney-shaped tables beside a silver wall for posters or magnetic poetry. Through another glass wall is a group study room with an oblong table and chairs, meant for six teens but often filled with a dozen or more. The only part of this 1,140-square-foot space that has windows, the study room overlooks the library lawn and busy Evergreen Road.

Collection: Metal wall shelving with green panels contains more than 6,000 items including hardcover YA fiction and nonfiction, picture books for teens, adult books for teens, paperbacks, and more than 500 graphic novels. Books on tape and CD as well as videos and computer-game CD-ROMs are included. Special compartmentalized shelving holds DVDs and music CDs. Flip-up magazine shelving allows storage of back issues underneath. Circulation is rising steadily, with 2005 figures expected to double the 2004 circulation. A few YA reference works are shelved in the adjacent Youth Room, but otherwise all library YA materials reside in Club Q & A. The teens' computers feature an online catalog, databases, word processing, filtered Internet access, and a printer station.

Young Adult Population and Community: Southfield is a city only ten minutes from Detroit, with roughly 78,000 residents; 60 percent are African American and the rest are a mix of Caucasian, Indian, Russian, Arabic, and Asian. The mostly middle-class and lower middle-class community contains many single-parent families. Large, profitable businesses pump much funding into the city. The library serves a total of 7,500 students from three middle schools and two high schools. It also serves many Detroit residents.

Hours, Staffing, and Teen Traffic: Club Q & A is open during all library hours: Monday through Thursday from 9:30 a.m. to 9:00 p.m., Friday and Saturday from 9:30 a.m. to 5:30 p.m., and Sundays from 1:00 p.m. to 5:00 p.m. from September to Memorial Day. Club Q & A is usually full by 3:30 p.m. on a typical

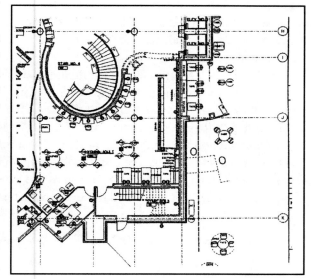

school day; as many as 200 teens, ranging in age from eleven to nineteen, come in and out. Weekend days draw about 100 teens. The computers are in constant use. Magazines, DVDs, videos, books, and computer games fly off the shelves. Many college students also use the space, as well as adults in mornings and later evenings.

The Youth and Teen Services Librarian is one of six full-time Youth Librarians (including a Youth Services Co-ordinator), assisted by one Youth Intern. The Youth staff shares duties, but everything related to teens is exclusively the domain of the Youth and Teen Services Librarian—with much support from the library's entire staff, including support, technical, and adult services.

Planning Process: The old library jammed thousands of patrons every month into its cramped 44,000 square feet. With little more than three shelf units of hardbacks and three spin racks, teens were the most overlooked age group. No designated teen specialist assisted them as they competed with children in the youth room and with the many business people and college students on the other two floors. Led by City Librarian Doug Zyskowski, the library staff worked hard to convince the community to build a new library. The bond issue passed on March 9, 1999. Focus groups planning the new building included teens who gave their input on what should go into the new teen room. Librarians visited children's museums and public libraries to get ideas for the youth area and the teen room. Phillips Swager Associates of Dallas, Texas, was hired, with project architects Denelle Wrightson, Eddie Davis, and Dirk Dalhauser incorporating the notion of Discovery as an indelible part of the library design. Construction began on April 11, 2001.

On June 15, 2003, the new library celebrated its Grand Opening with a Ribbon Cutting Ceremony. Ribbons and pairs of scissors hung from poles so that patrons could cut the ribbon along with the Mayor and City Librarian. In the circulation lobby was a huge cake in the shape of a stack of books. Librarians answered questions in each area of the building about its features, giving away magnets and color maps of the library.

Two new youth staff positions were added for the larger new library, one of which Shari Fesko filled in April 2003. Although hired as a youth generalist, Fesko focuses on the teen age group. In two years, with much support from coworkers, Fesko has dived into YA collection development and programming, roaming through Club Q & A each day to introduce herself to teens with overwhelmingly positive results; many return her greetings the next day or come back to participate in programs.

Youth Participation and Programming: Club Q & A has made such an impression on teens that many are eager to volunteer to become a part of the library community. To meet this demand, Fesko began a teen volunteer program in Fall 2003. Ever since, a revolving list of hard-working, highly motivated participants take their volunteering seriously. Attendance at new programs, including three Poetry Slams taped for the local cable station, has been high. A Readers Theatre Group presented their third performance in May 2005 with scripts developed from picture books such as *The Cat in the Hat*. Players must audition each time; 22 teens participated in the first performance and 28 appeared in the second, with teen crews who make props and costumes. The audience has grown to more than 100 parents and children.

In April 2005, a High School Battle of the Books began with nine teams reading five books and competing to answer questions about them. It is expected to grow like the long-running Middle School Challenge, which began with a small number of teams and grew to 55 teams, thanks to the support of school media specialists and teachers and an aggressive public relations campaign.

In conjunction with author Celia Rees's visit to the library, a discussion group about her book, *Pirates!*, is being held, with plans for an ongoing teen book group. To complement this year's teen summer reading game called "Do It Yourself Summer," unusual "DIY" sessions are planned on using duct tape, creating a functional item for a competition, redecorating bedrooms, and tinkering with cars.

True Confessions from Teen Services Librarian Shari Fesko

This is the YA space of my dreams because . . .

"It is a place just for teens, which the teens of this community truly appreciate. I love that it is a one-stop shopping spot; all teen materials are in one convenient location."

I still dream of these improvements:

"I know this area is huge compared to what they had before, but I would like to see it bigger. I also wish the TVs were more interactive and not just there to watch. Although we added track lighting after we opened, which has helped considerably, Club Q & A is still a bit too dark. As we grow and change, I know that lighting will be addressed."

Teen Patron Comments

A common comment from many teens who are flocking to the new space is "I wish this was my bedroom."

Southfield Public Library, 26300 Evergreen Road, Southfield, Michigan 48076, (248) 796-4200
http://www.southfieldlibrary.org/

Starbucks Teen Center

Seattle Public Library, Central Library
Seattle, Washington

J. Marin Younker and Amy Duncan

Description: Reflecting its role as part of one of the most spectacular new city libraries in the nation, the Starbucks Teen Center is all gleaming glass and 21st-century minimalism. Named for its city's famous coffee bar that donated $500,000 to the Libraries for All project that raised funds for the new library, it resides on Level 3 of the 11 levels of the 363,000-square-foot glass-and-steel Central Library in downtown Seattle. Among 25 neighborhood branches, the Central Library with its 400 public-access computers is a destination for teens from the entire city and county.

The 3,900-square-foot Teen Center is a long, thin rectangle stretching along the entire west side of Level 3. Its sunken floor is lower than other departments. With entrances at both the north and south ends, it opens into the Norcliffe Foundation Living Room that has comfortable seating for patrons of all ages. The Teen Center is reserved for teen use unless an adult accompanies a teen or uses the collection. At the south end, the long Teen Center Reference Desk, marked with "Teens" in large lettering, is visible from the entrance off 5th Avenue. A wall of glass extends upward at a 40-degree angle over the sidewalk below the Teen Center's west side. On the east side, a long counter holds a dozen black, flat-screen computers: two with the catalog and databases and ten with unfiltered Internet access and Microsoft Word. Teens can log on with their library cards for one hour per day. Thirteen study carrels complete the east wall. Posters with teen flavor are mounted on several support columns.

The Teen Center's bold color scheme contrasts its distinct orange floor with furnishings of gray and black. In the center of the space are three large, gray tables with black chairs for group study: Two tables seat four people each and the other seats eight. Along the western edge are seventeen orange, block-shaped foam cushions for casual seating. Behind a wall at the north end are two teen project rooms for special events. The larger project room seats fifteen at two tables and features a long storage counter with a sink. The smaller project room seats six at one table and contains a whiteboard and two Internet and Microsoft Word computers; one has Adobe Photoshop. On the eastern side of the project rooms is the Teen Services Librarians' workroom off the public floor.

At the Teen Center Reference Desk are program flyers and booklists. A bulletin board advertises teen library programs as well as community events and organizations. One low shelf near the desk displays graphic novels, comics, and reading recommendations.

Collection: Teen Center shelving totals 19.4 square feet containing 5,327 items plus 33 magazine titles. Seven metal shelves for magazines, books, and audiobooks occupy the north end. Current magazines are shelved face-out with back issues underneath. New YA fiction has its own section apart from older YA fiction—there are no adult books for teens outside the adult fiction collection (also on Level 3). Each teen fiction shelf includes a face-out display. New YA nonfiction—advice and popular culture titles of high interest, not homework-related—is the only nonfiction in the Teen Center. All other YA nonfiction is interfiled in the Books Spiral, a continuous run of adult nonfiction on Levels 6 to 9. Other Teen Center sections contain YA fiction audiobooks and YA series fiction. Next to the Teen Center is the adult science fiction and fantasy section, conveniently located for teen genre readers. Music and movie titles of interest to teens are found in adult collections.

In August 2004, three months after the library opened, 1,578 YA fiction titles circulated in the Teen Center—a 488% increase from 323 August 2003 titles. With more standard November 2004 traffic, Teen Center YA fiction circulation is still impressive: 813 YA fiction titles show an almost 200% increase since November 2003.

Young Adult Population and Community: The largest city in the Pacific Northwest, Seattle is in King County, Washington, between Puget Sound and Lake Washington, 108 miles south of the Canadian border. The Central Library serves teens from across the city, whose 2000 population was 563,374. Along with the King County Library System, Seattle Public Library also serves King County, the nation's nineteenth most populous county, whose 2003 population was 1,761,411. According to the 2000 census, 18 percent of the city's population is under age 20, with this breakdown: 50 percent Caucasian, 15 percent Asian, 12 percent African American, 9 percent two or more races, 8 percent Hispanic, 4 percent other races, 1 percent American Indian, and 1 percent Pacific Islander. The census also shows that 14.5 percent of children aged 17 and under live below the federal poverty level. In the 2003–04 school year, 39.2 percent of students received free or reduced price lunches at Seattle Public Schools.

In the downtown business district, the Teen Center serves a total of 1,543 students in two schools covering grades six to twelve and six diverse high schools, including a Catholic boys' school and another private school. Four Seattle School District schools serve special populations: One has a liberal arts focus, another is for ESL (English as a Second Language) students, one is in partnership with the YMCA, and one serves homeless teens in conjunction with YouthCare. Another school serves teens who are being treated or who have family members at the Fred Hutchinson Cancer Research Center.

Hours, Staffing, and Teen Traffic: Like the rest of the library, the Teen Center is open Monday through Wednesday from 10:00 a.m. to 8:00 p.m., Thursday through Saturday from 10:00 a.m. to 6:00 p.m., and Sunday from 1:00 p.m. to 5:00 p.m. Attracting primarily high school-age teens, after-school hours bring 20 to 75 users and weekends are filled with 40 to 100. Two full-time, professional Teen Services Librarians staff the Teen Center Desk, answering readers' advisory questions. They also do community outreach, programming and system-wide activities, and some collection development. They update the teen section of the library's Web site with teen reading lists, book reviews, librarians' book picks, teen program promotions, and links for teens at *http://www.spl.org/default. asp?pageID=audience_teens*. The Adult Fiction Department assists with desk staffing. Teen reference questions are answered in the all-ages Mixing Chamber on Level 5.

Planning Process: Because the former Central Library did not have a separate teen area, the Teen Center was a major priority for the new building. Teen and community input was solicited throughout the construction process. In January 2000, work groups were formed to plan spaces for specific populations; the Young Adult work group included teens. When the new Central Library opened on May 23, 2004, the Teen Center celebrated with a presentation by Book-It Theatre called "Baseball Stories" and invited students to attend an author visit by Isabel Allende. In coordination with the Mayor's Youth Council, teen input was requested concerning the library.

Youth Participation and Programming: Five teen volunteers participate in Teen Talk Time, a pilot program in partnership with the Chinese Information Services Center that brings new immigrant, low-English-proficiency teens together with bilingual teens who have grown up in the United States. The two book groups are Pizza and Pages, which discusses Best Books and Quick Picks nominees while eating pizza, and the Parent-Teen Book Group for middle schoolers who read and discuss a title with parents.

The Teen Summer Program consists of a series of programs plus the opportunity for teens to turn in a book review for a free book of their choice. Seattle Public Library partners with the local nonprofit Arts Corps to offer quality art programming based on the Search Institute's forty Developmental Assets. Library-produced programs include anime showings, computer lab drop-ins, and other events. This summer, "Catch Them Reading" targeted those who use the Teen Center but don't fill out reviews—librarians handed them colorful "flip pens" with the library's logo and Web address.

Central Library celebrates Teen Read Month, Banned Books Week, Black History Month, and Poetry Month through various programs held at the library and in local schools to strengthen partnerships. To fulfill the role of teen advisory boards, a series of bimonthly, topic-driven, drop-in Teen Input Forums (TIFs) is being considered, rotating between branches and the Teen Center.

True Confessions from Teen Services Librarians J. Marin Younker and Amy Duncan

This is the YA space of my dreams because . . .

The Teen Center is located in a building that has been nationally and internationally celebrated. The Central Library challenges teen stereotypes and notions of what a library is. Well situated on an entry-level floor, the Teen Center is very eye catching and visually distinct.

I still dream of these improvements:

We originally ordered two sound-dome listening stations for the Teen Center. Upon installation, we discovered that too much noise was leaking, which might disturb patrons. We would love to install replacements using innovative technology. We also hope to replace the foam cushions with seating that is more lounging-friendly. Lastly, we'd like an art installation on Plexiglas (or a similar material) that would create a distinct wall along the eastern edge of the Teen Center, further separating it from the general Living Room space.

Teen Patron Comments

"I come to the library every other day. Before the new Central Library, I never knew about the library. I like it because they help me find a book when I need it."—Jamie, 16

"I think the library is a good environment for doing school work. I get distracted at home. I come here three to four times a week. I like everything about it."—Jacqueline, 15

"The Teen Center is a wonderful place. A safe place. This is where teenagers can come to work on school projects and surf the net. I didn't come to the old library, but I come here three times a week. This library is much better because before there wasn't a place for teens."—Jason, 17

Seattle Public Library, 1000 Fourth Avenue, Seattle, WA 98104-1109, (206) 386-4636
http://www.spl.org/

The Teen Space

Carnegie Library of Pittsburgh
Pittsburgh, Pennsylvania

Karen Brooks-Reese

Description: It's almost "through the looking glass." An entrance in the decorated glass walls of the ground floor's adult popular collections in the newly renovated Carnegie Library of Pittsburgh–Main opens into the new Teen space. An eye-catching green "TEEN" sign in graffiti print greets customers as they enter. Beside the entrance, dynamic signage hangs above the Teen Librarian's desk: a shiny "Ask a librarian" sign with changing messages about library events. From the desk, almost every part of the Teen space is visible. This large trapezoid of 1,660 square feet divides into four areas: a lounge, computer workstations, a meeting room, and shelving areas. Closest to the desk are five flat-screen computer workstations, beyond which are two small, round tables with four seats each. Four additional stations sit against the glass wall. Computers contain the online catalog, databases, Word processing, and filtered Internet access. Four Mac workstations along the back wall offer Adobe Photoshop Creative Suite and other software to aid in the creation of film and video. In a back corner is another study table with four chairs.

The space is dominated by the large meeting room, reminiscent of a miniature building-within-a-building. The meeting room features a whiteboard (frequently written on), announcement postings, and enough room for larger groups to work at two tables with ten seats. One wall of glass doors can be opened entirely to make the meeting room an extension of the space. Closing the doors creates a quiet area for programs, meetings, or studying. Behind the meeting room is a staff office.

The rest of the space is a study in contrasts, with sleek modern furniture in bold, bright oranges, reds, and yellows; chrome and white tables; orange resin desks; and a soothing green carpet. The lounge area contains a coffee table, a sofa, and two comfy chairs with floor lamps near a door that leads to the stacks, where the majority of the teen fiction and nonfiction is shelved. Beyond that door, in a corner containing graphic novels, is another lounge area with two comfy chairs and a low table. Artificial skylights placed in the original ceiling create a bright, airy feeling, accentuated by the white walls. Despite all the modern features—including a signed poster of Neil Gaiman—the architectural beauty of the 1895 building shines through.

Collection: Space for the teen collection's 13,516 items (as of 2005) is divided between the 128 shelves of the stacks in about 312 linear feet, and the main room's 68 built-in, dark oak shelves that are original to the building, with 204 linear feet. Displays of new books, staff favorites, and titles relevant to special events highlight the stock of YA fiction, series paperbacks, picture books and adult books for teens, an extensive graphic novel collection, nonfiction cataloged with the Library of Congress system, magazines and zines, audiobooks, music CDs, Xbox games, reference, and curriculum support. In 2005, 40,650 teen items circulated.

Young Adult Population and Community: The Main library's Oakland neighborhood of Pittsburgh is home to the University of Pittsburgh, Carnegie Mellon University, Carlow University, and Chatham College as well as several hospitals. Oakland is a very diverse urban area, as its universities and hospitals attract residents from all over the world. In addition to serving the residents of Oakland, this Main Library of the Carnegie Library of Pittsburgh system is a resource for people throughout Allegheny County. Schools from southwestern Pennsylvania arrange for visits to the library for research and instruction. During weekends, teens from all over the county come to the library for materials and to hang out with their friends. As a result, the library's service population is difficult to measure. About 4,700 teens live in the Oakland area, attending one public high school and one public middle school, in addition to several local private and charter schools. But the public schools draw students from several area neighborhoods, and students at the private schools come from all over the county.

Hours, Staffing, and Teen Traffic: With the rest of the library, the Teen space is open Monday through Thursday from 10:00 a.m. to 8:00 p.m., Friday and Saturday from 10:00 a.m. to 5:30 p.m., and Sunday from 1:00 p.m. to 5:00 p.m. After school from 2:00 to 6:00 p.m., all computers and furniture in the Teen area are reserved for about thirty middle and high school students who use the space. Weekends attract about twenty teens at a time. The majority of users are between 13 and 17, but many adults seek out graphic novels and Xbox games, among other materials. Students from the MLIS program at the University of Pittsburgh often use the reference, fiction, and nonfiction collections.

Four full-time staff members work primarily in the Teen space: a Senior Librarian and three paraprofessional Teen Specialists. First Floor staff members sometimes cover desk shifts in Teen, while Teen staff members often cover desk shifts and are involved in First Floor programming.

Planning Process: To update the 1895 library building, a strategic planning process began in 2000. One of its goals was to improve services to young adults. Involved in the process were the previous library director, the previous manager of the Teen Zone—its former name—and several other librarians, who conducted community focus groups that included teens. Renovations began in 2002. The renovated First Floor of the Main library, including the Teen area, reopened in September 2004. During the interim, a very small space was allotted for teen materials on the library's second floor. Teen festivities for the official Grand Opening on October 3, 2004, included *Dance Dance Revolution*, Urban Legend storytelling, a graffiti artist, music, and food.

Youth Participation and Programming: At the request of its members, the Teen Advisory Council is called simply that. Its ten members help decide what programs to offer and make recommendations for materials as well as how to decorate the space. Several teen volunteers are involved in different projects: One is creating a database of all the zines with the goal of adding them to our catalog; several help with shelving and shelf-reading; and a group of eight designed and is implementing an early literacy program for young children called "Tell-A-Tale Theater." Although the library offers no tutoring, several tutors meet with their charges in the Teen area. The library subscribes to Tutor.com.

Teen programs range from the semiannual Teen Read Buffet to weekly programs such as the Monday Movie Matinee and *Dance Dance Revolution* every Friday. Filmmaking programs occur semiweekly in several yearly sessions. The Teen Summer Reading program is almost entirely online (*http://www.carnegielibrary.org/teens/tsr*). Teens log the books they read, and each week any teen who has logged is entered into a raffle. At the end of the summer, all participants who fill out a survey about the program are entered into a drawing to win a limo ride and tickets to a local amusement park for themselves and some friends. In addition, summer reading participants can have their fines waived once per summer. Increased summer programming includes weekly Teen and Tween Crafts and *Dungeons & Dragons*.

The teen section of the library's Web site, *http://www. carnegielibrary.org/teens*, is maintained by Teen staff, who also run a Teen blog for updates and reviews at *http://clpteens.blogspot.com*, created by Teen Specialist Karen Brooks-Reese; and a MySpace account for connecting with Pittsburgh teens at *http://www.myspace.com/clpteens*, created by Teen Specialist Joseph Wilk.

True Confessions from Teen Specialist Karen Brooks-Reese

This is the YA space of my dreams because . . .

"I never believed other librarians when they told me that teens 'hang out' in the library. Now, thanks to our new, vibrant space, they do."

I still dream of these improvements:

"More color—a mural on the wall, or artwork, or *something* to use up all the lovely white space. It would be great to have a successful book discussion and increase program attendance."

Teen Patron Comments

"There are a lot of opportunities presented in Carnegie Library's Teen area. Everything is easy to find, and the librarians don't hesitate to help you. Movie Mondays are fun (if I haven't seen the movie), and it's cool that they show them on the big screen."—Sonia, 15

"The Teen area has such a relaxed atmosphere and what makes it unique is it's fun here. People including myself go to the library every weekend to play Xbox and *DDR [Dance Dance Revolution]*—so the Teen area isn't just a place to read and do homework."—Aisling, 16

"The librarians are some reasons this library is one of my favorite places to be. They help to create and maintain this wonderful and supportive environment. The library is not just a place to borrow books and check your e-mail—it's a safe, fun, and invigorating place to learn, hang out, and have a great time."—Sarah, 17

"It's pretty sweet here. You can do your homework and play a few games every once in a while. I really like it here."—Nick, 15

"It's actually really awesome because you just come here and there aren't interruptions, and you can hang out with your friends, do work, and go on the computer. There are lots of resources for research, and it's easy to use. I definitely like coming here."—Phil, 15

Carnegie Library of Pittsburgh, 4400 Forbes Avenue, Pittsburgh, PA 15213, (412) 622-3114 *http://www.carnegielibrary.org/*

The New, Improved Best Cellar

Waupaca Area Public Library
Waupaca, Wisconsin

Peg Burington

The Best Cellar, Waupaca Area Public Library's original teen space built in 1998, was one of the first to be featured in *VOYA*'s "YA Spaces of Your Dreams." In 2002, when I became Assistant Director, teens already wished to make changes to their space. The teens I brought together eventually became the Student Library Advisory Group, (SLAG). They earned money to buy paint, added a decorative finish to the beige walls, and purchased a small refrigerator for drinks. They covered the oversized chairs with colorful fabric and lobbied for another computer. SLAG also planned teen activities and helped to select materials.

Increasing teen traffic was making the 616-square-foot teen room crowded and uncomfortable. The library's 2003 strategic planning process determined that the space allotted for young adults was "inadequate." Expanding into existing storage space would double its size. To design the new space, architectural designer Dawn Phillipsen and architect Bob Acord worked with SLAG members. A brainstorming session resulted in a wish list: more computers, an interesting paint job, quiet study space, a gaming system, comfortable seating, more tables, padded chairs, a drinking fountain, and a large refrigerator.

Plans were in place but budget constraints delayed the renovation. SLAG worked with the Library Foundation and Friends of the Waupaca Library to raise additional funds. Two teen SLAG members went through a grant interview process, speaking eloquently about the teen program and the relationships that they had formed through the library. Their obvious passion helped them win a $15,000 grant from the Fox Cities Community Foundation for computers, electronics, and furniture. When library staff and volunteers told patrons about the "wonderful community of teens" who used the Best Cellar, and their plans for a bigger space that more teens could enjoy, the community responded. The budget was approved and construction began in March 2006. The YA collection and activities were temporarily housed in the library's exhibit room.

New, Improved Decor and Furnishings

To brighten the storage area's twelve-foot unfinished ceilings, SLAG suggested painting the existing concrete structure, pipes, beams, and heating vents. SLAG members had chosen the flooring, paint colors, and cabinetry, and went shopping to pick out "funky furniture." Under my supervision, teens painted the walls apricot and added a decorative finish.

When teens arrived at the grand opening on Friday, April 28, 2006, to play games, use computers, and eat pizza, they found the neon "Best Cellar" sign from the old space hanging above the arched doorway to the Youth Department. The new 1,400-square-foot teen space prompted many "WOWs." In one corner, a red vinyl restaurant-style booth seats six. In the opposite corner, a gaming area holds three upholstered cubes and a large-screen TV. Both booth and TV are connected to sound-localizing speaker systems whose "sound domes" look like inverted acrylic salad bowls, allowing gaming and listening without disturbing others. Beside the gaming area is a twelve-foot computer bar with eight stools, four computers using the library's wireless connection, Ethernet cables for four laptops, and a printer.

Black metal shelving lines the walls, holding YA fiction and nonfiction, careers, biographies, magazines, DVDs, and videos. Music CDs have their own carousel. Double-sided oak shelving contains audiobooks and graphic novels. Red bell-shaped hanging lamps illuminate the wall shelving, while track lighting and fluorescents light the room.

In the center are two round tables for four, a large red-and-black sectional couch, an oblong display unit, and the staff desk. A three-tiered storage system wraps around a structural column, designed by the architect for belongings such as backpacks and jackets. The drinking fountain in SLAG's original plans required costly plumbing; instead there is a bottled water dispenser. Acoustical sound clouds help absorb the sound. Blue-and-black checkerboard linoleum brightens the floor. Entirely different from the rest of the library, this unique space has its own look and atmosphere.

A Room Just for Programs

A glass door between two large windows leads into a separate room for teen programs, SLAG committee meetings, study groups, and quiet reading. The TV's five-foot screen is perfect for gaming, movies, and computer activities. Snacking is easy with a refrigerator, microwave, and cupboards. Two six-foot tables can be folded, and twelve folding chairs can be tucked away in the cupboards. Two oversized chairs, pillows, a lamp, and a rug add comfort. The program room's walls are painted in vibrant blue, highlighted by a lighter blue pattern.

Staffing

As Young Adult Coordinator, I oversee all activities planned for the Best Cellar, order materials, and serve as SLAG's advisor. Because I am also the library's Assistant Director, the room is staffed by two part-time Young Adult Library Assistants when school is not in session. One is a high school student and one has graduated, planning to pursue a library degree. Both are avid readers who readily offer readers' advisory and reference help to the teens who enjoy relating with peers who supervise their space.

Building Teen Library Services and Spaces: A Recipe for Success

The Waupaca Area Public Library serves a population of 17,000 in central Wisconsin, in the city of Waupaca and the towns of Farmington, Dayton, Waupaca, and Lind. Sometimes I am asked how my small community library can offer such a phenomenal teen program. Here's my recipe for success:

1. Get teens involved and get involved with teens. Start a teen advisory group to help plan and facilitate programs. Be prepared to respond when you ask what activities and space they want; they assume you will act on their suggestions. If you cannot provide what they ask for, explain why. Learn your teen patrons' names and spend time talking with and listening to them. Encourage their involvement as advocates, employees, participants, and volunteers! My SLAG members call themselves "library junkies."

2. Place the right person at the helm. The person in charge of teen services must enjoy teenagers, be tolerant but able to set limits, be a good listener, be ready to get her hands dirty, and have a great sense of humor.

3. Provide opportunities for everyone to feel included by offering a variety of activities and programs. One size does not fit all! The teens who come to a book discussion might not be the same ones who join an Anime Club.

4. Be visible and verbal. Library staff and teens who use the library are your greatest advocates. Go out into the community to talk about your program or proposals for a new teen space. Rotary, Lions Club, City Council, school assemblies, and radio or local cable TV shows provide venues for getting the word out.

5. Gain advocacy across generations. Don't limit your library talk to teens and families. Evidence indicates that having more adults in young people's lives is a predictor of their well-being and success. Connecting teens with others, by teaching crafts to young children or computer skills to senior citizens, offers them the opportunity to be leaders and build relationships throughout the community.

6. Gain the support of all your stakeholders: your administrator, Library Board of Trustees, Friends of the Library, and other organizations associated with your library. Encourage them to adopt excellence in library services to teens as a common goal.

7. Don't use lack of money as an excuse. Foundations and community organizations are interested in funding youth programs. You, too, can win a grant.

8. Create a unique space! The teen space does not need to mirror the rest of the building. Go beyond library walls to look at interesting spaces in all different kinds of buildings.

9. Be flexible. The teens who assist you with planning programs and spaces will move on. A whole new batch of teens will appear in five years or less. Trends change; expect teens to make changes. Your furniture doesn't have to last for twenty-five years!

10. Embrace and respect teen culture and technology. Use it to attract teens to your space and programs. Technology plays a large part in teens' lives. Familiarize yourself with IM, gaming, and other trends.

Teen and Staff Comments

"It's freakin' awesome! The library teen room offers opportunities for teens to socialize and use library resources. It's better than any library I've ever been to."—Kyle, 13

"This library is my home away from home. I love it because everyone gets along. I check out about twenty books at a time and it meets all my reading needs."—Alison, 15

"The best part about this new space is that it was designed by the teens who use it. It's exactly what they wanted. Their ideas weren't edited or watered down by adults. Compared to the old room, it is a much more comfortable place to work—more elbow room!"—Jessi James, Young Adult Library Assistant.

Waupaca Area Public Library, 107 South Main Street, Waupaca, WI 54981, (715) 258-4414 *http://www.waupacalibrary.org/*.

Columbus Public Library
Columbus, Georgia

Brijin Boddy

Description: To reach the Teen Department, teens walk through Popular Materials, passing the library café. Just outside the large glass wall with double doors marked "Teen Room," teens find graphic novels and popular series on low shelves. Inside the glass wall that maintains an open feeling while containing noise, the focal point of the rectangular 1,779 square-foot space is irresistible: an electric-blue surfboard computer table more than ten feet long. Ten flat-screen computers are reserved for teen "surfing," homework, listening to music, or online chat. Ten green and purple rolling chairs with adjustable height levels are ranged around the surfboard.

An oasis of color and light, the room has its own spacious energy. Overlooking the back lawn, the outside glass wall allows natural sunlight to fill the space and reflect off the vibrant orange wall paint. Along that outside wall, teens lounge in chic and comfortable swan chairs of yellow or orange, curling up with a book or chatting with friends. Interspersed with the chairs are three low, round coffee tables that showcase new books, bookmarks, and flyers. Sleek, stain-resistant cork floors add a rich brown color to the décor. Even the little things in the Teen Department support its fun, eclectic theme. The clock is a large, colorful sunburst on the back wall. The light fixtures are star shaped. Retro-inspired oblong cutouts in the wall relieve its orange expanse.

As teens enter, they face the octagonal metal display sheet on the wall—a unique showcase for upcoming events. Along the back wall, three tall rows of metal shelving house audiobooks and teen fiction. Although the Teen Department has a square, wooden study table with four chairs that overlooks Popular Materials, it also offers two quiet study rooms: one just inside the entrance and the other, near the fiction, designated for "Homework Help" and containing the teen reference collection. Each room has a long study table and six purple or green rolling chairs. Glass doors allow visibility into the rooms while restricting noise flow. These study rooms are one of the Teen Department's most popular features, used by about eighty teens per month and frequently booked in advance for group projects, social meetings, or individual study.

Between the two study rooms is the staff area. A glass door leads to a spacious office for the teen librarian, with ample shelving, storage, and plenty of floor space to spread out works in progress. Outside the office door, a short shelving unit holds rotating book displays. A public staff desk faces the Teen Department's entrance, where staff members greet teens as they enter, field questions about computers, and provide reader's advisory for YA fiction, graphic novels, and series.

Collection: The Teen Department's collection contains 8,456 YA fiction books, 383 audiobooks, and 309 reference books as well as magazines and board games. More than half of the 400-plus volumes in the graphic novel collection are usually circulating. Less than a year after moving into the new library building, YA fiction circulation skyrocketed from 8,123 books in the old building's last year to 30,630 in the new building, a 277 percent increase. Circulation of 2,322 volumes of YA nonfiction, intershelved with adult nonfiction, more than doubled in the new building. Young adult DVDs and CDs are also in adult collections.

Through GALILEO (**G**eorgi**A** **LI**brary **LE**arning **O**nline), teens' computers access more than a hundred databases and more than 2,000 journals with full-text articles, encyclopedias, and government publications. The library also subscribes to Learn-a-Test, an interactive online learning platform with practice tests and courses including SAT, AP, GED, ASVAB, and many others. All computers have Microsoft Word, Internet-based computer games, and Internet access filtered by the Secure Computing Smart Filter. Using CD/DVD drives with headphones, teens listen to music and watch DVDs or Internet videos. The Teen Department also plays requested, approved music on Friday afternoons. One separate computer is an online catalog and another is a reservation station for booking computer time.

Young Adult Population and Community: The Columbus Public Library is the main library of the Chattahoochee Regional Library System, located in Columbus, Georgia, in Muscogee County, an urban area with 186,291 citizens. According to the 2000 Federal Census, the county's population is 50.4 percent White, 43.7 percent African American, 4.5 percent Hispanic, 1.5 percent Asian, and 0.4 percent Native American. Median income is $34,798; the home ownership rate is 56.4 percent. Just six miles from the library is Fort Benning, one of the largest Army posts in the United States, housing around 100,000 soldiers and dependents who are eligible for library cards and services. In Muscogee County, the library reaches 18,360 students in 23 middle schools and 16 high schools. Beyond the city of Columbus and Muscogee County, the Regional Library System serves four other Georgia counties: Chattahoochee, Marion, Quitman, and Stewart. In the five-county area, the library's Teen Department serves approximately 23,837 teens. More difficult to count are teens in eight additional Georgia counties and three Alabama counties where the library issues free library cards.

Hours, Staffing, and Teen Traffic: The Teen Department is open during regular library hours: Monday to Thursday from 9:00 a.m. to 9:00 p.m., Friday and Saturday from 9:00 a.m. to 6:00 p.m., and Sunday from 1:30 p.m. to 6:00 p.m. After school, the Department draws an average of 102 teens, ages twelve to eighteen, per day. On weekends, teen traffic increases to an average of 117 teens per day. Staff includes one full-time professional librarian as Teen Department Head, one full-time public service staff member, and two part-time public service staff members.

Planning Process: In 2000, a comprehensive study of what people wanted in their library found that the community shared a service vision that included an up-to-date building with an expansive print collection and online services as well as a role for the library as a cultural center for the city, with meeting rooms, study rooms, computer training classes, and lectures. After many open community meetings invited feedback from teens and adults, the final plan was set. On April 24, 2003, ground was broken for the new Columbus Public Library. Construction of the 100,000-square-foot building took less than two years. The library's grand opening occurred on January 3, 2005; the Teen Department opened on January 7.

Youth Participation and Programming: In November 2006, the Teen Department conducted the first meeting of its Teen Advisory Board, which will have an opportunity to influence programming and develop the future Teen Web Page. In addition, 108 teens volunteered throughout the library system this past year; five volunteers work in the Teen Department.

Ongoing programs include a monthly Teen Writer's Workshop and a Homework Help program that meets three nights a week and weekend afternoons. The Teen Department teaches three monthly computer classes with varying fun and educational topics. Each month, the Department hosts a Saturday matinee movie in the library's auditorium, which boasts a large screen, surround sound, and comfortable seating for 128 people. Recent movies include *The Sisterhood of the Traveling Pants* and *Coach Carter*. One newer program is a Teen Book Discussion Club at a local high school. Every other month, participants meet with the Teen Librarian during lunch period to discuss the book they have chosen to read. In keeping with Teen Read Week's Get Active @ Your Library theme in October 2006, a Get Active with Your Friends program included an online gaming event in which teens shared tips and secrets about their favorite online games.

In 2005, the first Summer Reading Program in the new building, "I'm with the Band @ the Library," was a great success, drawing 592 teens who read 923 books. Teens who read five books earned an invitation to a Murder Mystery Night at the end of the summer and a chance to win one of five iPod minis. In 2006, a comic book-themed Summer Reading Program enjoyed equal success. A Winter Reading Program ran from December 1, 2005, through January 13, 2006; reading ten books earned a chance in a drawing for a portable DVD player.

True Confessions from Teen Department Head Brijin Boddy

This is the YA space of my dreams because . . .

"it offers a unique and fun area that is just for teens. They have their own computers, study areas, lounge area, and their own books. It's a great space for teens to be teens in the library."

I still dream of these improvements:

"I would love to see more seating and desk space. And of course more shelving is always wonderful."

Teen Patron Comments

"I like it because it's comfortable. You're around people your own age, and it's easy to talk to friends and still get things done. It's very organized."—Amber, 16

"I like the set-up of everything being separated into different sections."—Jasmine, 17

"You get to meet new people, talk amongst yourselves. You get peace of mind and quiet."—Whitney, 17

"I like the anime books and getting on the computers and sitting and reading the books."—Devin, 12

Columbus Public Library, 3000 Macon Road, Columbus, GA 31906, (706) 243-2669
http://www.cvlga.org/branches/columbus

A Teen Library at the Mall

Palos Verdes Library District
Rolling Hills Estates, California

Alison Orr

Located in a retail space next door to the Palos Verdes Library District's main library, the Annex teen library was conceived by PVLD Director Kathy Gould as a way to meet the demands of our active teen patrons, who had outgrown our small YA area. Limited by the building's layout, a larger, more private YA space inside the main library was impossible. So when a storefront opened up in the mall next door in spring 2006, planning for the Annex began. Just six months later, on September 15, 2006, we opened our doors. Although developing an independent teen space beyond the confines of the library may seem daunting, the Annex is proof that it can be done. By partnering with a local nonprofit organization, building community support, and most important, listening to our young adults, we created a unique and successful teen space.

The teen-designed Annex logo hangs above the circulation desk.

Maximum lounging: vintage Herman Miller chairs, couches, and open floor space.

In the back corner, the computer bar is a popular spot.

How the Annex Got Started

Palos Verdes Library District operates three public libraries on the Palos Verdes Peninsula, a residential community outside of Los Angeles, California. Local teens often complain that "there's nothing to do on the hill," (as Palos Verdes is called). Although many use the PVLD main library, the small YA space cannot accommodate the boisterous energy of a large teenage crowd.

To develop a fun, safe hangout space for teens, PVLD partnered with Freedom4U, a local nonprofit that promotes healthy activities for teens. Together with library board members and local parents, PVLD and Freedom4U planned the framework for the project.

The mission of the Annex is to provide students in grades six to twelve with a supervised, dedicated space that complements the services of PVLD and Freedom4U's programs and offers:

- Opportunities for safe, constructive interaction in a comfortable environment

- A collection of high-interest, up-todate, circulating library materials such as paperbacks, magazines, comics, graphic novels, and other formats of special interest to teens

154

- Access to games, computers, and other sources of information and entertainment

- A place where teens can meet, talk, hang out, and have fun

- Activities sponsored by PVLD, Freedom4U, or other community organizations

The Annex is funded by the Peninsula Friends of the Library as well as Freedom4U donors. Local businesses supplied furniture and carpeting at a discounted rate. Local interior designer Stacey Green generously donated her services to create a stylish yet comfortable atmosphere on a limited budget.

Description: The Annex is a 1,500 square-foot retail space between a barber shop and a golf shop in a shopping center next door to the library. An L-shaped room with one restroom and a staff room/storage area, the space officially can hold more than 100 people, but it begins to feel crowded with more than 50. With a cool blue and green color scheme and the clean lines of modern furniture, the Annex exudes a hip, coffeehouse feel. It contains four round tables with chairs, two couches, and four vintage Herman Miller chairs (which had been sitting in storage at the main library for years).

In the back of the Annex, the 42-inch flat-screen TV (donated by a parent) is usually surrounded by teens perched in beanbags and playing the Playstation 2 or Nintendo GameCube consoles, purchased with funds from our teen-run bake sales. Our ceiling-mounted LCD projector shows movies against the back wall. In the corner, a custom-built "computer bar" houses five computers with

Teen volunteers were involved in every aspect of Annex development—even painting!

flat-screen monitors. Each is equipped with Internet capability, word processing programs, and our PC reservation management software.

The entire Annex collection of books, graphic novels, and magazines is housed on outwardfacing, slat-wall shelving. We reused slat-wall panels that were left by the previous tenant and purchased wire holders that display the collection in a bookstore-like fashion. To maximize floor space, we avoided freestanding shelving and spinning racks. For ease in rearranging furnishings to accommodate programs such as live performances and movie nights, all the Annex furniture is on casters or wheels.

The reference desk is in the back of the room and the circulation desk is up front, allowing the staff an uninterrupted view of the entire space. On the wall behind the circulation desk, a four-by-six foot canvas features a reproduction of the Annex logo, which was designed by thirteen-year-old Amanda Ho, winner of the Logo Design Contest in the summer of 2006. Her logo is also featured on the outside of the building and on all Annex publicity material.

Collection: The Annex collection complements the existing, comprehensive Young Adult collection of more than 3,200 items at PVLD's main library. Although a few items support school curricula, the exclusively paperback Annex collection features high-interest recreational reading: more than 600 popular fiction titles, some nonfiction titles, and more than 150 comics and graphic novels. Twenty-five magazines cover a range of topics including sports, fashion, gaming, entertainment, and world events. All paperbacks, graphic novels, and magazines

Looking in from the entrance, the hip style and attractive paperbacks draw many teens daily.

Teens can find their favorite magazines and even a guitar to play.

are available for checkout. A growing collection of CDs, DVDs, and video and board games are not circulated. The video games are in almost constant use.

Hours, Staffing, and Teen Traffic: The Annex is operated by PVLD on Monday to Thursday from 3:00 p.m. to 9:00 p.m. Freedom4U operates the Annex on Friday from 3:00 p.m. to 10:00 p.m., Saturday from 1:00 p.m. to 10:00 p.m., and Sunday from 1:00 p.m. to 6:00 p.m. The PVLD staff includes one part-time Annex Librarian and two part-time Annex Library Assistants. The Freedom4U staff is largely parent volunteers. At least two staff members are in the Annex during all open hours. The Annex is open only to young adults in grades six through twelve. Upon entry, all patrons are required to show a student ID or some other form of identification that includes their age. Adults and children in fifth grade and below are not permitted to use the Annex.

Approximately 50 students frequent the Annex on weekdays. Many of these teens also visit the main library, alternating between the two spaces. We were very pleased with the Annex door count of 577 for the first full month of operation, and expect that more programs and word-of-mouth publicity will increase our numbers.

For Teens by Teens

Teens might cite the video games, relaxed atmosphere, or hip design, but I think that the most exciting thing about the Annex is the high level of teen involvement during its development. Beginning in April 2006, we visited local middle and high schools and led brainstorm sessions with the teens. As leader of the library's teen volunteer group, the Peninsula Teen Activity Council (PTAC), I encouraged discussion of the Annex at every semi-monthly PTAC meeting, asking the teens' ideas, opinions, concerns, and expectations. I was met with insightful, creative, and mature responses that were integral to the Annex's development. At the main library, I led another Annex brainstorm discussion that was open to the public. Teen volunteers recorded suggestions from the group on posters mounted around the room. Many items on those long lists of books, magazines, CDs, graphic novels, DVDs, and video games are now part of the Annex collection. During frequent brainstorm and discussion sessions, teens also helped to develop the Annex rules, design the physical layout of the space, and plan events for the grand opening.

Our teens' involvement wasn't limited to discussion. With the help of our enthusiastic Facilities department, we hosted the Annex Painting Party in August 2006. Teens arrived early on a summer morning to spend the day painting the interior walls. Equipped with rollers, brushes, and a lot of energy, the teens enjoyed the work and developed a sense of ownership over the space. When these volunteers come into the Annex today, they like to point out which walls they painted. In September 2006 as the Annex opening approached, teen volunteers labeled, organized, and shelved the entire Annex collection. Our grand opening party featured games, music, pizza, and prizes, and was attended by more than 65 teens, many of whom helped the Annex take shape. Teen volunteers continue to support the Annex by suggesting and participating in teen programs such as our teen zine, teen craft activities, and semi-monthly Anime Club.

Hard Work Pays Off

With partnerships, community support, teen involvement, and resourcefulness, libraries can make independent teen spaces a reality. Since the recent opening of the Annex, we have received a positive and enthusiastic response from our community and we look forward to a bright future for our new teen space.

Teen Patron Comments

"The Annex is a great place to hang out after school. Even as an eleventh grader, I enjoy the specialty and entertainment provided by this convenient place. I like the fact that there is nobody who is going to tell you that you are being too loud unless you are literally yelling."—Scott, 16

"The Annex is a great place to socialize with friends and make a couple of new ones. There are lots of things to do, and I think that's why it appeals to a wide variety of teens. And the occasional party/event keeps it interesting!"—Andrew, 12

Palos Verdes Library District, 701 Silver Spur Road, Rolling Hills Estates, CA 90274, (310) 377-9584
http://www.pvld.org/

Knowasis: Thunderbirds Charities Teen Learning Center

Scottsdale Civic Center Library
Scottsdale, Arizona

Medina Zick

Description: When you cross the stainless-steel threshold of Knowasis, you enter a different universe. From the main hall of Scottsdale's Civic Center Library, you pass through an etched glass enclosure featuring the lightbulb-and-lightning Knowasis logo. You step onto a woven carpet of silvery grey plastic vinyl (Plynl). Dominating the room is the ceiling, an amazing piece of artwork with drop panels covered in scrim fabric, backlit with color in five sections. You hear music playing in surround sound and the chatter of busy teens at the cyber circle or lounging on bright, geometric-shaped foam furniture while watching a 52-inch plasma TV. Glass, steel, and concrete highlight this 4,000-square-foot teen space.

Teens watch the plasma TV in the living room area.

To the left of the entrance are three glass-walled study rooms with cork flooring. Four tables seat sixteen. A glass wall slides open to convert two small study rooms into one larger room. Beyond these study rooms are movable foam chairs and ottomans of lime green, sky blue, hot pink, raspberry, taupe, and grey. Five listening domes are scattered throughout the room. In the living room area, the foam seating focuses on the huge TV, flanked by a steel display area. On the wall, 22 clear acrylic frames hold teen artwork and photos.

Near the living room is a circular table with fourteen flat-panel computers. With wireless access, the computers offer Microsoft Word, Excel, PowerPoint, filtered Internet access, databases, and the library catalog. Games include *SimCity*, *Zoo Tycoon*, and *Rollercoaster Tycoon*.

The etched-glass Knowasis entrance shows its logo and donors' names.

Opposite is a translucent white staff desk for two, with changeable tube lighting at the bottom and a standing express computer station for teens. Wrapping around the desk is the homework area, with five glass-top tables and two computers containing SAT software. Sixteen retro-style plastic chairs in red and baby blue mirror the table design with silver metal bases.

In the back, a café area has two metal tables seating a total of six, two vending machines, and a stainless steel bar and sink. The café will eventually include an outside shaded patio with additional seating. Eating and drinking is permitted throughout Knowasis.

Study rooms near the Knowasis entrance.

Busy teens in the cyber circle; the staff desk is in the background.

Collection: Shelving for the collection of 6,500 items covers the entire right wall of the room. Beside the entrance, zigzag shelves hold manga, anime, and popular DVDs. Next is the teen fiction collection of 2,500 books. A college and career reference section of about 100 items is near the service desk, followed by a collection of 450 classics from local school reading lists. The graphic novel browsing section and audiocassettes complete the shelving range. Teens help staff to update the graphic novel collection of more than 1,000 items. A custom shelf attached to the steel display space holds forty-five magazine titles. Circulating back issues are shelved in cubes around the room. A rolling, steel display unit holds some of the 1,500 music CDs as well as special displays. Nonfiction is shelved with the adult collection; Knowasis displays new nonfiction in plexiglass cubes.

Young Adult Population and Community: Near Phoenix, the City of Scottsdale is Arizona's fifth-largest city, with a population of more than 226,000. Surrounded by the Sonoran Desert and the McDowell Mountains, Scottsdale is known as an affluent area and a tourist attraction. The Scottsdale Public Library consists of four libraries scattered throughout the City; a fifth will open in 2008. Civic Center Library's new teen center is in the oldest part of Scottsdale, which contains the City's highest concentration of teens as well as the lowest income levels. Nearly 25 percent of residents are minority families; many have no computer access at home. The library serves more than 21,000 youth ages 10 to 19, including 13,836 students in 7 middle schools and 5 high schools in the Scottsdale Unified School District, as well as teens in the area's charter and private schools.

Hours, Staffing, and Teen Traffic: Knowasis is open during regular library hours: Monday to Thursday from 9:00 a.m. to 9:00 p.m., Friday and Saturday from 10:00 a.m. to 6:00 p.m., and Sunday from 1:00 p.m. to 5:00 p.m. After-hours teen events occur on Friday evenings. Knowasis draws 125 to 400 visitors daily during after-school hours, and 500 teens on weekends. The door count has reached 9,000 visits in a month! Adults and children may visit briefly to retrieve materials, but the 12 to 18 age limit is enforced. Staff includes a full-time Teen Coordinator and a Librarian as well as a part-time (30-hour) Librarian. Paraprofessionals include one full-time Library Assistant and one part-time (20-hour) Library Assistant.

Planning Process: Planning and construction of the teen center in the main branch became an official goal with the library's 2001 Strategic Plan. The project was enthusiastically adopted by the Friends of the Library, who raised more than $500,000 from donors. During the planning phase, staff visited local schools to invite teens to participate in focus groups to help design the teen center. Attendance ranged from ten to fifteen in small groups up to the largest meeting with 82 teens.

At their first meeting with the architects, the teens were encouraged to talk about where they felt comfortable spending time. They were given disposable cameras and asked to photograph places or things that they liked. Many photographed elements from nature, such as backyards or landscapes. Most submitted photos of their bedrooms or living rooms. Other photos included popular hangouts such as Starbucks, McDonald's, and the mall. One young man snapped the inside of his refrigerator. At the second meeting, teens began to discuss what elements their library space should have. Many answers related to their photos: Comfortable seating, skylights or an outdoor area, food, and a relaxed and friendly atmosphere were rated highly. The architects compiled a list of the teens' priorities. At subsequent meetings, the teens discussed technology, looked at furniture catalogs, and created floorplans. They also worked with

Suspended light and listening dome.

a graphic design firm to create the name Knowasis (oasis of knowledge) and a logo to go with it.

During the summer before the opening, teen meetings focused on materials selection and policies for the room. The teens helped to create the graphic novel collection, selected more than 1,000 music CDs, and submitted DVD suggestions. They continue to play a vital role in materials selection and programming.

Knowasis celebrated its grand opening on February 23, 2006, with a Mardi Gras theme that featured flashing balloons, jingle jesters, and chocolate coins and beads sporting the Knowasis logo. Teens made decorations and gave speeches. A local high school drum corps marched down the hallway to lead the crowd into Knowasis for the mayor's ribbon cutting. More than 250 people attended the opening; an after-hours party for teens lasted until 10:00 p.m. as a deejay kept 165 teens dancing under a disco ball.

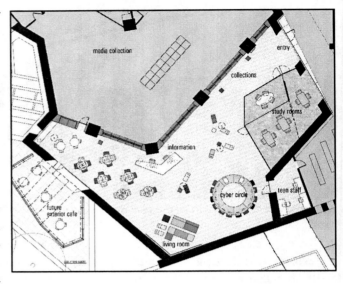

Youth Participation and Programming: The library has two active teen boards: Civic Center Teen Advisory Board and Mustang Teen Advisory Group. The grant-funded Teen Library Advocates publicized Knowasis with their own PowerPoint presentation and worked as peer mentors. More than 125 teens serve as library system volunteers. The Teen Summer Reading program draws about 1,600 teens. Other activities include the Scottsdale Teen Idol program, poetry contests, craft programs, book discussions, and daily gaming. After-hours events include costume parties, scavenger hunts, and dances. Knowasis also offers practice SAT exams and workshops, after-hours study nights during exams, Job Skills workshops, and volunteer tutors.

True Confessions from Teen Coordinator Medina Zick

This is the YA space of my dreams because . . .

"I was lucky enough to participate in the process from design to completion. While working in the youth and adult areas, I noted the gap in service to our teen population. They didn't feel comfortable in the children's room, and their style didn't blend with adults. Their need to travel, snack, and socialize has given teens a bad reputation in library land. Visiting other Teen Rooms, working with the focus groups and the architect, helping to fundraise, and watching the project develop was both challenging and exciting. It was an amazing experience to see our dream become a reality! I enjoy walking into Knowasis each day and seeing teens just hanging out. Many in our diverse crowd had never considered the library to be a fun place until Knowasis opened. We are serving an almost entirely new population in a relaxed and supportive environment. We have food, chatter, music, and laughter in huge doses. We're meeting some amazing teenagers as we build positive relationships and programs to suit their needs and interests. We've faced a number of challenges both in changing paradigms and guiding teens' behavior, but we've learned a lot in the process. Having staff who are truly dedicated to serving teens makes all the difference. Our policies and procedures continue to develop, and the teens rarely give us the opportunity to sit back and relax. It will never be the easiest job in the library, but it might just be the most rewarding."

I still dream of these improvements:

"We hope to finish fundraising for a shaded patio that will give the teen space an outdoor area. We'd love to have more computers and additional staff for evenings and weekends—who wouldn't?"

Teen Patron Comments

"The room is really cool now. The people are nice. It's a good place to meet friends and use the computers."—Daunte, 16

"I helped with the planning, and it's really great to come here now and see the room. I love the way it turned out, and I am really glad I had the chance to help."—Lindsey, 17

Civic Center Library, 3839 N. Drinkwater Boulevard, Scottsdale, AZ 85251, (480) 312-7323
http://www.scottsdalelibrary.org/content/locations_and_hours

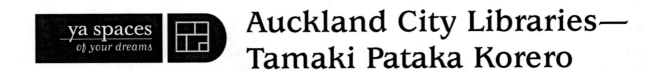
Auckland City Libraries— Tamaki Pataka Korero

Central City Library, Aukland City Libraries
Auckland, New Zealand

Annie Coppell

A Visit to New Zealand

In March 2006, I travelled to the other side of the world for a splendid vacation in New Zealand, one of the most beautiful places on earth. I spent much of my busman's holiday visiting teen spaces in Nelson and Christchurch on the South Island, and in Auckland on the North Island. I was impressed with the international scope of teen collections: Because New Zealand's publishing industry is small, libraries purchase directly from English-language publishers around the world. British and American editions of *Harry Potter* are shelved side by side with books from Canada and Australia. My biggest surprise: Every teen librarian I met was hooked on *VOYA*. They rolled out the red carpet for its editor, inviting me to tea with local authors and an all-day tour of Auckland's libraries by librarian/literary agent Frances Plumpton. I am so grateful to Frances and everyone who gave me their kind attention.

When Frances introduced me to Annie Coppell, the teen librarian at Auckland City's Central Library, Annie confided that she had always dreamed of seeing her teen space in *VOYA*. Now Annie's dream comes true! I asked Annie to describe her whole library, not just the teen space. We retain her "Kiwi" spellings, expressions, and terms in the language of the Maori, New Zealand's indigenous people. All New Zealand library signage is in English and Maori.—Cathi Dunn MacRae.

Welcome to Auckland

Known as the City of Sails, New Zealand's largest city has 1.3 million people, three harbours, two mountain ranges, 48 volcanic cones, and more than 50 islands, according to its official Web site (*http://www.aucklandnz.com*). A third of New Zealand's population lives in the Auckland region's four cities; each has a separate library system.

Auckland City Libraries serve one of those cities' population of 401,500 in sixteen community (branch) libraries, a Central Library, a mobile library, a service centre on Great Barrier Island, and an extensive Web site (*http://www/ aucklandcitylibraries.com*). The Central Library on Lorne Street parallels the Central Business District's (CBD's) main Queen Street, near two private secondary schools for years 9

Facing the enquiries desk: beanbags, just returned, and non-fiction.

Rocket ships

Teens read.

Looking into the teens' space from near the children's area.

to 13, the equivalent to U.S. grades 8 to 12. The library serves a teen population of 37,700, aged between 12 and 18 years. Auckland City's diverse population includes more than 180 ethnic groups. The majority (65 percent) are of European descent. The Asian population (around 12 percent) is growing. Significant Maori and Pacific Island populations make Auckland City the biggest Polynesian city in the world.

Redeveloping the Central Library

Opened in 1971 with a second half in 1982, the Central Library was refurbished in 1996. In May 2006, the new-look Central Library was unveiled after a two-year redevelopment project. Part of a strategy to revitalise the city's CBD into a vibrant and dynamic business and cultural centre and to transform the library into a key destination attracting more than one million visitors each year, the project was a key initiative in Auckland City's CBD into the Future.

Along with physical changes came a realignment of library staff structure, moving away from specialist collections and staffing to a layout based on customer usage. The children's and teens' sections (known as CaTS to staff) had always been on the first floor. (Note that New Zealand's ground floor is America's first floor, our first floor is your second, and so on.) One of our major relocations was to move CaTS downstairs, separating teens' from children's as much as possible whilst enabling specialist staff to be close to both areas.

Now the ground floor is the "Read & Relax" area. It houses circulation, adult fiction and graphic novels, world languages, the News Zone (playing TV news channels on a screen), lending magazines, children's, teens' and the café.

The first floor holds adult non-fiction, music, and a learning centre. The second floor houses the heritage and special collections department—among its extensive treasures is a Shakespeare first folio. Spread through the three public floors are 56 computers for customer use.

The third floor contains administration and bibliographic services. The basement has two levels of stack storage. In May 2007, Central was the home library for 36,725 patrons who made 93,185 visits and issued [checked out] 72,110 items, with 32,534 books and magazines issued on our four self-checkout machines. Customers know that they have successfully issued their books when they hear James Brown sing, "I feel good."

The Teen Services Role

As Teen Services Librarian, I am part of the Community Outreach Team, which covers services and collections for children, teens, seniors, and users of our world languages collections. My role is many-faceted: direct customer service as part of the Central Library staff; oversee the teens' collection and services within the Central Library; work with community libraries to support teen services, collections and areas; and prepare the teen Web pages. I also work on school holiday programmes (focused on primary/elementary schoolaged children), other children's events, and preschool Storytimes. I have a close working relationship with the teens' collections buyer.

In the wider world, Auckland City Libraries is a foundation partner of AnyQuestions/UiaNgaPatai (*http://www.anyquestions.co.nz*), in which libraries across New Zealand staff virtual reference desks and chat online, real time, with school students from around the country.

The Central Library Teens' Area

Under the escalators, the teens' area has a cave-like atmosphere. It is bordered by the DVD collection, world language magazines, and the console games lending collection. Across the floor are the children's area and world languages collections. Further along is adult literacy and adult fiction. The ground floor enquiries desk is staffed by two teams, Readers' Services and Community Outreach.

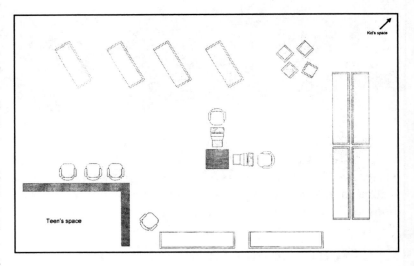

The teens' furniture is designed for lounging with much-favoured beanbags and a red swivel chair reminiscent of *Dr. No.* We love our "rocket-ship" shelving stand! Two computers placed on coffee tables have Microsoft Office applications and free Internet access. Near the area is a block of six more computers. In this cosy, welcoming space, it's not unusual to find groups of teens sprawled on the beanbags reading, using a computer, or flicking through magazines. The area is obviously theirs. Says fourteen-year-old Annaliesa: "The teens' area is so cool. I can just sit and relax and read my books."

The Teens' Collection

Targeted at 12- to 16-year-olds, the collection includes fiction, partially divided into genres: Fantasy, science fiction, and horror are shelved together, as are action and crime. New Zealand authors are separated out, as well as romance and popular series. The last three groups are shelved in our rocketship stand. Non-fiction is organised by Dewey, with an emphasis on recreational reading. We also have lending magazines, graphic novels, and audiobooks. Teen fiction and graphic novels are floating collections that can be returned to any Auckland City library, where they are shelved until issued again. Our January 2007 summer holiday was a bumper time—our 2,140 teen fiction items (including all genres and graphic novels) had an 82 percent turnover [circulation], with a 33 percent turnover in non-fiction. The Central Library's teen collection averages 1,557 issues per month.

Recent Teen Events

In October 2006, we trialled a programme of teen events in the Central Library, kicking off with a Murder Mystery. We offered study skills drop-in workshops before end-of-year exams and at the beginning of the school year, which runs from February to December. (Learn about the New Zealand school system at *http://www.minedu.govt.nz.*) Craft workshops included cards, beaded jewellery, and scrapart. First-floor staff ran two technology workshops for teens. In March, we presented a Winter Looks Workshop in conjunction with the local Body Shop and SUPRÉ, a girls' fashion chain from Australia—six of our community libraries also held these workshops. In April, two artists and the manager of a comics store, Gotham Comics, led a workshop on getting into the comics business.

The highlight was definitely the Winter Looks workshop, and the craft workshops went down well. The most rewarding outcome has been the personal relationships that I have built with the teens attending, particularly those who came to nearly all the programmes.

Where to Next?

The library's business plan for 2007–2008 has a strong emphasis on services to children and young adults, giving us the opportunity to focus on outreach to schools, advertise our expanded collections, and organise more events. In conjunction with community libraries, I'll be visiting the 28 secondary schools in the area to raise awareness of our services and collections. With other staff, I participate in networks of secondary school librarians run by New Zealand's National Library School Services (see *http://www.natlib.govt.nz*).

Before the end of the year, we'll be getting a new study support collection containing study guides for all subjects taught in secondary schools and the different years, to complement materials for teens in our adult non-fiction collections.

Another challenge is the redevelopment of the library Web site. The teens' pages have an average of 25,850 hits per month (the site as a whole averages 313,556 hits per month). We're planning to move into the space of our target audience by having a library presence in *Bebo* and *MySpace* and by utilising Web 2.0 technology.

Our future focus is on getting out there, physically and virtually.

Auckland City Libraries, PO Box 4138, Shortland Street, Auckland 1140, New Zealand
+63 (09) 377 0209
http://www.aucklandcitylibraries.com/

Summers Young Adult Center

Otis Library
Norwich, Connecticut

Jennifer Rummel

Description: When you're standing in Otis Library's atrium, look for the door frame to the left of the main circulation desk on the first floor and you'll find the brand new Summers Young Adult Center. Step off tiles and onto blue, grey, and purple carpeting as you walk through the entrance to this sizeable (1,276 square feet) and relaxing teen hangout. Take a look at the easel in the foyer for news of upcoming events and then check out the new books on display behind the easel. Colorful party lights decorate the column walls and ceilings. The curved teen information desk is to the right, covered with teen newsletters, bookmarks, and other relevant information; a helpful staff member awaits teens' questions and concerns. The YA Librarian's office is behind the desk in the back corner of the room.

On the wall opposite the doorway, alongside two metal bookshelves and one L-shaped range shelf, two long wooden tables with gray counter-like tops host six flat-panel computers strictly for teens. The computers offer word processing, filtered Internet access, databases, and the library catalog. Along the wall to the right sit two blue and tan restaurant-style booths with matching tables underneath windows overlooking the staff courtyard. To the right, a lounge area offers five abstract-patterned, light green/pink/purple/blue/tan-colored chairs and one loveseat surrounding a wooden coffee table. In the right corner sits the study area—two tables with four chairs each that match the computer furniture—and a massive shelving unit. Posters of Jack Sparrow, Spiderman, Yoda, and Shaquille O'Neal, among others, adorn the painted white walls, along with a bulletin board where future teen events as well as "library in the news" and town information are posted.

Collection: Young adult books are shelved among three units, holding a total of 4,803 titles. Near the study area, a smaller shelving unit contains new titles while a taller unit contains a growing number of audiobooks, magazines, and video games. Curriculum support/ homework help and college/career books are peppered throughout the shelves. Graphic novels and comics are shelved together in a separate location in this otherwise Dewey arrangement. Many of the books have genre stickers on them to make browsing easy for teens. In the two-month period of May and June 2007, immediately

The YA area entrance helpfully greets teens with an upcoming events easel and an information desk.

Flat-panel computers are readily available for teens only.

following the new library's opening, YA circulation was 3,337. Some testing and career materials as well as media and reference books are housed in a separate section of the library. The Jim Lafayette Collection, consisting of new fantasy and science fiction, is shelved elsewhere but will eventually be placed in the teen area.

Young Adult Population and Community: Located in the southeast corner of Connecticut, twenty minutes from the historic seaport of Mystic, the city of Norwich—nicknamed the "Rose of New England"—has a population of 37,040. Founded in 1659, it appeals to city lovers. Forty

Brilliant party lights and decorations adorn the display area.

minutes from Connecticut's capital, Hartford, and two hours from New York City, diverse Norwich is home to Italian, Polish, Greek, Native American, French-Canadian, Haitian populations, and more. Large area employers include two casinos, a medical research company, a builder of nuclear submarines, and the Navy's submarine base. Norwich's working-class environment is currently undergoing revitalization. Otis Library, located downtown, is the city's only library, connected to many other libraries in the state that fulfill book requests. Otis also has several book drops around

Comfy lounge chairs welcome teens who want to relax.

The new book section near the entrance serves as a great study area.

the area. The library serves approximately 4,775 students from two middle and two high schools. Most schools are not within walking distance, yet it still draws teens after school and in the evenings.

Hours, Staffing, and Teen Traffic: Summers Young Adult Center is open from 2:00 p.m. to 8:00 p.m. while school is in session, and during regular library hours for the summer and weekends: Monday, Tuesday, and Thursday from 9:00 a.m. to 8:00 p.m., Wednesday from 10:00 a.m. to 8:00 p.m., Friday from 9:00 a.m. to 5:00 p.m., Saturday (September through June) from 9:00 a.m. to 5:00 p.m., and Sunday (October through April) from 12:00 p.m. to 4:00 p.m. The YA center is used by 30 to 50 teens on weekdays and evenings after school, and on weekends by 50 to 70 teens. The space is intended for patrons in grades 6 to 12 only; a staff member at the information desk will kindly remind others of this policy if it becomes a problem. Two staff members are assigned to Summers Young Adult Center: a full-time, professional YA librarian who is the department head, and a part-time, high school student who serves as assistant librarian.

Planning Process: The old 1960 building had no young adult space. After two years of renovations, the new 36,000 square-foot Otis Library opened to the public on April 30, 2007. The eight million-dollar building, complete with large meeting spaces, new children's area, courtyard, and twenty-first-century library technology, was expanded to better serve Norwich and its adjacent communities. The planning process occurred with the previous director, Linda Summers, for whom the YA center was named.

Youth Participation and Programming: With the library's first Young Adult Center in the new building came an effort to "diminish perceived barriers" and "cultivate the next generation of library users and supporters," according to Library Director Robert D. Farwell. A teen advisory council was developed to fulfill these goals: "making our young adult patrons part of the decision-making process; helping cultivate new library supporters; and introducing younger patrons to libraries and librarianship through active participation in programmatic planning."

The new Teen Board meets once a month over pizza to discuss improving the library, including updating the graphic novel, biography, and video game collections. Other monthly programs include an anime club and Monday movie nights. This past summer, teens competed in the reading game using the YNK (You Never Know) @ your library theme. The six-week mission, full of code breaking and agent tracking, led to a prize for the lucky winner. Other programs have included crafts such as making bath salts and molding chocolates, playing library clue (a game based on the actual Otis Library with its employees acting as suspects), and a murder-mystery dinner titled "Death of a Book Nerd," using characters from teen books. September 2007 saw the addition of a bimonthly mother/daughter book club, with a father/son book club hosted in the off months.

The restaurant-style booths against the wall overlook the courtyard.

Each summer, teen volunteers assist with programs and circulation in the children's room.

True Confessions from Young Adult Librarian Jennifer Rummel

This is the YA space of my dreams because . . .

"It shows teens that the library is not only for selecting books, but it is also a place for fun. We have something for the book lover, but also we have video games, magazines, and graphic novels that some teens primarily come into the library to select. I love seeing teens leave the library with an armload of books or a cool-looking video game, but mostly with big fat smiles on their faces!"

I still dream of these improvements:

• More computers.
• More video game equipment to hold gaming nights.

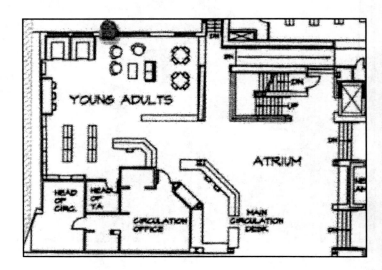

Teen Patron Comments

"OMG! It's great!"—Jenn, 17

"Off da hook."—Anonymous

"Has a lot of taste."—Anonymous

"It's a great place to sit and read a book."—Stephanie, 11

"I like it, it's nice."—Dulce, 19

Otis Library, 261 Main Street, Norwich, CT 06360, (860) 889-2365
http://www.otislibrarynorwich.org/

600 Pod: Learning Resource Center and Library

Juvenile Detention Center Branch, Pima County Public Library
Tucson, Arizona

William Bevill

Description: Life is different on the inside. Locked doors and concrete block walls separate the Pima County Juvenile Court (Detention Center) from the rest of the world. Video surveillance is constantly monitored. Teens are expected to clean their ten-by-twelve-foot living space daily. The Juvenile Detention Center (JDC) Branch of the Pima County Public Library (PCPL) and Learning Resource Center, tagged the "600 Pod" by staff because of its location in the building, is a haven for the teens of the center. Situated inside a former "living unit" (an area where there are individual rooms for each youth and a communal space), it is entered from a hallway that connects to other living units through locked doors. The center's cold, concrete floors end abruptly at the library's entrance, replaced by a brilliant blue carpet with splashes of yellow, green, purple, and red. Three beautiful murals, painted by former JDC youth from images of actual totems around the world, decorate the area. The wall of windows on

The sun welcomes library visitors as they walk through the entrance.

the east side of the 775-square-foot space welcomes the rays of sun to brighten the room. A glass door among the windows opens to a large, secure outdoor area with basketball hoops and picnic tables. Fiery red metal bookshelves line the perimeter, and two double spinners with lower shelves on wheels move freely in and around the space. The two laminate tables and twelve plastic yellow chairs provide adequate seating for the small number of youth allowed in the library at a time.

A mobile spinner is situated next to the magazine rack for teens' perusal.

An orange bookcase shaped like a rocket ship stands to the left of the Learning Resource Center's entrance. This area is a computer lab run by the Court Alternative Program of Education (CAPE) to supplement the educational services it provides. The librarian's and library associate's desks sit to the right of the entrance; their computers are the only ones in the space. Green doors, labeled with numbers and letters, lead to storage rooms and two offices. Posters of Spiderman, Shaq, *Pirates of the Caribbean*, and more hang from the walls and doors, as well as a slat board for magazines in the far right corner.

Security issues are important in the library so pencils, staples, and scissors are prohibited when the teens are present. All staples must be removed from magazines and comics.

Bright-colored shelving lines the door to the learning resource center.

JDC teens contently read their books in the library.

Collection: Shelving around the four walls and a few strategically placed spinners hold the library's approximately 7,000 to 8,000 titles. The number is difficult to estimate because nothing is cataloged. The collection is geared exclusively toward incarcerated teens; there are very few adult and children's books. Every volume is a paperback—hardback books are not allowed. Furthermore the collection is censored for content and images. There is no Dewey Decimal System or Library of Congress arrangement. Instead the general fiction section is organized alphabetically by author's last name; SF, Fantasy, Classics, and Westerns sit on separate shelves. Books on similar subjects are grouped together and put where they fit best. For example, magazines are kept on slat boards, series fiction is held on a moveable spinner, and the girls' fiction and nonfiction collection is kept on another spinner. This spinner is rolled into the main library space only when the girls are present. The Spanish-language collection fills an entire cart for the many Spanish-speaking youth in the detention center. Another cart containing a variety of materials is assigned to the maximum security living unit because youth there are not allowed to physically visit the library. The space also houses graphic novels, early readers, and reference books including college/career books and curriculum-support material.

Instead of checking out books electronically, the teen's identification number is written inside the back cover. When returned, books are checked for gang markings and other damage. Prior to the move to the new site, the detained youth checked out 1,500 books per month. By April 2007, circulation increased to 2,000 per month, and by June the number reached 3,000. When books are requested but not available in the library, the youth can reserve them from PCPL's main branch, accounting for another 150 to 200 books circulating per month. In addition, each living unit has at least one permanent cart of books.

Young Adult Population and Community: Located in the south central region of Arizona and stretching all the way to the Mexican border, Pima County, Arizona, is home to one million people. Most of the population lives in Tucson, the state's second largest city, whereas the rest of the outlaying areas are quite rural. Pima County includes the San Xavier Indian Reservation and a large part of the Tohono O'odham Nation. The majority of the population is white and Hispanic or Latino. The population of incarcerated youth in Pima County mirrors this statistic—37 percent are Caucasian and 47 percent are Hispanic. The youth that the library serves read two to three years behind grade level

Hours, Staffing, and Teen Traffic: Although the Pima County Juvenile Court Center never closes, the library is only open Monday through Friday between 8:00 a.m. and 4:30 p.m. The library staff sees a steady stream of teen traffic between those hours as detention officers bring different groups of teens from the various living units at their scheduled times. The teens are only present when brought by the officers. At any given day, there can be 100 to 140 youth staying in detention, with 10 to 20 youth per living unit. Most of these youth come to the YA space every day of the week to attend class in the Learning Resource Center. After they use the computer lab, a handful of teens at a time—never the whole pod at once—are allowed to browse the collection. Four times a week youth are also allowed to visit the library and check out books. Each month there are around 1,200 total teens using the library; this figure is easy to ascertain because attendance is tallied for each visit. The female detainees have a separate learning center so special arrangements are made for them to visit the library twice a week for book checkout. The staff includes one full-time professional librarian, one full-time paraprofessional library associate, one part-time paraprofessional page, and two part-time homework tutors.

Planning Process: In 1999, the PCPL started bringing books to the incarcerated teens, thus opening the JDC library. It was originally a tiny, cluttered room that housed the book collection. Teens were not able to physically go to the library; the books were put on carts and wheeled around to the different living units, enabling the teens to browse only a small part of the collection at a time. In 2006, the Juvenile Court decided to move the library to a bigger space to make it more accessible. Joint funding from PCPL and CAPE made this transition possible. Six months later, on March 1, 2007, more than one hundred community members, including judges, probation officers, and library staff, celebrated the grand opening of the new library space and the CAPE Learning Resource Center.

The highly secured courtyard outside the library is a favorite hangout spot for teens.

Youth Participation and Programming: Youth in the detention center are assigned to four levels of behavior and privilege, with those in level four exhibiting the most excellent behavior. Level four detained youth receive the privilege of participating in a volunteer program in which they are occasionally allowed to spend one hour in the library checking books for damage, assisting in the necessary book repairs, and shelving books.

In addition, the teens of individual living units can choose to participate in monthly book discussion groups based on the *Bluford Series* (Townsend Press). Youth also enjoy the special summer activities provided to them, including classes on juggling and beading, root beer float parties, and a planetarium activity.

The detention center, the CAPE school, and PCPL have worked together for the past ten years to bring poets, singers, workshops, presentations, and classical musicians to the incarcerated teens. The youth usually gather inside one of the empty living units for these programs. The female teens have been involved in the Inside/Out Chapbook program. The program, for both detained youth (inside) and non-mainstreamed youth (out) at Pima Vocational High School, builds connections and awareness by shared writing between the two sets of teens. Themed workshops contribute to the content of the chapbooks—collections of poetry and illustrations—which can be viewed on the library's Web page for the JDC at *http://www.tppl. org/services/jdc*.

True Confessions from Library Associate William Bevill

This is the YA space of my dreams because . . .

"The JDC library is all about books and all about readers. The youth here will read on their spare time, sometimes twelve books a week or more, and their love of reading really shows and makes it special for the library staff. One youth, a young man who claimed to not be a reader before he came to JDC, spent several weeks reading full-length books. It was after he finished the book *Eragon* that he told us 'Reading is like watching a movie. But with books, you see the images in your head.' What he said has reflected [the thoughts of] many readers here, many who are eager to continue reading on the outside, and who ask us every week if they will get a library card on the outside so they can visit the public library. This is a wonderful environment to work in having youth who are open to all kinds of books and learning and opening their minds to worlds that were once unknown to them."

I still dream of these improvements:

"To have every book that every youth asks for. When a youth comes in and realizes what a library has to offer them, they start thinking about all kinds of subjects and stories. There are dozens of books in a week that we can't find because they are out of print or just don't exist; we want every child to have every book that would enlighten and delight them."

Teen Patron Comments

"You got a great library here. You have more books here that I like than I can find at my own library!"—male, 16

"This place is sweet. I like coming up here. Reading books in here is my favorite thing to do."—female, 15

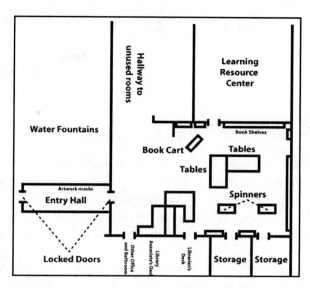

Juvenile Detention Center Branch, Pima County Library, 2225 E. Ajo Way, Tucson, AZ 85713
(520) 740-4565
http://www.library.pima.gov/about/jdc/

EPL Teen Department

Elizabeth Public Library
Elizabeth, New Jersey

Kimberly Paone

Description: Enter Elizabeth Public Library (EPL) and pass the children's department on the first floor and the adult reference/ readers' advisory on the second floor, climb the stairs to the third floor, and there, next to the periodicals department, is 3,400 square feet of space entirely devoted to teens. The large L-shaped lounge area doesn't have its own door, but it is practically a separate room because it is sectioned off from the elevated periodicals department by a short staircase. Even the staff on duty occupies a separate 180-foot office space behind a wall of windows. Teens are greeted by splashes of color throughout the space, including a purple welcome sign and other cutout labels to denote different sections of the department. The basic color scheme contains classic grays and blacks, with chest-nut brown wood tables and bookshelves. Near the entrance, a large bulletin board advertises programs, school news, events, contests, and book information. The books and other materials line the walls of the room, leaving a humungous space in the center for eight tables with four chairs each, a sectional leather couch that can comfortably seat eight or nine teens, two leather bucket chairs, an oversized love seat that fits four, and two large ottomans that can be used as seats or workspaces. To the left sit eighteen Internet-access computers and two catalog/ database terminals, equipped with word processing and computer games. Along the back wall, Garden State Teen Book Award nominees are prominently displayed next to the manga spinning racks.

The staff office is separate from the teen department, giving teens a sense of freedom and ownership of their space.

Collection: The teen department hosts 15,424 young adult titles, excluding magazines and audiovisuals, on an impressive 841 feet of shelving space. Some shelves are still empty to accommodate a growing collection. Elizabeth teens can enjoy thirty non-circulating magazine subscriptions, such as their favorites *Shonen Jump, MAD, Wizard, CosmoGirl,* and *J-14.* Fiction, including adult books for teens and paperback series (which have red dots on their spine for easy finding), are shelved alphabetically by the author's last name. Graphic novels and manga are cataloged with Dewey numbers but are shelved by series or author title and contain blue dots on their spines. YA circulation figures for 2007 were 18,497. Teens can find audiobooks, videos, music CDs, and Playaways in the audiovisual department on the second floor. Also on that floor are nonfiction materials and reference for teens, which are interspersed throughout adult titles. The library's online resources, including curriculum support and homework help, are available in the teen department.

Teens leisurely read the manga, graphic novels, and magazines that surround them in this section.

With eighteen computers on hand, teens are always able to get online for research, homework help, games, and social networking.

Many high school students like to come here after a hard day of school and unwind with a good book.

Young Adult Population and Community: Originally called "Elizabethtown," this history-rich city was the first colonial English-speaking community and the first capital of New Jersey. Located south of Newark and only sixteen miles from New York City, Elizabeth was named one of America's greenest cities in 2008 by **Popular Science** magazine. It is the birthplace of famous YA authors Edward Stratemeyer and Judy Blume. A large number of non- English speakers reside in Elizabeth; the majority of the population is Hispanic or Latino so many residents speak Spanish or Portuguese. Most patrons walk or take public transportation to Elizabeth Public Library's main branch because of its urban setting. The library serves a total of five thousand-plus students from the public high school alone—one of the largest in the nation. There are also private schools and more than thirty middle schools. The teens come mostly from single-parent homes or working-class families and have responsibilities outside of school, including caring for younger siblings and/or holding part-time jobs to help support their families.

Hours, Staffing, and Teen Traffic: Elizabeth Public Library is open Monday through Friday from 9 a.m. to 9 p.m. and Saturday from 9 a.m. to 5 p.m. The library is closed on Sundays. The teen department is staffed at all times when the library is open. At around 5 p.m. on weekdays, the teen area sees thirty to forty teens. A fairly large crowd of teens will show up on Saturdays after lunch, but more teens come after school unless there is a special program planned. Most teens are older because of the proximity to the public high school and nearby parochial school, but teens aged thirteen to nineteen are encouraged to come by and hang out. Adults are allowed and use the space mostly during the day. The YA area staffs one full-time supervisor and two full-time library associates who split their hours between the teen, reference, and children's departments, and the other branches. Other EPL fulltime librarians occasionally help staff the teen department when needed.

Planning Process: The planning for the new teen space began in January 2008. It was decided that the teen department would move up to the third floor to swap spaces with the reference department. Kimberly Paone, supervisor of the teen department, says the primary goals were to centrally locate the adult materials and services on the library's main floor and to create a space for teens that was not situated in a high-traffic area. Library Director Dorothy Key, Assistant Director Monica Eppinger, Head of the Reference Department Robert Barbanell, and Paone were involved in the initial planning stages, and then staff members

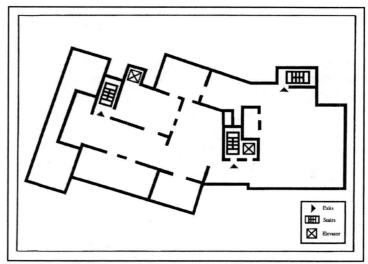

gave their input. Teen volunteers as well as other library staff were instrumental in executing the actual move; for instance, the teens physically moved all of their materials from the second floor shelves to the third floor shelves!

On Saturday, June 7, 2008, Elizabeth Public Library combined the teen space's grand opening with the Teen Summer Preview, an annual event in which the teen summer reading club (SRC) theme is announced. The library served teen-friendly refreshments—Doritos, Ring Pops, juice, and candy bars—and gave the fifty teens in attendance the opportunity to participate in a scavenger hunt throughout the new teen department.

Youth Participation and Programming: Community service hours are required for Elizabeth high school students so the library maintains a very healthy teen volunteer program. In 2007, 85 teen volunteers served a total of 578.5 community service hours, shelving and straightening books and completing clerical tasks. In addition, the Teen Advisory Council (TAC) members receive community service hours for time spent at meetings and participating in TAC-sponsored activities.

A teen Book Discussion Group gathers monthly; the members recently finished their second (and final) term as a YA galley group, so there has never been a lack of new and exciting books from which the readers can choose. The teens are fortunate that the library is very near Manhattan because it provides the opportunity to host many won-

When Teens Get Too Comfortable in Their New YA Space
by Kimberly Paone

When we moved the teen department to its new home on the third floor, added comfy leather furniture, and provided room in which to move around, our goal was to create a welcoming environment where teens could congregate, do homework, read, and relax. That goal was accomplished . . . a bit *too* well. Our teens claimed the room as their own, which meant that soon after the initial newness wore off, there were frequent instances of eating, kissing, sleeping, running, shouting, and other no-no's occurring on a regular basis. Our group of regulars knew these infractions were wrong, but the new space gave them a sense of freedom that made them seemingly "forget" those old rules. We had to start kicking teens out so we applied the "three strikes" rule that we have used in the past. Youth breaking the rules first get a warning, explaining that their behavior needs to stop. If they continue, they get a second warning and are told that a third time will mean they need to leave the library for the day. There absolutely needs to be follow-through with that third strike. I hate telling them to take a walk, but it seems to be the most effective way to keep the peace. Of course, we're not running a military state here—the noise level is decidedly higher than any other place in the building, and if noise complaints come our way, adults are invited to move themselves to an area away from our teen department. We try to make sure that teens—even the ones breaking the rules—are always treated with respect, both by staff and by other patrons. Strikes are never yelled across the room; rather, staff members approach the offendor(s) and calmly explain the situation. Teens asked to leave are invited to come back the next day, and *almost* always they not only come back but return without continuing the behavior that got them bounced in the first place. It's not a perfect world, and some days staff members feel like pulling their hair out, but there is some order in the chaos and that's important.

derful teen authors. The Anime Club also meets monthly. In July and August of 2008, EPL's teen department hosted sixty-two programs—movies, crafts, special guests, Project Runway, game nights, karaoke, and much more. A favorite among teens is the "Talk Your Way to a Ticket Day," an opportunity for youth to tell a staff member about a book they've read to earn a ticket toward the end-of-summer raffle.

True Confessions from YA Librarian Kimberly Paone

This is the YA space of my dreams because . . .

"The teens and I feel a real sense of pride in this space. It feels like a second home to many of them, and I am so happy that we are able to provide it."

I still dream of these improvements:

"Eventually we hope to have a closed-off, quiet study area, which will be very useful for both our teen and adult patrons. We're also planning on posting READ posters featuring the Teen Advisory Council members, and I'm looking forward to accomplishing this goal."

Teen Patron Comments

"The old teen department was good but the new one is way better. In the old teen department we had less room, and it looked just like any other part of the library. Nothing really made it stand out like our new one. Now it's more spacious and we can move around more easily. We have couches, and the place looks a lot brighter and more colorful than our old teen department. More and more teens are showing up. The library is now known as the new chill spot for all kinds of teens."—Mariana, 18

"I like the new teen department. It's my home away from home. Compared to the old one, this one is cloud nine."—Robert, 17

"The new department is better, like we have more space and we have more independence."—Janice, 17

Elizabeth Public Library, 11 South Broad Street, Elizabeth, New Jersey 07202, (908) 354-6060
http://www.elizpl.org/

Teen Rooms

Northwest Library, Columbus, Ohio
Old Worthington Library, Worthington, Ohio

Sarah Cofer and Ann Pechacek

Description: Located in the northeast corner of Old Worthington Library (OWL), adjacent to the living room area containing audio visuals and new books, the 1,097-square-foot OWL teen room welcomes patrons inside using a homey, store-front appeal. With a wall full of blue- and green-colored windows, an aluminum awning that hangs above the French door entrance, and a sunny yellow paint job with purple trim, it is not difficult for teens to feel that it is the front of their very own building. A computer bar with five stations—ten stools included—runs along the wall facing the entrance. To the left is a group study room with four tables put together in the shape of a giant football for increased seating. Through a glass wall is another study room—this one specifically for teens, which can only be accessed from the teen area—that includes two tables and seats six. The staff roving station is in the corner nearby. On the adjacent wall, two oversized purple and silver round booths complete with brushed laminated steel tables sit in front of huge arched windows. Most of the collection is held on the remaining wall. The carpeted floor with alternating squares of red, orange, blue, green, and purple complements the primary color scheme. The lounge area in the middle of the floor contains six comfy chairs with three stools that are dark red, light red, and orange. A portion of the ceiling is painted black and left open, exposing the wiring and pipes. A perforated vaulted floating fixture hangs from the high ceiling and lets in light from above.

Don't be fooled by its appearance; the teen area at OWL really is connected to the library.

Approximately seven miles west on Interstate 270, another newly renovated Worthington teen room dwells in the Northwest Library (NWL) branch. This 970-foot square space is adjacent to the technology area and next door to two group study rooms. Fortunately for NWL teens, their requests were heard and the teen room is as far away from the children's section as possible. Upon entering the fully enclosed space, it is impossible to miss the brilliant red, orange, blue, green, and purple hues. The carpet and walls, including the exposed rafters and air ducts, match this color scheme. All eyes are drawn to a garage door with blue, green, and purple glass panels, which can also serve as an entrance, depending on the teens' needs: The door can stay open during the day while teens are in school but closes in the evenings and for teen programs to give teens privacy. This huge glass

The renovations at NWL included putting the teen space immediately next to the technology area.

The proximity of the booths to the books makes studying a breeze at NWL.

Every wall in NWL is a different color: one is purple, another blue, and the others have accents of red and cream.

door keeps the area open and easily monitored while blocking noise to avoid disturbing patrons. New books sit on either side of the entrance to this space, which looks similar to an artist's workshop. The center of the floor is the lounge area, home to five futuristic chairs, a boomerang-shaped coffee table, and two side tables that can double as chairs. There is a study table with two chairs to the side of the lounge space for studious teens. Along the back wall alcove are six computer stations situated on a bar in front of a large floor-to-ceiling window. Along the wall holding audio books and the nonfiction collection are two café-style yellow booths, which can seat twelve and are perfect for studying alone or in a group. The staff roving station is also placed in this area. The majority of the collection sits near the adjacent blue wall.

Collection: Old Worthington Library's teen section contains 7,000 items, including hardcover YA fiction and nonfiction, adult books for teens, paperbacks, comics, reference books, and at least 500 audio books. Seventy square feet of stainless steel Opto shelving hold the graphic novel collection and magazines. One mobile shelving unit houses new teen books and other titles for display. Annual circulation is 36,050, and the stock turnover ratio is 5.78, which means each item circulates an average of five to six times per year. Music CDs and DVDs are located either in the adult or children's area. All other YA materials reside in the teen room. The teens' computers feature an online catalog, databases, word processing, unfiltered Internet access, unrestricted gaming, and the ability to view videos and listen to music.

The 8,500 volumes at Northwest Library are held by 204 square feet of stainless steel Opto shelving, four mobile double-sided shelving units that give approximately forty-six square feet of shelving each, and an additional thirty square feet of new book displays. The types of materials are the same in both spaces, but in addition to the CDs and DVDs found elsewhere, adult books for teens are housed in the adult fiction collection. Annual circulation is slightly higher at 39,315, and the stock turnover ratio is 7.105. The computers at Northwest offer the same features as those at Old Worthington Library.

Young Adult Population and Community: The city of Worthington, a suburb of Columbus located in the center of Ohio, was one of the Midwest's first planned communities. It enjoys the conveniences of a big city without losing the charm of small town living. Worthington Libraries serve a suburban community of roughly 61,000 Franklin County residents. Worthington has one of the most ethnically diverse student populations among suburban school systems in the county; approximately 7 percent of students are Asian, 6 percent are African American, 2.7 percent are Hispanic, 2 percent are multiracial, and 0.2 percent are American In-

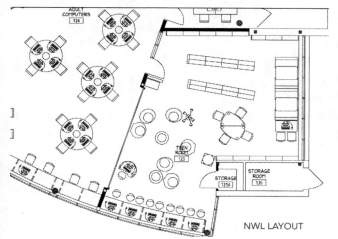

NWL LAYOUT

dian. The district has almost three hundred students with limited English proficiency who speak approximately thirty different native languages. OWL serves a total of 2,225 students from two middle schools and one high school, and NWL serves 4,500 students in three middle schools and two high schools. The city has worked hard to keep the library at its heart; it paid off in 2007 when Worthington Libraries was recognized as the National Library of the Year by *Library Journal* and Gale.

Hours, Staffing, and Teen Traffic: The YA areas are open during regular library hours: Monday through Thursday from 9 a.m. to 9 p.m., Friday and Saturday from 9 a.m. to 6 p.m., and Sundays from 1 p.m. to 5 p.m. from Labor Day to Memorial Day. Teens ranging in age from twelve to eighteen start coming to the library around 3:30 p.m. on a typical school day and 11 a.m. on the weekends; the OWL teen area sees 20–40 teens daily whereas NWL sees 6–12 teen users. The Worthington Libraries Patron Code of Conduct includes the strictly-enforced policy, "Designated Teen areas are designed for patrons ages 12–18 years old. Adults and younger children are encouraged to use other areas of the Library." Almost all of the adult and children's staff, including fourteen librarians and eighteen library associates are scheduled periodically for a shift in the teen rooms. No one librarian is "fulltime," although the teen librarians at each branch are scheduled more frequently. This scheduling allows the teen rooms to be staffed during their busiest times of 4 p.m. to 9 p.m. on weekdays and 11 p.m. to 6 p.m. on weekends.

Planning Process: The current Old Worthington Library opened its doors in 1979; the Northwest branch followed seventeen years later thanks to a unique partnership agreement with the Columbus Metropolitan Library. Although both had spaces set aside for teens, they were not separated by walls and were adjacent to either the children's department or the adult services area. Worthington saw increased usage and decreased revenues in the early 2000s, until a grassroots campaign was enacted to save the struggling library. In 2005, Worthington Libraries succeeded in passing a $2.6 million property tax levy to continue and improve services of the library. Part of this plan recognized that teens are a unique group in the community and specifically cited improving young adult services.

Teens can relax with a book or check out the latest computer games in the lounge area at OWL.

Teens looking for quiet can use this study room or the teen-only one behind the glass wall at OWL.

The oversized tables and deep-set booths at OWL are great for group hangouts and study sessions.

The teen librarians started brainstorming sessions with the teen advisory boards to find out what the teens wanted in their new area. As the renovation plans came together, the architects held focus groups with the teens to ask them questions about colors, themes, layouts, and such. During the past two years, the teen librarians have had frequent meetings with the architects to plan the teen area in its entirety. Throughout the planning process, they would report

Teens absolutely love the trendy but functional garage door in NWL.

The floor-to-ceiling windows in NWL provide ample light to computer users.

back to the teens and ask for feedback. For instance, when trying to decide on the right lounge furniture, the teen librarians posted a quick poll on the *Worthingteens* blog (*www.worthingtonlibraries.org/teen/blog*) and asked the teens to vote on their favorite furniture. (The library's third branch, Worthington Park Library, opened in April 2008 and is a 5,280 square foot storefront facility in a retail shopping center. Because it is a new library, a teen area was incorporated into its design. Given space limitations, it is not as large as the teen rooms at the two other libraries.)

Youth Participation and Programming: The libraries have a very active Volunteen Corps, which provides assistance all year long but also plays a big role during the summer reading program. Volunteens serve as an informal advisory board and are often asked to provide input into programming and other matters including the renovation of the teen room. Most of the official advisory boards' members graduated in 2008, so for the time being, different library teen groups handle the tasks of a traditional board.

Worthington Libraries launched an online book discussion group to meet the demands of teens who were more interested in chatting about books on the teen blog than having in-house discussions. OWL still provides this service to teens, hosting a Book and Bag group with the middle school across the parking lot and coordinating a Book and Bagel group at the local high school twice a month before school begins. The libraries have an active presence on MySpace, lots of options for homework help, and monthly drop-in programs with activities like DIY crafts, anime movie showings, and Wii gaming. Both branches have quarterly teen-only TGIF programs on Friday nights after the library closes.

Worthington Libraries subscribe to tutor.com and provide Live Homework Help, aka Online Tutoring, to students through the vendor. The library is also part of the statewide service HomeworkNow in which students can chat one-on-one with a reference librarian 24/7. Students can also access both Online Tutoring and HomeworkNow from home via the library Web site and a valid library card number.

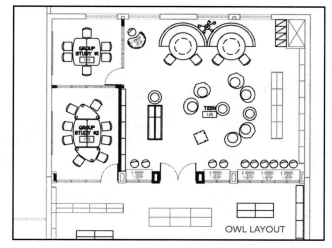

True Confessions from Teen Librarians Sarah Cofer and Ann Pechacek

This is the YA space of my dreams because . . .

"When I started my career at Worthington Libraries, my teen area was basically one wall, a collection on a single bay of shelving, some seating, and two computers. Now I have an entire room with four walls and six computers and lots of seating. I love that there are different types of seating for the different types of activities the teens do while they are here in the library. The teens can study independently or in groups, lounge around while reading, or hang out at the computers. I love all the natural light that comes in from the two walls of windows. The mobile shelving is awesome because it allows us to make the teen room a multipurpose room. Not only does it hold a teen collection, but if we move the shelving, it also becomes a fabulous meeting space. I feel so lucky to have such an awesome teen space. The garage door is just a dream come true because it allows the teens to have four walls so that they can be themselves and not disturb other library patrons. The teens love being in the teen room!"—Sarah Cofer, Northwest Library

This is the YA space of my dreams because . . .

"When I started at Old Worthington the teen room was a corner in the fiction/audio visual area. We had a few computers, but the area was entirely open for anyone to come in and included bean bags that attracted little kids. Now we can close the doors after school and teens can be teens. We have so much more room and the area is well lit. Many days when school is in session, I do my off-desk hours in the teen room just to enjoy the atmosphere—it is the most inviting area in the library and is incredibly quiet. I love the booths, the colors, the group study room just for teens, and the way it feels like you are entering an entirely new building. To hear teens who see the area for the first time say 'wow,' 'killer,' 'this is the teen room?' or 'I can't believe this is our room?' makes me proud to be a teen librarian and proud to make the teens feel like they fit in the library."—Ann Pechacek, Old Worthington Library

I still dream of these improvements:

"The one thing I will always dream about is more space for collection growth. I would also like to add a way of playing music in the teen room in the future and a fabulous sign above the garage door that screams 'teen!' to our non-teen patrons. I would also like to have a fun name for the teen space."—Sarah Cofer, Northwest Library

I still dream of these improvements:

"I would love to have music playing in the room, a great sign [that] says this is the teen room!"—Ann Pechacek, Old Worthington Library

Teen Patron Comments

"I love the new teen area of the library. The old area wasn't really conducive to comfort—it was too stiff and open for me to be comfortable chatting over homework without worrying I'm laughing too loud. But the new teen area gives teens their own (bright, colorful, cheerful) space that is designed for us and by us. I'm more likely to spend time at the library now that I have this space."—Rachel, eleventh grade, Old Worthington Library

"The previous teen area was okay, but there wasn't much privacy for people doing homework, or much space to sit . . . the current area is cooler and more secluded, with more comfortable seating arrangements. Thanks."—Bennett, ninth grade, Old Worthington Library

"The new space is much more comfortable and teen friendly. The organization is good and the computers are convenient.—Alex, eleventh grade, Old Worthington Library

"I thought the teen area was okay before, but I love it now! The new furniture is cool, and it's cool that the area has walls and a door. I also like the new computers."
—Melissa, tenth grade, Northwest Library

"Before the renovation, it was clear that a generation in the library was missing. Whether it was the children curled up in the corner to read or play with puppets or adults with their heads buried in their own world with their books, the teens did not have a place in the library where they [felt] that they belonged. Now with the new addition of a teen room in the library, I know that I can safely come to the library where I feel that I don't have to sit in the little stools or big plain tables with unforgivingly hard chairs. Now I have a new sense of belonging in the library." —Wendy, eleventh grade, Northwest Library

"The teen area before was very small, and it was very plain. And it really wasn't that much of a separate space. The new teen room is nice because it is separated from the rest of the library with a garage door, which is interesting and much more modern than a regular door. The furniture is also a bit funkier, which is the style of teenagers today, and instead of just study tables, we get booths, which is a much easier way to work as a group on a group project. My favorite thing about the new teen room is the furniture. Before we had the same chairs as the rest of the library. Now we have bright colored and oddly shaped chairs which are much more comfortable to study in."—Rachel, tenth grade, Northwest Library

Northwest Library, 2280 Hard Road, Columbus, OH 43235, (614) 807-2626
http://www.worthingtonlibraries.org/visit/locations/northwest

Old Worthington Library, 820 High Street, Worthington, OH 43085, (614) 807-2626
http://www.worthingtonlibraries.org/visit/locations/oldworthington

Young Adult Room

East Meadow Public Library
East Meadow, New York

Frances T. Jackson

Description: In the back of the reference department at East Meadow Public Library, visitors can peer through the looking glass into the brand-new Young Adult Room. Five large rectangular windows on a curved wall let onlookers check out the wave-like wooden bookshelves, bright green and warm blue walls, and sunshine streaming from the alcove windows—unique attributes to the 1,400 square-foot YA area. Also unique is the teen-picked rug; with its blue, green, and gray dots and grids, it looks more like binary code with flowing data than a carpet. The sound-proof room's sole entrance is on the corner of this curved wall; on the other side of the wall are four window seats alternating between shelves of paperback and boardgame collections. Adjacent to the entry way is another curved wall covered by metal shelving that holds the college and career books and leads to a wall-mounted OPAC computer. Two librarians' desks sit in the left center of the room and behind these stations are two project rooms that can each seat six teens. On the far wall, teens congregate in their lounge area, a small alcove in front of a floor-to-ceiling bay window, which hosts three green, swivel easy chairs. Next to the alcove, the display area hosts a bulletin board and a gallery hanging system for four large paintings or eight smaller pieces of art. A dropped ceiling, shaped like a rowboat, hangs in the center of the room; the area's lighting illuminates the table and computer area below. Flanking one side of the rowboat is a long, custom-built bookshelf for fiction titles. The remaining walls hold metal, adjustable shelving units that contain the special collections. A tiny room in the back of the work area serves as a staff office. The room was designed to be multipurpose for also hosting gaming events, movies, or bibliographic instruction with easily movable, wooden tables and chairs. For a video tour of the YA Room, check out *http://www.eastmeadow.info/tourYA.html*.

Collection: More than 600 linear feet of shelving hold the YA area's 13,200 titles. Custom wood shelving holds fiction, short story, paperbacks, text books, classic works, and *CliffsNotes* collections. Metal shelving hangs around the room for college, career, reference, graphic novels, biographies, and periodical collections. Popular paperback series and required summer reading get their own shelving

The curved bookshelf, computer desk, and all other furniture were custom-built for this space.

The rowboat-shaped drop ceiling illuminates the young adult room; on the right is the curved wall with fiction and window seats.

184

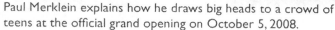

Paul Merklein explains how he draws big heads to a crowd of teens at the official grand opening on October 5, 2008.

Teens enjoy the lounge area by the window alcove.

units—a rack that sits near the custom wood shelving and a four-shelf, double-sided, metal book truck. The room is simply arranged by format and/or genre with separate areas for hardcover and paperbacks. The YA area's three computer workstations contain an online catalog, databases, word processing, and unfiltered Internet access. The library is in the process of adding three or four laptops to accommodate the growing number of teen users. Audiobooks and videos are still housed in the media area, and the majority of nonfiction is interfiled with the adult material to better serve the entire community. The average annual circulation for the last eight years is 16,246, which includes 2007–08 when much of the fiction collection was boxed and stored due to renovations. The 2008 summer circulation figure was 3,950, which gives an optimistic view of high numbers for the 2008–09 fiscal year.

Young Adult Population and Community: The East Meadow Public Library community is located in central Nassau County, Long Island, New York, about twenty-five miles east of New York City. There are approximately 52,000 residents in the East Meadow School District, which encompasses all or parts of four different postal areas, East Meadow, Levittown, North Bellmore, and Westbury. The community is home to fifteen churches, five synagogues, and one mosque. The school district's racial diversity breaks down as follows: 70 percent Caucasian, 15 percent Asian, 13 percent Hispanic and 2 percent African American. The library serves a total of 4,600 students in two middle schools and two high schools, and another approximately 300 students from several parochial institutions that are outside of the East Meadow School District.

Hours, Staffing, and Teen Traffic: The YA areas are open during regular library hours: Monday, Tuesday, Thursday from 9 a.m. to 9 p.m.; Wednesday from 11 a.m. to 9 p.m.; Saturday from 9 a.m. to 5 p.m. from October to May; and Sunday from 1 p.m. to 5 p.m. from October to May. Summer hours are Saturday 9 a.m. to 1 p.m. and closed Sunday. The room is open to the general public for quiet study when school is in session, but any adults or children not accompanied by a teen must vacate the room at 2 p.m. The young adult

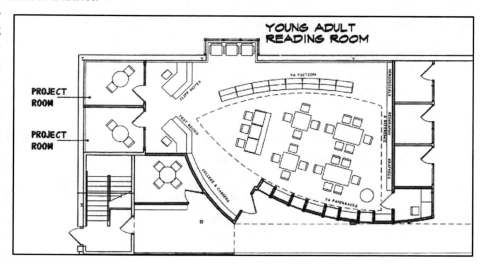

computers are kept offline until this time, when 40–50 teens from grades 6–12 start trickling into the space. On weekends, this number increases to approximately 90 youth. The YA Staff monitors the room to ensure the strict teen-only policy and encourage the older teens to use the space. A team of seven staff members rotate desk shifts, working two at a time to cover the room: this staff includes two full-time and three part-time professional librarians, and two paraprofessional pages.

Planning Process: The East Meadow Public Library began as a store-front library in 1955 until the current location opened on September 11, 1960. A few years later the library received expansions, but the YA section was not added for another forty-two years. At this time, the library began seeing a need for a separate YA space because of increased programming and plans to renovate the area behind Reference Services were formulated. It was decided to use a reputable architect whose work the Acting Library Director and Head of Young Adult Services liked. These two, along with the Assistant Director and the Young Adult Services staff, had input in the initial stages of creating the YA area. After finding out what they wanted and needed, the architect came up with three plans and one stood out as the clear choice. The actual renovation took place a year later, in October 2007, because the entire roof needed to be replaced first. In the interim, the team of five worked on finding appropriate furnishings and used the Teen Advisory Board whenever possible for help in decision making.

The YA space technically opened in June 2008, void of any fanfare, but necessary to accommodate teens in the busy summer ahead. The Grand Opening took place on October 5, 2008, the day Sunday hours began for the new school year. The room was dedicated in the memory of John Franzen, Library Director of EMPL from 1987–2006 and a wall plaque with this dedication was revealed to onlookers. Teen presence was felt as a local high school jazz choir played and the library hosted the high school art show. Teens were also invited to participate in two programs offered: Paul Merklein demonstrated his talent for drawing Great Big Faces and two anime artists led "Create Your Own Anime Character Workshop."

Youth Participation and Programming: The EMPL TAB was very instrumental in raising funds and awareness of the new teen room by writing letters and spreading the word to local and state politicians, local businesses, and the community. They continue to be a positive force, helping choose color and design for the teen space and guiding the direction of programs and events. The library also has an active Book Buddies volunteer group and a successful summer reading program. In 2008, an astounding 199 youth participated in Metamorphosis, the summer reading game.

During the soft opening of the YA area, young adult services held a six-week Wii Olympics using *Wii Sports* and *Deca Sports* to celebrate the 2008 Olympics in Beijing. Six sports were selected—Tennis, Bowling, Baseball, Archery, Snowboard Cross, and Kart Racing—and each week the teens competed in a different sport. Each competition had sixteen brackets for sixteen contestants, similar to NCAA Basketball's Final Four Tournament. The top two competitors played for gold and silver, and the bronze was decided from the losers in the semi-final matches. A week before the 2008 Beijing Olympics, a New York City news program, a regional newspaper, and a local cable news show ran stories on the library's successful teen program. The Wii has become an integral part of programming during school holidays, and next summer the library will have a countdown to the now annual Wii Olympic games.

Many teens take advantage of the library's Web site (*http:// www.eastmeadow.info)*, which provides a Teen Talk section, including links to New York State Regent Exams; colleges, scholarships, and homework help; updates about what is going on at the library; book reviews for new and old titles by YA staff and community teens; and a YA Librarian Chat section for instant communication.

True Confessions from Head of Young Adult Services
Frances T. Jackson

This is the YA space of my dreams because . . .

"It is a positive, safe place for teens to gather, a place where parents don't need to worry about their [youth], and a place where the teens can come to be themselves."

I still dream of these improvements:

"The teens of the twenty-first century are more media oriented than ever, so I still would love to bring the YA media, including the audiobooks and DVDs, into the room. I still dream of surround-sound music in the space and listening stations in the window seat areas. There is an overwhelming need to create a video gaming collection for the teens. Of course, I would love a bigger area for my staff and storage for prizes, booklists, and the extra stuff we need to run an exciting and creative space."

Teen Patron Comments

"First of all the room is gorgeous and it meets all your needs to learn more and [has] lots of books to read." —Christine, eleventh grade

"The YA room is a great, fun, safe place where teens can just hang out and be themselves. It has a very comfortable and relaxing atmosphere to hang out, do homework, or just read. Before the YA section didn't feel like it was just for young adults, now it's a place they can call their own." —Monisha, eleventh grade

"When the teen room was made, my friends and I finally had somewhere to hang out over the summer. It was a place that had an unlimited amount of things to do. We could stay there for hours and never get bored. We did everything from playing Boggle to flipping through magazines. Sometimes we even sat down to read a good book. Whether we were surfing online or simply just talking, we had a lot of fun at a place we call our second home." —Angelica, eleventh grade

East Meadow Public Library, 1886 Front Street, East Meadow, NY 11554-1700, (516) 794-2570 *http://www.eastmeadow.info/*

Oakland TeenZone
Humming a New Tune

Oakland Public Library
Oakland, California

Anthony Bernier and Nicole Branch

On January 17, 2009, after years of planning, fundraising, and construction delays, the Oakland Public Library (OPL) finally overcame all obstacles and opened its much-anticipated, newly remodeled TeenZone Department. Planning began in 2001 with the vision that OPL TeenZone would accommodate, educate, and celebrate the city's youth; eight years later this teen space is fulfilling that mission.

Oakland, California, one of the most diverse cities in the nation, sits across the bay from San Francisco and hums to its own tunes. A city of more than 400,000, Oakland teams with populations of Chinese, Vietnamese, African, African American, and diverse Latino communities, both foreign-born and native. Although the area boasts several colleges and the eighth most highly educated citizenry in

The living room area in the center of TeenZone.

the United States, high housing costs and urban challenges place many families on the fringe or below the economic middle-class mainstream. Consequently Oakland is also known for its radical political activism; the Black Panther Party, Free Speech, and anti-Vietnam war movements of the 1960s and 1970s all trace their origins to Oakland.

Oakland's unique legacy reverberates through its youth as well. Young people are a force here. Home to the famed Youth Radio, downtown hosts more than a dozen nonprofit youth services agencies. Oakland is also on the cutting edge of educational reform. The small school and charter school movements have already produced thirteen middle and high schools downtown alone. Most of these schools, however, cannot offer young people the full complement of conventional resources. The Oakland Public Library's TeenZone, located in the heart of downtown, now responds to the diverse and vital needs of its urban youth.

Before.

After.

A study area separated from the main space by magazine and game racks.

The study rooms are sectioned off with translucent partial walls to give privacy but still have an open, spacious feel.

Adhering to the idea that young adults add value to space design processes, they have been thick contributors to the Zone from the start. The library's Youth Leadership Council (YLC), heavily involved at every point from the design process through construction, participated in interviews to select and meet regularly with architects; revised many versions of the conceptual plans; led five small design charette groups in an all-day review process with architects, administrators, Foundation staff, and seventy-six other teens; and contributed to the furniture and technology selections. The commitment to youth leadership and transparency is evident in the YLC's minutes (posted prominently in the Zone) and in photos and movies on the TeenZone Department Web page (*http://www.myspace.com/mainteenzone*).

TeenZone Design

Tucked up on the second floor of the two-story, 1951 Main Library building adjacent to the picturesque Lake Merritt, the Zone is sited near the highly regarded Oakland history room. The placement is both practical—the space is rather secluded—and symbolic—the close proximity to the history room conjures the community's activist roots and connects youth to them.

Tall exterior windows line the west and south-facing walls, bathing the 2,415-square-foot space in natural light. Although the room is conventionally rectangular, it does not "read" that way anymore; creative design elements consciously break the typical monotony of horizontal and vertical lines with dynamic curvature and varying heights. In opposite corners along the east wall, translucent acrylic partial walls rise like an origami crane's wings to define two small, semiprivate tables and chairs. The in-between space is separated from the main room by chest-high magazine shelves. The Zone's western edge frames additional semi-private seating with skyline views of downtown.

In the center of the room, an oval dropped ceiling showcases stylish lighting to distract from institutional fluorescents. Mirroring the dropped ceiling are two recycled terrazzo computer counters that wrap around structural pillars and a longer computer crescent that offers twelve Apple iMac stations and movable stools. The Zone also accommodates disabled youth with two additional adaptive stations. Defining the center of the Zone, a curved, corrugated metal wall hugs another rounded communal seating area featuring three comfortable couches and a large ottoman. The space achieves flexibility, a sense of movement and choice, and entices a variety of youth activities.

Four dedicated staff members (three full-time Young Adult Specialist librarians and one part-time paraprofessional Library Assistant) freely roam the space un-tethered to a traditional reference desk. Staff offices are adjacent to the Zone. A staff computer, located in the middle of one counter, keeps staff online and constantly in the mix.

The TeenZone is decorated in muted grays and blacks with pops of red, orange, green, and blue throughout. The high-tech color scheme echoes in the sophisticated carpeting, a gray background with orange and blue ovals. The color and design schemes combine youth-friendly aesthetics and evoke varying tastes, styles, and time periods. The Zone's east wall features a gigantic floor-to-ceiling world map. Exaggerated size is one common aspect of youth aesthetics, and the huge map signals how the library can simultaneously launch personal and global imaginations. In addition to these interior design features, OPL enhances the library user's experience by offering a rotating youth-produced art exhibit along the wall leading to the TeenZone entrance.

Seating Matters

The Zone's commitment to developing a purpose-built and developmentally appropriate YA space is also apparent in design choices that address the teens' anatomical comfort. This goal is achieved primarily through offering a wide variety of seating options: couches, sofa chairs, task chairs, stools, countertops, and even sturdy window ledges. Seating variety allows young adults to rework much of the space's furnishings as they like as well as provides a range of posture positions for the many ways in which youth prefer to sit, stand, and even recline. Likewise, the chalkboard walls in meeting areas, a large whiteboard, and a variety of video games encourage a range of physical movement and interaction. The wide selection of choices dramatically contrasts conventional and institutional table-and-chair-only options.

The movable shelving units are labeled clearly by genre.

Collection

The collection of more than 2,800 printed volumes and 750 media titles is displayed on seven movable shelving units and three wall units. Users borrow materials at the main entrance on the first floor. These measures ensure more flexibility in the Zone and more space for teens, thus avoiding the privileging of library infrastructure and materials over the age-appropriate needs of YA library users.

The Zone's collection is geared to meet the recreation and information needs of the city's young people. Thus the space is not a school library by another name but rather a space to explore personal interests, new materials, and information curiosities. As a result, the Zone collection features only the latest graphic novels, manga, fiction, urban fiction, movies, and video games among many other materials.

Similarly the Dewey Decimal System is being phased-out in favor of a more youth-preferred classification system to reflect user-driven prerogatives. The staff finds that this new scheme better meets the information behaviors of local youth. Most items are categorized and shelved by genre and title. The superhero collection is shelved not by author or title but by superhero. When resource needs exceed the Zone's collection, the staff helps young adults make bibliographic connections with the rest of the Main Library's formidable holdings. Launching from the Zone into the larger library encourages more confident intergenerational mixing in the adult spaces and offers retreat back to the young adult space. Thus youth select for themselves the best dose of intergenerational mixing appropriate for them.

Lessons Learned

The previous OPL "YA space" was little more than six bookshelves. When YA services began a strategic planning process with a new YA Coordinator in 2001, the staff quickly recognized the need for a more professional profile and truly separate space. Although these goals were met, the transition to the redesigned Zone presented several unanticipated challenges. Not long after having developed the new space plan, the library's Foundation disbanded and thus did not contribute anticipated funding support. The project also endured several false starts in securing a contractor. Both of these issues tremendously delayed the project, which in turn affected previous staff and youth relationships. During the extended construction phases, the library's capacity to host class visits, conduct programming, and maintain community connections was considerably limited. Consequently staff must now re-establish relationships and refuel dormant outreach activities. Given the dramatic augmentation of technology, staff must also improve their own connections to technology and the ways youth currently use it.

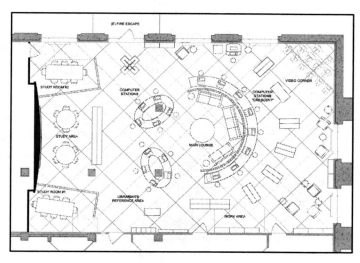

As more libraries seek improved spatial equity with young adults, unanticipated consequences can present challenging new service questions: How can libraries ensure continuity of service during renovation? And how can libraries anticipate changes in interpersonal dynamics as new resources are introduced. It is easy in a redesign project to become engrossed in the constant demands of planning and construction. But a remodeling project should carefully and realistically re-prioritize departmental service objectives to reflect these circumstances and perhaps even temporarily suspend some aspects of normal operations. Certainly some additional technical training would seem reasonable for a staff increasing their computer work stations from zero to twelve.

What's Next?

Although the TeenZone now represents a powerful advance in youth services, the project did not achieve every aspect of an ideal YA space. Several features did not make the final cut. A self-check machine, which proved too costly, would not only have furnished users with their own convenient check-out path, avoiding the longer lines on the ground floor, but it would also have maximized privacy for borrowing materials on health, sexual identity, and other sensitive subjects. The current project was also completed without backpack storage. Finally, with the Foundation's collapse, the project lost the ability to exploit otherwise superior donor recognition opportunities throughout the space.

Now that the TeenZone is operational, a number of post-occupancy considerations are in order as well. The library should design, collect, analyze, and regularly report data about what will most assuredly cause dramatic usage increases. Another task that should be undertaken within the next year is a user-centered, post-occupancy study similar to the one conducted on a YA space at another OPL branch, which can be found at *http://www.ala.org/ala/ mgrps/ divs/pla/plapublications/publiclibraries/novdec2006pl.pdf.*

After achieving all of its founding objectives, young adults now fill the Zone—a responsive and purpose-built space designed to meet their needs and preferences. As one young adult shared, "I feel as though the space has now become a room (for us)." They use the computers to find comics, video clips, and curricular materials. They gather in corners, share magazines, and make new friends, all while keeping an eye on little brothers and sisters playing board games. Outside, Oakland's downtown streets continue their unique rhythm.

Dr. Anthony Bernier is a full-time faculty member at San Jose State University's School of Library and Information Science, and Project Director of both the first Institute of Museum and Library Services (IMLS) Leadership Grant to examine YA space and YouthFacts.org.

Nicole Branch is an MLIS candidate at San Jose State University, an ARL Diversity Scholar, and has worked with Bay Area youth for the past ten years. She is currently a Research Assistant working on the first IMLS research grant.

Oakland Public Library, 125 14th Street, Oakland, CA 94612, (510) 238-3134
http://www.oaklandlibrary.org/index.html

Photos courtesy of Dave Adams Photography. *http://www.daveadamsphotography.com.*

The Library Commons:
Informal Social Interaction for Teens and Adults

McMillan Memorial Library
Wisconsin Rapids, Wisconsin

Ron McCabe

Finding a way to balance conversation and quiet study has been a perennial problem for public libraries. This dilemma is often most apparent after school when teens need to unwind and talk with friends after a long day of structured activities. McMillan Memorial Library in Wisconsin Rapids, Wisconsin, found a solution in the form of The Library Commons. The Commons supports informal social interaction for both teens and adults. For teens, it provides a gateway to the full range of library services, including their own young adult collection area. The Library Commons provides a large area for conversation and in turn allows the library to effectively zone larger areas as traditional quiet settings. Our commons area has been the single most important thing we have done to make the library a teen-friendly institution.

The Public Library Tradition and Innovations Since the 1960s

Public libraries are natural social gathering places but have traditionally provided little support for informal social interaction. In the classic public library, areas adjacent to collections were quiet study areas. Meeting rooms supported formal social interaction. Informal interaction was tolerated in lobbies but not encouraged anywhere in the library. Since the 1960s, many libraries have reacted against the conventional rule of silence. Some have encouraged informal social interaction throughout their facilities, limiting quiet areas to small designated spaces such as study rooms. Library users who want larger areas for quiet study often object to this solution. In the more recent past, public libraries have begun to support informal social interaction by providing coffee shops; academic libraries have developed informal social environments through their concept of the "information commons." Our Library Commons is a successful experiment that builds upon these recent innovations.

Teens have a variety of seating options in the Library Commons.

The Beginnings

The Library Commons was the culmination of a 2002–2003 space needs analysis by consultant Anders Dahlgren, followed by a 2003–2004 feasibility study conducted by the architectural firm of Meyer, Scherer, and Rockcastle, Ltd. The space needs analysis recommended a major expansion of the building; the feasibility study determined that such a major expansion was

Teens love having access to the adult DVD collection.

193

not financially possible. To keep the facility improvement process moving forward in the summer of 2004, the library staff and architects worked to find a way to add public service space without expanding the facility. The Board of Trustees approved the idea of developing a 5,000-square-foot area that was underutilized at the time.

The idea of using this space as a commons area came from the concept of the "information commons" from Ray Oldenburg's book, *The Great Good Place: Cafes, Coffee Shops, Community Centers, Beauty Parlors, General Stores, Bars, Hangouts and How They Get You Through the Day* (Paragon House, 1989). My assistant director Andy Barnett was instrumental in planning collection and seating areas, and architect Rhys MacPherson and his staff at Meyer, Scherer, and Rockcastle gave us a brilliant design for the space. We spent the fall of 2004 emptying the storage area and then were in construction until September 2005 when the Library Commons opened to the public.

These computers at the entranceway fill up quickly after school.

The coffeehouse area gives patrons a relaxed, home-like atmosphere.

The McMillan Library Commons

After passing self-check machines and a service desk, patrons are surrounded by nine different bright-colored strips on the walls and also in the room's rubber flooring. On the right side of the 5,000-square-foot area is a row of four public computers with barstyle seating; four more computers occupy space on the opposite wall in a similar fashion. The entire commons area has wireless Internet access. Continuing along the right wall is a lounge area featuring soft chairs and booths followed by a magazine and newspaper section that hosts a vending machine and traditional lounge furniture and tables. There is enough seating in the commons area for eighty people. Angled bookstore-style shelving houses audiovisual materials in the center of the room. Colorful hanging ceiling ellipses frame the lounge area with the booths and the coffeehouse area in the front corner of the room.

The coffeehouse is an important and favorite feature of the commons area. It was initially run by private vendors who later went out of business; it is now managed by library staff and doubles as a staff workstation for checking in materials. Although this method works well, our extremely tight staffing means limiting the hours of the coffeehouse from 9:00 a.m. to 1:00 p.m. When our finances permit us, we will include after-school hours and offer services specifically designed for teens.

In creating this large social area, we were careful to include collections that would either not be used at the library or collections that tend to be browsed rather than studied. We included computers in this area as well because many computer users are not bothered by background noise. We encourage conversations at normal volumes and allow people to enjoy food and beverages in the commons area.

The vending machine serves up tasty food and beverages to teens after school.

During the school day, the commons area is used mainly by adults; after-school hours see between thirty and eighty junior high students joining the adults in the commons. Many teens socialize, browse collections, or use computers here. Others take advantage of library programs such as *Guitar Hero, Rock Band*, crafts, or films that are offered in the adjacent All Purpose Meeting Room or the Fine Arts Center auditorium. Teens who want a quiet study atmosphere can go upstairs to the adult services department where the young adult collection is housed. Teens may also choose to use the youth services department, which is also located on the upper floor. We decided to house the young adult collection—selected by one of our youth services librarians—in the adult service section because we have found that most teens do not want to be in the same room as the younger children. We have ample room to place the teens' collection there as well as sixteen additional public computers.

An interesting and important effect of the commons area has been that it has allowed us to zone the upper floor of our 45,000-square-foot building as a quiet area. In the past, the afterschool student rush filled the upper level with noisy conversations that were difficult to control. Creating a library commons has been a great help to both adults and teens seeking a traditional library environment.

Discipline

We have found that discipline has been greatly improved since opening the Library Commons. By segregating informal conversation to the commons, our adult services department is so quiet after school that even traditional library users are satisfied. In the commons area, we prevent shouting, pushing, running, and other unsafe or disruptive behaviors. It is easier to respond to these extreme behaviors, however, than to try to create a quiet environment in a situation where fifty students are talking in normal tones. In the commons area, our response to these extreme behaviors is understood and accepted by most teens.

We do, of course, occasionally have problems so staff is required during after-school hours to make sure that the commons area can be effectively used by everyone. Since we opened the commons, we have experimented with using teachers, teacher aides, and security guards for this work. Our professional staff will step in when a student's behavior is so egregious that he or she needs to be barred from library use for a period of time.

Another discipline-related problem is the need to respond to adults who believe that all parts of the library should be quiet whenever the library is open. We respond first by suggesting that these adults move to the adult services department. For those not satisfied with this response, we explain the need for students to have a safe place to go after school, the developmental importance of informal socializing for young adults, and the right of young adults to use the library in ways they find meaningful. We note our disciplinary efforts and explain that we are teaching civility to our young people.

The Library Commons as a Key to Serving Teens

We find that the use of a large commons area removes the most important barrier to effective teen service—the absence of a place to talk with friends. Socialization is natural and contributes to the health of both individuals and the community. We believe that the public library's role as a community center requires facility support for informal social interaction. Our Library Commons is the best way we could integrate this support into the larger service program of our library. If we were to dedicate a social area to young adults only, it would be too small to accommodate the many students who come to the library. Combining this area with collections and services for adults allows us to make efficient use of our available space. A commons area provides teens an informal, comfortable gateway to all of the library's services—services especially designed for that age group as well as services for the adults they are becoming.

Teen Comments

"I like hanging out downstairs in the Commons rather than upstairs because I can talk to friends."

"I enjoy using the wireless Internet access and booths in the Commons."

"All the colors are cool. I like how it's set up."

"We come here after school to sit in the booths. It's social down there with the CDs and DVDs and stuff. We like to sit and read magazines."

McMillan Memorial Library, 490 East Grand Avenue, Wisconsin Rapids, WI 54494, (715) 422-5136
http://www.mcmillanlibrary.org/index.shtml

House Calls: Teen Space Makeover:
Teens and Local Newspaper Collaborate for Affordable Changes
Montgomery County Public Libraries
Maryland

Kathie Weinberg

The *Washington Post* has a national reputation for excellence in political reporting. Locals also know it for the popular "House Calls" column that runs every Thursday in the Home and Garden pages of the Arts and Living section. Readers can send in drawings or pictures of a living space that is in need of a drastic change or has a design challenge, and with luck, the project will be selected by the newspaper to receive expert design tips and complete redesign concept. So what does this feature have to do with libraries and teen space? On a whim, teen service librarians from

Teens take a break from reading to chat in Bethesda Teen Space.

the Montgomery County Public Libraries (MCPL) in Maryland submitted a request to the newspaper for a redesign of public spaces, specifically, the teen spaces in our branch libraries. We added an additional criterion, that teens be involved in the process from beginning to end. To our surprise, a reporter called us back! The result is three redesigned and implemented teen spaces at the Bethesda, Chevy Chase, and Quince Orchard branches. We received complementary professional design input for each of these libraries. Funding for the project came from local Friends of the Library groups, grants, and of course, the library system. The best part about the project is the teens' involvement during all the planning and implementation stages, including expressing their views on the space required, signing off on design features, and furniture and accessories shopping and assembly.

To begin the process, the *Washington Post* reporter met with MCPL's Teen Advisory Group (TAG). These teens were emphatic that they wanted clearly defined teen space in branch libraries, but had many views on what this space should look like. Some of the ideas they agreed on included:

- Comfortable chairs for lounging, including bean bag chairs or space on the floor for sitting.

- Space for both individual and group work.

- Message board walls with current information, fun posters.

- Wi-Fi access, plus networked computers.

- Good signage defining the space for teens.

- Fun colors, but not to the point that they clashed with the rest of the library.

Teens love to lounge on the floor of their new area.

197

The *Washington Post* makeover column then put out a call for design groups that might be interested in participating in the projects. Typically these design groups work gratis, although they do receive publicity when the project results are reported. The designers are not responsible for implementation, and it is up to the subject to decide whether to actually follow through with the design suggestions. All three design groups chosen for the branch projects were most generous with their time, however, and fulfilled their promise to follow the projects through to completion.

The Bethesda Library Project

Tuscan Blue Design, the group selected for the Bethesda Library project, first came to look at the library space and then to meet with the TAG and other Bethesda teen patrons in spring 2008. These teens again expressed their views on how the library space should look, and the designers listened with open minds. Tuscan Blue then took the design requirements, their notes, and their drawings, and developed the plans. Meredith Ericksen and Laura Cassese, principals of the design group, met with teens on a Saturday morning with free donuts as "bait" and shared their design proposals.

Vibrant hues of green and blue meshed well with the library interior and small round rugs provided splashes of orange to individualize the space. Furnishings were comfortable, utilitarian, and well-priced. Window treatments were added to help personalize the area. Floor lamps and a large "TEEN" sign added the final touches. Shelving was almost doubled, and placed in such a way as to define but not enclose the area. To complement the Wi-Fi offered to users, two computer workstations were added with two additional carrels.

Kay Bowman, Agency Manager for the Bethesda Library, and the teens made revisions, and a consensus was met. The design was finalized, and we moved on to the next step, MCPL Executive Committee approval. The Committee, which includes MCPL Library Director Parker Hamilton, was enthusiastic about the design ideas and accepting of the teen input, so the project was approved with few modifications. Hamilton is a firm believer in library space for teens; her support made an otherwise slow-moving entity pick up speed and go full force ahead for the teen project.

Funding was the next hurdle. Library budgets are being cut everywhere, and MCPL is no different. It was clear that with book budgets and staff cuts, major purchasing of new furniture and other resources in the teen areas would not be possible. Knowing this fact but having the luxury of the Friends of the Library Bethesda Chapter's support, we presented the project to this group with clearly detailed information on the estimated total cost. Tuscan Blue had been most respectful of our price limitations—it focused on keeping the furniture and accessory budget low—but neglected to factor in the cost of the shelving. For the Bethesda project, the total cost was approximately $6,000, with shelving being the greatest expense. Much of the furniture was to be purchased at the local Ikea store. The Bethesda Friends group was very enthusiastic about the project and gave us the go ahead.

Shelving was ordered, lists were made, and a shopping trip to the local Ikea was planned. By then it was August, and we had the pre-school attention of the teens. Several carloads of teens accompanied the *Washington Post* reporter and photographer, librarians, designers, and a few parents to the store. We even had an Ikea representative at our disposal, so the trip was efficient but fun and more than a little wild. We paid the bill with Friends funds and headed back to the library. The next step was furniture assembly. To no one's surprise, teens have many more assembly skills than librarians. Everything was constructed and put in place. The show *Design on a Dime* would be proud to employ these teens. Although the teens were willing, the library system handled the painting, furniture moving, and computer rewiring. Our local Friends group also supplied volunteers to help with installation of the window treatments, bulletin boards, and decorative fabric. The teen sign was installed, and we were ready for teens to enjoy this space.

Teens sort through the many fabric choices for the wall hangings and windows.

Quick Facts for Chevy Chase Library

8005 Connecticut Ave., Chevy Chase, MD 20815, (240) 773-9590

Designer: Charles C. Almonte

Vision: To have the space fit in with colonial style of building yet be inviting to teens. Agency Manager Mildred Nance wanted "to add a teen twist to a very traditional colonial designed building."

Teen Ideas: Wanted their own separate space, an area that they could lounge in and get work done, and colors that were fun but didn't clash with the rest of the library.

Major Items Purchased: Because of the ample shelving available, most items purchased were for seating: one lounge chair, one wicker-swivel chair, two "slipper" chairs, two stools, two tables, and small desk and chair.

Color Scheme: Shades of green and orange to match the rest of the building, with a large metallic teen sign to complement the area.

Square Footage: 15' X 16'

Duration of Project: Began August 2009; finished October 2009

Overall Budget: $5,000

Quick Facts for Quince Orchard Library

15831 Quince Orchard Rd., Gaithersburg, MD 20878, (240) 777-0200

Designer: Dan Banks, Project Design Company

Vision: To meet the needs and interests of teens, including expanding and relocating the Young Adult Collection, and to make them feel more welcome in the library.

Teen Ideas: Wanted modern urban feeling, a space that fit in with the rest of the library, comfortable chairs and seating, and places to plug in laptops.

Major Items Purchased: 4 interlocking kidney shaped tables with 16 chairs. Mobile in center, 4 plush armless sofa chairs with tables attached. Newspaper-type stand for graphic novels.

Color Scheme: Green, orange, gray, with black walls.

Square Footage: 30' X 45'

Duration of Project: Began at the same time as Bethesda project in spring 2008, but because of the requirements of a DEMCO grant, it wasn't finalized until June 2009 (with the exception of the mural which is still in its planning stage).

Overall Budget: $10,000 from the DEMCO Room Makeover Prize that the library won and an additional $7,000.

We had an official ribbon cutting ceremony during Teen Read Week in October 2008 with director Hamilton doing the honors. Teens were present, along with the Friends and the public. The Bethesda Library discovered quickly that if you provide a welcoming space, teens will enjoy it. We have had to put up signs reserving this space for teens weekdays after 3:30 p.m. and on weekends. There is a constant flow of teens enjoying our makeover.

The experience at the Bethesda Library has taught us several lessons. First, do not be shy about approaching local community groups and businesses for assistance. The worst they can do is decline, and in the case of the *Washington Post*, the designers, and the Friends of Bethesda Library, they may offer more support than ever imagined. Typically, interior designers who work on "House Call" projects only submit the designs to the *Washington Post*. In this case, however, Tuscan Blue worked with us through the whole library project, including installation. In addition to supplying us with funding, the FOL Bethesda volunteers also helped with installation. Second, teens are the best resource in planning an area in your library solely for their use. They are full of wonderful and innovative ideas yet respectful of the library as a whole. We have learned at the Bethesda Library that if we build the space, they will come.

Bethesda Library, 7400 Arlington Road, Bethesda, MD 20814, (240) 777-0970
http://www.montgomerycountymd.gov/apps/libraries/branchinfo/be.asp

TEENSPOT:
"It's Where You Want to Be"

Public Library of Cincinnati and Hamilton County
Cincinnati, Ohio

Jennifer Korn

Description: In the southeast corner on the second floor of the Main Library's North Building, a glass wall containing the painted words "TeenSpot: It's Where You Want to Be" invites teens to take a closer look at the resources and freedom the library has awaiting them. Patrons can get to TeenSpot either by climbing the spiral staircase or taking the elevator from the first floor, or by crossing the enclosed breezeway that connects the library's North and South Buildings. The L-shaped, 8,147 square-foot space has an open entryway lined with glass display cases that advertise programs and events, a silver book display cart, and a giant magnetic poetry board, all leading into a spacious, atrium-like reading lounge. TeenSpot's brilliant hues of black, blue, red, green, silver, and gold can be found everywhere from the wave-like carpet to the accent walls and furniture. The many windows surrounding the ceiling of the third floor let plenty of sunlight shine down to this area, which contains seven comfy, movable chairs and plenty of space to install temporary displays for contests and programs. Beyond the reading area is a circular service desk that is surrounded by display shelves and leads into the main computer area. On the left side of the computer area and general fiction is the Manga and Graphic Novel nook, bordered by two floor-to-ceiling windows and containing more comfortable lounge chairs. Another nook to the left is the café area that is home to two diner-style booths and two vending machines as well as plenty of high-top and regular-style tables and enough chairs to seat 44 teens. A retractable screen lowers from the far ceiling for watching movies and playing video games. This dining area is one of only two areas where food is permitted in the building and is essential to the department's success. On the opposite side of TeenSpot are three meeting rooms with awesome glass walls that have special panels the teens can use as dry erase boards. The large meeting room, used for programs and school visits, seats 25, and the two smaller, quiet, study rooms have one round table and four chairs each.

The entrance shows the glass wall of one of the programming rooms.

The chairs in the computer area are lightweight and on wheels so teens can easily move around.

A view of the atrium-like reading lounge in the center of TeenSpot.

The café area is a favorite hang-out spot among teens.

Collection: The YA department's 28,693 volumes are held on 3,416 feet of shelving throughout the space. Fiction titles are arranged alphabetically on standard metal library shelving, but each genre and type has its own section. Paperbacks are also alphabetized and sit on three, freestanding, spinning racks. Nonfiction is arranged by collection—biographies, new titles, and general nonfiction—using the Dewey Decimal system. Graphic novels and manga are shelved by their Dewey Decimal numbers as well, but these titles are kept on a combination of face out and regular metal shelves in the Graphic Novel nook. Magazines and serial comics are shelved on opaque plastic racks that are mounted to structural posts throughout the room. Anime DVDs and audiobooks round out the collection and can be found in their own sections alphabetically by title and author name, respectively. The Outreach Department holds a greater selection of large print teen materials and various popular and classic teen items that are used for classroom collections and visits to special needs schools. This department is not accessible to the public, so books must be retrieved by staff. Adult books with teen appeal and music CDs for teens can be found on the first floor of the South Building in the Popular Library. YA circulation for January through November 2009 was 50,715 titles, or 4,610 per month. Twenty-two full service computers include the online catalog, databases, Microsoft Office 2007 Suite, filtered Internet access, and capabilities to listen to, watch, edit, and download music and videos. There are two express terminals at the entranceway that allow only Internet and library catalog access and can be used for a maximum of fifteen minutes.

Young Adult Population and Community: Known as The Queen City, Cincinnati, Ohio, is north of the Ohio River at the Ohio-Kentucky border. Because the Main Library is located in the heart of downtown, the department serves approximately 10,000 teens from a large regional area encompassing the city of Cincinnati (~332,252 pop.) and the surrounding Hamilton County (~832,396 pop.). This geographic location also means that the Main Library serves schools not only from Hamilton County, but also Butler, Warren, and Clermont Counties in Ohio, and Boone, Campbell, and Kenton Counties in Kentucky. For example, from January to June 2009, the library served 925 teens visiting from twenty-one different schools. According to TeenSpot Manager Jennifer Korn, on a daily basis, the teens served are predominately black and living close to, if not under, the poverty level.

Signage hangs above the different sections so teens can easily browse books.

Hours, Staffing, and Teen Traffic: The YA area is open during regular library hours: Monday, Tuesday, Wednesday from 9 a.m. to 9 p.m.; Thursday, Friday, Saturday from 9 a.m. to 6 p.m.; and Sunday from 1 p.m. to 5 p.m. TeenSpot is designed for teens ages 12–18, but young adults (ages 18–25) occupy the room heavily during school hours, and younger siblings seem to enjoy tagging along. Programming in the TeenSpot is exclusively for teens. An average of 35 teens hang out at any given time during after-school hours, increasing to 40 on weekends, with 100 or so youth wandering in and out of the department through the day. A team of nine staff members is assigned to the YA area: six full-time employees consisting of one manager, three teen services librarians, and two library service assistants, and three part-time workers, including two library service assistants and one student shelver.

Planning Process: The teen space was created in 2008 when the Main Library decided to do a complete overhaul, later dubbed as Main Library 21st Century (ML21). The library was formerly arranged by subject specialty, grouping the teen fiction collection in the fiction department. The many different subject departments were combined into fewer, more generalized sections, and the teen department and the technology department were created. Administrators and library staff met for several months to plan the proposed changes, including where the teen department would be located, how it would be staffed, and what materials would be included. The library hired an architecture firm, which gave suggestions on floor plans and design schemes. The Official Teen Advisory Board had the most say regarding décor, furniture, displays, and other accents for the teen room. The OTAB also worked together to come up with the department name. In January 2008, TeenSpot was officially opened, but without any furniture other than shelves, a desk, and computers. The rest of the furniture arrived bit by bit, and by April of the same year, TeenSpot became the fully operational haven it is today.

Youth Participation and Programming: TeenSpot is home to a variety of great activities thanks to OTAB teens who are responsible for generating program ideas, setting the criteria for and judging the teen library programs and contests, and creating content for the Library's teen Web site (*http://teenspace.cincinnatilibrary.org*). Although the site is maintained by the Web Coordinator, teens add things like weekly survey questions and book reviews. The library also employs teen volunteers to help with programs and general upkeep of the teen department.

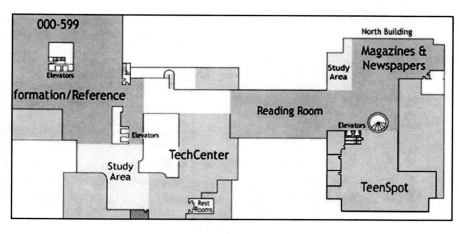

In addition to a wide variety of monthly programs and gaming events, TeenSpot also hosts a very popular Cosplay twice a year. This event includes costume and Cosplay contests, ramen noodle and Pocky-eating competitions, anime viewing, and a DDR tournament. For the last Cosplay, TeenSpot brought in the local Japanese American Society to lead origami and calligraphy workshops. TeenSpot also hosts a yearly teen Poetry Contest in April and Photography Contest in October, complete with award ceremonies for family and friends. OTAB selects the winners from hundreds of submissions all over Hamilton County.

Every week a volunteer from the Cincinnati Youth Collaborative College Resource Center comes to TeenSpot to give free advice on preparing for college. Teens are free to drop in during the regularly scheduled visit hours or can make an appointment to meet separately with the volunteer. A Homework Central Department is conveniently located directly below TeenSpot, which offers free printing, free tutoring, and homework assistance to all students.

True Confessions from Teenspot Manager Jennifer Korn and Teenspot Librarian Martha Camele Earls

This is the YA space of my dreams because . . .

"It demonstrates the level of dedication the library has to serving teens. This space was created by teens, for teens, and is staffed by people who enjoy working with teens. Whether teens visit to receive research and homework assistance, find a good book, or socialize, this space is designed to meet those needs. My favorite part of TeenSpot is its ability to respond and adapt to the needs and wants of the teens who use this space and who are ultimately making the Library's space their own space."—Jennifer Korn

"I think that TeenSpot is the space of our dreams because it is a department that provides a real space for teens. The physical environment, the collection, and the programs and services are all geared toward welcoming teens. And I think the staff is a big part of that; having a staff that wants to work with teens, specifically, makes all the difference in the world. A library can have the best collection, programs, and services in the world but without a staff dedicated and passionate toward teen services, none of the rest matters much."—Martha Camele Earls

I still dream of these improvements:

"I would like for more area teachers and schools to be aware and take advantage of the awesome services TeenSpot provides for education and entertainment to teens. TeenSpot staff would love enhanced technology and training so we could offer programs on media production [because] our teens are very interested in it." —Jennifer Korn

Teen Patron Comments

"My favorite thing about TeenSpot is the people who work here."—Jessica Rashid, 12

"Before TeenSpot opened, I only came to the Library if I had to, not to hang out. Now, I like hanging out in TeenSpot after school. I like that I get to be around people my own age and not adults. There's lots to do. I can go to a quiet area if I want, or I can participate in a program. I also like to bug the staff!"—Asia Felton, 17

Public Library of Cincinnati and Hamilton County, 800 Vine Street, Cincinnati, OH 45202-2009, (513) 369-6900
http://www.cincinnatilibrary.org/

New Green Teen Space

Battery Park City Branch, New York Public Library
New York City, New York

Jeremy Czerw

Description: Less than a five minute walk from Stuyvesant High School, a public magnet school for academically gifted students, is the new two-story, ten-thousand square-foot Battery Park City Branch Library, a certified green project. The building, opened on March 15, 2010, has low-flow water fixtures, automatically dimming lights, and a heating and cooling system designed to use less energy than traditional systems. The carpets are made from recycled truck tires, the circulation desk is made from recycled cardboard, and the terrazzo staircase is made of recycled glass chips. The space is filled with light streaming through floor-to-ceiling windows. The YA collection and adult collection are next to each other on the first floor, in an open area patrons enter after they've moved past the DVD collection, public computers for adults and teens, and the information desk.

The reading lounge tucked below the "Stairway to Heaven."

The YA space is a rectangular area of approximately one thousand square feet. There is seating in the rear of the space that borders the CD collection and the YA book collection. There are also teen-friendly, comfortable lounge chairs and work tables on the second floor of the building overlooking Lower Manhattan. The second floor also has an area for adult and teen programs—it currently has a flatscreen TV, and a Nintendo Wii is on its way.

The library's accent colors are pale green and vibrant orange. There is a magazine display in the YA section that is also used for book displays and special projects. The top of about four hundred linear feet of waist-high standard shelving throughout the YA section provides display space for recommended books, reviews, art, and other items. Two tables, seating four to six people, are located near the YA collection, and over a dozen other lounge chairs are near the tables and in other seating areas throughout the building. One hundred twenty linear feet of wall-mounted, angled shelving display DVDs, and approximately twenty-four linear feet of magazine display racks are reserved exclusively for YA materials, with storage behind the shelving for back issues.

The second floor features desks with power outlets for laptop users that look out onto the streetscape below. Ten laptops can be checked out and used anywhere in the building, and free Wi-fi is available throughout the building. There are also twelve PCs for adult and teen use and an additional two express PCs with fifteen-minute appointments. All of the PCs allow access to dozens of online databases through *http://www.nypl.org/*, including many not available to users who aren't actually in the building, and include Microsoft Office software. Two additional computers are dedicated to catalog searching. The library offers filtered Internet access—patrons can request a filtered site to be unblocked. All patrons are welcome to play games online, and headphone jacks are available for those wishing to hear media content.

Collection: The YA collection consists of approximately four to five thousand items, including fiction, picture books for teens, adult books for teens, graphic novels, magazines, and nonfiction. Teen requests to develop a comics collection are currently under consideration by the collection development office. The collection also includes audio books, videos, music CDs, college and career information, and paperbacks. The collection provides recreational reading and curriculum support, with homework help and reference.

Generally, arrangement is by Dewey. Manga is separate from other graphic novels, and urban fiction also has its own section. CDs and DVDs are shelved by title (for movies, TV series, and other videos) or alphabetically by the artist's name (for music CDs). Currently, teen urban fiction, DVDs, CDs, and graphic novels are interfiled with adult materials. No YA circulation figures are yet available.

Study tables are located by floor-to-ceiling windows near the DVD and graphic novel collection.

Young Adult Population and Community: The Battery Park City Branch serves New York City's Community District 1, comprised of several downtown Manhattan neighborhoods with a total population of 34,420 in 2000, and new residential construction in the past decade has sharply increased that number. In 2000, approximately 67 percent of the population was non-Hispanic White, 7 percent Black, 14 percent Asian and Pacific Islander, 4 percent multiethnic, and 8 percent Hispanic. Also, approximately 25 percent of the total population was born outside the United States. The teen population as of 2000 was approximately 2,050, with many more students coming into the area to attend school each day. The branch serves 8,610 students in one junior high school and six high schools.

Hours, Staffing, and Teen Traffic: All areas of the building are open at the same times: Monday, 10–6; Tuesday, 12–8; Wednesday, 10–6; Thursday, 12–8; Friday, 10–5; Saturday, 10–5. At least a dozen younger teens are coming in right after school each day, and about twelve to twenty visit on the weekends, mostly with their parents. So far, the branch has attracted mostly younger teens—predominately twelve- to fourteen-year-olds. Patrons of all ages have asked for materials from the YA collection. The main information desk, staffed by the library manager, one adult librarian, one teen librarian, and one children's librarian, serves adult and teen patrons.

Waist-high shelving provides plenty of display space.

Youth Participation and Programming: The new teen space hasn't been named yet, and a name-the-YA space contest is planned once the teen advisory group (TAG) is up and running. There was a grand opening the first week, and the library will have an official welcome party for teens after the staff gets to meet more of them. Video gaming events are planned, and the high school has been informed that the library is looking

Perilously comfortable chairs welcome teen readers.

for teen volunteers. Online homework assistance is available through *http://www. homeworknyc.org*, and the library hosts a teen Web site at *http:// www.nypl.org/help/getting-oriented/resources-teens.*

True Confessions from Senior Librarian Jeremy Czerw

Battery Park City is one of the pilot NYPL branches testing a new portable staff PC that we can use in the branch and anywhere else with wireless Internet. We can use the PC to register patrons for library cards, take pictures, search the catalog and the Internet, and circulate materials. I can't wait to take our staff tablet PC to the neighboring waterfront park and other hangouts in Lower Manhattan—to intercept downtown commuters heading for New Jersey or the Staten Island Ferry. We're in a densely packed, high-rise residential neighborhood of Manhattan that has been clamoring for a library for over a decade. Most residents are from wealthy households, but the library attracts tourists and New Yorkers of all backgrounds and income levels. In the weeks since we've opened, I'm thrilled to report that the library's patrons and staff reflect the diversity and intellectual curiosity of New York at its best. It's a great place to work.

This is the YA space of my dreams because . . .

"we have a beautiful space with great computer access and great books, right next to local schools and amazing parks. Also, even though we're in traffic-choked Lower Manhattan, you can bike to our library on a car-free bike path that runs the length of the island. The community waited a long time for this library, but according to our patrons, it was worth the wait."

I still dream of these improvements:

"I can't wait to start visiting local schools and getting to know the teens better. I'm looking forward to starting a TAG and helping the teens plan programs for the summer."

Teen Patron Comments

"It's really cool, with a lot of areas for homework. It's really well designed and modern."—Olivia, 11

"I like that it's quiet. The old library that I went to was too noisy. There's a good feeling here."—Isabel, 11

"At my house, I have a little brother and sister who can be loud and annoying, especially when I'm trying to do my homework. It's great to come here and do my work in a quiet place. And I can help my friends with their work, too."—Cora, 12

> Battery Park City Branch, New York Public Library, 175 North End Avenue, New York, NY 10282, (212) 790-3499
> *http://www.nypl.org/locations/battery-park-city*

Teen Space

Martin Luther King, Jr. Memorial Library
Washington, DC

Elsworth Rockefeller

Description: The Teen Services Division has moved around the Martin Luther King, Jr. Memorial Library throughout its history and has shared space with numerous service areas. During the recent renovation, we were housed in the corner of the Business, Science, and Technology Division on the first floor. The swing space (which was never seen as a permanent location) was about six hundred square feet. We had five computer stations and about one hundred seventy linear feet of shelving. The close quarters created some obstacles in serving our population, but we knew a completely renovated, purpose-built space was in process, so we focused on the future during the interim period.

Now, we're on the second floor of a four-floor building, across the hall from the Art, Music, History, and Biography Division. Our other close neighbors include the Adaptive Services Division (a great programming and service ally) and the Children's Division.

View of Teen Space seating, stacks, and train graphic.

Seating and TV.

View from "back door" to "front door."

Another view of back wall.

Catalog computers.

Teen customers using computer workstations.

Moving sidewalk graphic, shelving.

The new Teen Space has 3,836 square feet with two entrances. The space includes a quiet study room with glass doors, a vending/printing/ lockers room, a lounge area with a flat screen TV, a separate media-editing booth, and two computer banks. There is a separate staff work space (with workstations/computers for each staff member). We went with a shared workspace for the service desk, which includes six computers for teen customer use and two stations for staff. The shared space works very well for us and has allowed for some dynamic customer service.

In contrast to the Ludwig Mies van der Rohe style of the larger library building, the Teen Space was designed to feel contemporary and teen friendly, with striped grey carpeting, stainless steel tables, white countertops, multicolored soft seating, and a red accent wall behind a patterned resin panel where the fifty-two inch flat screen TV is mounted. We added graphics of birds on a telephone wire on a horizontal bulkhead and DC Metro trains on the end panels of the low shelving in the reading room for visual interest. The quiet study room has fabric-covered walls for sound muffling.

The space includes nine stainless steel square tables (each about two and a half feet by two and a half feet), forty-four plastic Herman Miller seats at tables and computers, six steel stools at the shared workstation, three white stools/ tables in the lounge area, three soft seating cubes in shades of red (each about three feet by three feet), and my personal favorite, a low white plastic console for media equipment. Our shelving has expanded with two T-shaped thirty-three inch high shelving banks (each T is approximately ninety linear feet), and approximately seven hundred linear feet of traditional library shelving (seven feet high with adjustable shelves). We had the shelving built to accommodate face-out books; we do not use book ends with fiction.

The computer area holds twenty fully functional iMacs, and we have a mobile laptop lab with twenty machines. There are two catalog computers in the space as well. Internet access is filtered and computer games are available.

The teen collection has 4,600 print items (fiction, nonfiction, magazines, graphic novels, manga) and 1,200 non-print items (music CDs, PlayAways, audiobooks on CD).

Our nonfiction collection is considered "high interest," so we have books on topics like celebrities, sports, sex, and human development, etc., but not resources on academic subjects. The children's room houses the academic nonfiction for youth up through high school level. For older teens or teens looking for more in-depth research, the adult collections are found in the adult reading rooms. The nonfiction is arranged by Dewey, fiction and graphic novels by authors' last names. The materials are separated into the following sections: fiction, non-fiction, audiobooks, fiction in Spanish, reference, manga, and graphic novels. About 1,007 items are circulated each month. There is a "shelved with adult" section of graphic novels and lots of music of interest to teens in the Popular Library.

Young Adult Population and Community: We are located in the center of Washington, DC, so we serve a wide variety of teens. The majority of our users are African American, though we see lots of diversity. Some of the teens

Back wall of teen space.

One of the two computer banks.

EVENT FLYER

we serve live in the neighborhood of Penn Quarter (where the library is located), others live in more distant parts of the city; a group of our teen customers currently stay in shelters or transitional housing, and some come in from the suburbs to use our facility. Some of the teens live in multi-million-dollar condos and others live in rent-controlled communities. We're gifted to be a place where all DC youth can come and find the resources they need.

Being in an urban area, we also have the opportunity to serve many youth from places throughout the U.S. and abroad who are touring the area. We recently had an opportunity to work with a group of sixty teens stuck in the area for a week and a half because of travel restrictions to Europe (due to the volcanic ash). There are a total of over eighty thousand students in DC, and we serve approximately five thousand youth from middle and high schools in the immediate downtown area. We work with lots of charter schools and home school groups, too.

Hours, Staffing, and Teen Traffic: Teen Space is open the same hours as the main library: Monday and Tuesday 12:00 p.m. to 9:00 p.m., Wednesday through Saturday 9:30 a.m. to 5:30 p.m., and Sunday 1:00 p.m. to 5:00 p.m. Thirty-five to sixty teens frequent Teen Space after school and fifty-five to eighty on the weekends. Teen Space is designed for teens aged 12 to 19, but most of our users are young men between 16 and 19. All library customers are welcome to explore our collections and work with staff. We currently operate with two full-time Teen Services Librarians, one full-time Library Associate, and two part-time Teen Aides who work twelve hours a week each.

Planning Process: The Martin Luther King, Jr. Memorial Library building opened in 1972. Dedicated teen services began in 1982, and the current Teen Space opened in 2009. Teen Space was designed by the library administration, a team of architects, the teen services manager, and the Capital Projects department of the library. Teens were asked for input on several components of the space. The process was lengthy—at least two years—and changes were made throughout the process. The actual building of the space only spanned a few months.

Teen Space opened in September 2009, and two opening events were held in October. One event was for teens and featured local radio personalities, athletes, and other guests, along with teen programming and snacks. The second was for adults who serve teens, and drew educators, care providers, employees from youthserving agencies, and others invested in youth development. We distributed information about our services and collections, registered users for Educator Cards, and scheduled group visits.

Work was just finished in the media-editing booth connected to the Teen Space. Our next step will be training all youth services staff, after which we will begin using the booth with customers. It will be a place for teens to create and edit music and video files. It contains really cutting edge equipment, and should be a major draw.

Youth Participation and Programming: Teen Space hosts a group of twelve high school students from a local Charter school each year as volunteers and accommodates other

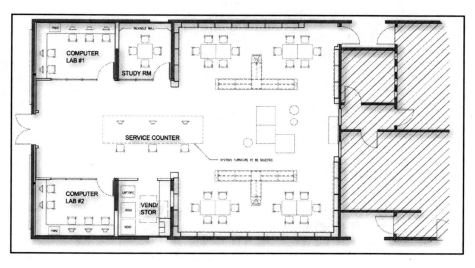

youth volunteers as appropriate. The District of Columbia Public Library (DCPL) has a Volunteer Coordinator who coordinates teen community service. We regularly provide space for local nonprofit groups to meet, including agencies working with HIV/AIDS prevention and education, academic skills and college prep, and general teen health and wellness. We host a teen summer reading program which include reading incentives, programs, and recreational events.

The Library's Web site (*http://www.dclibrary.org/teens*) includes special information for teens about jobs, homework help, book recommendations, real world issues and events. Teens can comment on or add to the Teen Space Facebook page, called Teenopia (*http://www.facebook.com/pages/Washington-DC/TEENOPIA/54057663732*). Teen Space offers an electronic tutoring service called Tutor.com. Youth regularly access this from the computers.

Teen Space also offers a very popular cupcake decorating program twice a month, regular gaming activities (Wii and Xbox), lots of technology programs (create and edit videos and music for social networking sites, etc.), and weekly movie nights. We also have chess classes every Saturday, intermittent college prep workshops, and book discussion groups. We offer lots of high interest programs during the summer months and host large-scale programs in conjunction with ALA/YALSA initiatives, cultural celebrations, and special occasions.

True Confessions from Children's and Teen Services Manager Elsworth Rockefeller

The whole staff was nervous about the shared-space service desk. It limited the storage area to two tiny drawers and gave staff almost no privacy for telephone and in-person reference. Once the decision was made, however, and the desk installed, everyone loved it. The closeness of staff and customers lends itself to collaborative work and more informal relationships, and we've learned that we can function without all of our "stuff" at the desk. It also makes the room feel contemporary and welcoming; there is no sense of the old fashioned "reference desk" standing between staff and customers. The design also encourages staff to walk around the room to provide roving reference and really take an active interest in what teen customers are doing.

This is the YA space of my dreams because . . .

The technology is amazing. We are lucky to have great innovators supporting us, including Chris Tonjes, Director of Information Technology for DCPL, and Eric White, Manager of AV and Television Services. Mr. Tonjes made sure we could offer our teen customers the best technology and continues to advocate for our customers and the needs in the library and in the community. Mr. White has helped us make decisions about media equipment and helped us maximize the use of our tech tools.

I still dream of these improvements:

Is it hot in here? As with any renovation, we continue to improve the space. Temperature control in the room has proved something of a challenge (imagine eighty-seven degrees in the winter), but I think we have found a sustainable solution; it's a comfortable seventy-five degrees right now (and I know more about air conditioning systems than I ever thought I would. I can explain how a chiller works and even compare it to an evaporator-free system). We'd also love some "room to grow," since our use numbers are going up monthly.

Teen Patron Comments

"The new Teen Space is better than before because we can be louder . . . and there are more computers that always work now." —Drew, 18

"Teen Space is a good place to hang out and talk to your friends or play games. My mom lets me come here because it's not 'on the street' but you can still have a good time. It's cool that food is allowed."—MiHailia, 14

"I can edit music on the computers and use Facebook all I want. I found a job on the computers, too, and it's okay to have the volume on."—Isaiah, 19

"Video games you can play for free, magazines, and a place to bring friends . . . I like coming here."—Michael, 16

Martin Luther King, Jr. Memorial Library, 901 G Street N.W., Washington, DC 20001, (202) 727-0321
http://www.dclibrary.org/mlk

Appendix

Resource List

Selecting materials and products is made so much easier with today's Internet shopping than when libraries began experimenting with purpose-built YA spaces. The following lists suggest many standard and creative options for a wide range of budgetary considerations. While few manufacturers and vendors specialize on products and services for young adult spaces or libraries, those appearing in this list have been scrutinized for relevance to YA aesthetics.

The lists feature seven general categories:

- Designers and Consultants

- Furniture

- Textiles, Upholstery, and Textures

- Displays, Merchandising, Shelving, and Storage

- Flooring and Ceiling Treatments

- Standard Library Suppliers

- Aesthetic Amenities: Art, Posters, Decoration

Because our survey demonstrated a need for expanding the library vocabulary with respect to YA seating, the vendors and products appearing in this list especially emphasize creative seating (such as ottomans, stools, benches, and booth products) to maximize the range of YA seating options in libraries.

Designers and Consultants

BiblioTECH Associates
http://www.bibliothequedesign.com
Library consultant specializing in school library facilities design.

Creative Arts Unlimited, Inc.
http://www.creativeartsinc.com
Expert planners and destination space creators.

DEMCO Library Interiors (DLI)
http://www.demcoservices.com
Consulting and design services.

Library Consultant's Online Directory
http://www.libraryconsultants.org
A listing of library consultants, searchable by name, state, and expertise.

Longo Libraries: Complete Library Planning
http://www.longolibraries.com
Consultation, planning, budgeting, project management, construction, and installation services, along with library furnishings.

Furniture

AGATI
http://www.agati.com
Group study ensembles for educational spaces, including a library division.

Arcadia
http://www.Arcadiacontract.com
Innovative design and quality manufacturing.

BFI
http://www.bfionline.com
Creative commercial interiors.

Brandrud
http://www.brandrud.com
Furniture retailer for a variety of environments.

Brayton International
http://www.brayton.com
Furniture manufacturer that specializes in European and custom design.

Bretford
http://www.bretford.com
Furniture and equipment.

Community Furniture
http://www.communityfurniture.com
Chairs, tables, and lounge seating for institutions. Specializes in wood.

Cranberry Clouds
http://www.cranberryclouds.com
Stylish seating designs.

Danko Design
http://www.peterdanko.com
Eco-friendly seating and tables in fun designs.

Design Public
http://www.designpublic.com
Inspiring, functional, aesthetic-driven, modern furniture.

Design Within Reach
http://www.dwr.com
Retailers for the "Prince Aha Stool."

Diner Booths
http://www.dinerbooths.com
Booth seating options.

Embury Ltd.
http://www.emburyltd.com
Specialists in library furniture design.

Emeco
http://www.emeco.net
Durable aluminum chairs, made out of 80 percent post consumer and post-industrial metal.

Febland Group Ltd.
http://www.febland.co.uk
Stool specialists.

Fixtures Furniture
http://www.fixturesfurniture.com
Seating and tables.

The Foof Store
http://www.thefoofstore.com
Giant comfier-than-beanbags, including rockers, ottomans, and themed cushions.

Funky Sofa
http://www.funkysofa.com
Stylish and unique sofas, loveseats, chairs, sectionals, ottomans.

Furniture Lab
http://www.furniturelab.com
Inventive, extremely customizable tables, seating, booths.

IKEA
http://www.ikea.com
Inexpensive, stylish furniture and accessories.

Izzydesign
http://www.izzydesign.com
Seating and other furniture with a focus on practicality and flexibility.

Loewenstein
http://www.loewensteininc.com
European-style environments and furnishings.

LoveSac
http://www.lovesac.com
A beanbag-sofa-pillow hybrid.

LumiSource, Inc.
http://www.lumisource.com
Stylish furniture, accessories, contemporary and novelty lighting.

Metro
http://www.metrofurniture.com
A furniture designer and manufacturer specializing in stylish seating.

Modus Furniture
http://www.modusfurniture.co.uk
Contemporary and creative stools and benches.

Nienkamper
http://nienkamperlibrary.com
High quality, European-inspired seating and shelving.

Sparkeology
http://www.sparkeology.com
Durable ottomans.

Turnstone
http://www.turnstonefurniture.com
Sleek, modern, and simple business-style furniture.

Versteel
http://www.versteel.com
Tables, chairs, seating, personal workstations.

Vitro Seating Products
http://www.vitroseating.com
Specializes in retro fifties-style chairs, stools, booths, and tables.

Worden
http://www.wordencompany.com/Brix?pageID=213
Furnishings for libraries, from seating and tables to circulation and technical furniture.

Work Chairs
http://www.workchairs.com/
One of many dealers of the "Swooper" chair: "Sitting in motion."

Textiles, Upholstery, and Textures

Architex
http://www.architex-ljh.com
Innovative small scale, solids, textures, and coordinate upholstery.

Carnegie
http://www.carnegiefabrics.com
Fabric and upholstery for furniture, walls, and windows.

CF Stinson
http://www.cfstinson.com
Commercial fabrics, including upholstery, panels, leather, and vinyl.

Crypton
http://www.cryptonfabric.com
"Super fabrics" that protect against stains, spills, mildew, odors, mold, and bacteria.

Maharam
http://www.maharam.com
Stylish textiles from commercial spaces.

Mayer Fabrics
http://www.mayerfabrics.com
Comprehensive product line and service.

Momentum Group
http://www.themomgroup.com
Woven fabrics, vinyl, panel, and cubicle and cloth.

Robert Allen
http://www.robertallendesign.com
Fine fabrics with innovative design and construction.

Displays, Merchandising, Shelving, and Storage

DisplayCase Depot
http://*www.displaycasedepot.com*
Standard and customized display cases, kiosks, showcases, and exhibit booths with European designs.

Facements
http://www.facements.com
File coverings, cushions, and tackboards.

Franklin Fixtures
http://www.franklinfixtures.com
Standard, modified, and custom display fixtures.

JD Pacific Rim Inc.
http://www.jdstore.com
Various custom-capable shelving, fixtures, showcases, signage, accessories.

Library Bureau Steel
http://www.librarybureaushelving.com
Custom end panel and displays.

Library Display Shelving
http://www.librarydisplayshelving.com
Modular, clear, acrylic display shelving.

Lift Systems
http://www.liftsystems.com
Merchandizing and display units.

MJ Industries
http://www.mjshelving.com
Shelves and shelving accessories.

PB Teen (Pottery Barn Teen)
http://www.pbteen.com
Furniture, lighting, and decorations with teen appeal.

Professional Store Design Group
http://www.tpsdg.com
Creative art end paneling (stock or custom).

Siegal Display Products
http://www.siegeldisplay.com
Floor displays, plastic frames, tabletop displays, sign holders, wall displays, kiosks.

Specialty Store Services
http://www.specialtystoreservices.com
Creative shelving and display ideas including mini grid cubes, various natural wood displays, creative lighting alternatives, banners, signs.

This Into That
http://www.thisintothat.com
Shelving, displays, and art from decommissioned books.

Flooring and Ceiling Treatments

Acoustical Solutions, Inc.
http://www.acousticalsolutions.com
Soundproofing and noise control.

All Noise Control
http://www.allnoisecontrol.com
Noise barrier and absorption products.

Armstrong
http://www.armstrong.com
Acoustical and design products for floors and ceilings.

Centiva
http://www.centiva.com
Standard and custom flooring designs with colors, textures, and finishes.

Decorative and Area Rugs.com
http://www.decorativeandarearugs.com
Rugs in contemporary, classic, modern, kid's, shaped, and retro styles.

Eco Friendly Flooring
http://www.ecofriendlyflooring.com
Environment-friendly wall and flooring options (featuring recycled metal tiles, bamboo, cork, recycled glass titles, linoleum, stones, and reclaimed or sustainable wood).

Forbo
http://www.forboflooringna.com
Commercial floor coverings and surface solutions.

InterfaceFLOR
http://www.interfaceflooring.com
Environmentally responsible modular flooring.

Joy Carpets
http://www.joycarpets.com
Carpet, modular carpet, and area rugs in fun patterns and customizable designs.

Milliken Flooring Covering
http://www.millikencarpet.com
Carpet construction and designs.

Nora Rubber Flooring
http://www.norarubber.com
Rubber floor coverings in traditional, innovative, and customizable styles.

RugsRugs.com
http://www.rugsrugs.com
Modern, contemporary, classic, and unique area rugs.

Aesthetic Amenities: Art, Posters, Decoration

AllPosters.com
http://www.allposters.com
The world's largest poster and print store.

Art.com
http://www.art.com
Retailer of art prints, including movie, music, and sports-themed posters.

AS Hanging Systems
http://www.ashanging.com
Producers of hardware for mounting artwork on walls.

Blik Surface Graphics
http://www.whatisblik.com
Oversize, self-adhesive, removable wall decals for quick and creative decoration.

Derksen Projection Systems
http://www.derksen.com/
Interior lighting projections and displays.

Kling Magnetics
http://www.kling.com
Custom magnets and magnetic products, including paint.

Lifesize Celebrity Cutouts
http://www.cardboardcutouts.com
Cardboard stand-ups of celebrities, popular icons, and animated characters.

Magnetic Poetry
http://www.magneticpoetry.com
The original poetry kit, plus related kits and word-themed products.

RetroPlanet.com
http://www.retroplanet.com
Provider of cool retro products.

Salemi Industries
http://www.salemiindustries.com/
Commercial-grade sound-resistant cell phone booths

Stretch Wall
http://www.stretchwall.com
A unique finishing solution that uses stretched fabric as décor.

Standard Library Suppliers

Brodart
http://www.brodart.com

DEMCO, Inc.
http://www.demco.com

Eurway
http://www.eurway.com

Gaylord
http://www.gaylordmart.com

Highsmith, Inc.
http://www.highsmith.com

Library Interiors, Inc.
http://www.libraryinteriorsinc.com

Library Index

Allen County Public Library - Fort Wayne, IN, 114-116

Auckland City Libraries - Central Library - Auckland, New Zealand, 162-165

Avon Lake Public Library - Avon Lake, OH, 130-132

Base Line Middle School - Boulder, CO, 117-118

Bemis Public Library - Littleton, CO, 50-52

Blue Island Public Library (Tech Annex) - Blue Island, IL, 85-88

Carnegie Library of Pittsburgh (Teen Space) - Pittsburgh, PA, 145-147

City of Mesa Library - Mesa, AR, 128-129

Columbus Public Library (Teen Department) - Columbus, GA, 151-153

Crandell Public Library - Glens Falls, NY, 30-32

Cuyahoga County Public Library (North Royalton Branch) - North Royalton, OH, 43-44

Cuyahoga County Public Library (Solon Branch) - Solon, OH, 58-59

Cuyahoga County Public Library - Beachwood, OH, 3-4

Delray Beach Public Library – Delray, FL, 81-84

East Meadow Public Library - East Meadow, NY, 184-187

Elizabeth Public Library - Elizabeth, NJ, 174-177

Fortuna Library (Tiny Space) - Fortuna, CA, 26-29

Frederick County Public Library (C. Burr Artz Library) - Frederick, MD, 11-12

Glendale Public Library – Glendale, AR, 62-64

Hammond Public Library - Hammond, IN, 18-20

Hampton Bays Public Library (HBAY Teen Services) - Hampton Bays, NY, 97-101

Harris County Public Library - High Meadows Branch; Aldine Branch; Tomball College and Community Library; Barbara Bush Branch; and Clear Lake City County Freeman Branch – Houston, TX, 76-77

Hays Public Library - Hays, KS, 133-135

Hennepin County Library (Franklin Library) - Minneapolis, MN, 93-96

Houston Public Library – Houston, TX, 9-10

Knowasis Scottsdale Public Library - Scottsdale, AR, 158-161

L.E. Phillips Memorial Public Library - Eau Claire, WI, 122-124

Lancaster Public Library (The Hub) - Lancaster, PA, 21-25

Lindbergh Middle School - North Long Beach, CA, 119-121

Los Angeles Public Library - Los Angeles, CA, 107-108, 112-113

Martin Luther King, Jr. Memorial Library - Washington, DC, 208-212

Mastics - Moriches - Shirley Community Library- Shirley, NY, 45-47

McMillan Memorial Library - Wisconsin Rapids, WI, 193-196

Middleton Public Library - Middleton, WI, 73-75

Montgomery County Public Library - Bethesda Library; Quince Orchard Library; Chevy Chase Library - MD, 197-200

Natrona County Public Library - Casper, WY, 70-72

New York Public Library (Battery Park City) - New York, NY, 205-207

Newport Beach Public Library (Central Branch) – Newport Beach, CA, 136-138

Oakland Public Library - Oakland, CA, 188-192

Orrville Public Library - Orville, OH, 48-49

Otis Library (Summers Young Adult Center) - Norwich, CT, 166-169

Palm Harbor Library - Palm Harbor, FL, 33-36

Palos Verdes Library District (Annex) - Rolling Hills Estates, CA, 154-157

Phoenix Public Library – Phoenix, AR, 125-127

Pima County Public Library (Juvenile Detention Center Branch) - Tucson, AR, 170-173

Pinellas Park Public Library - Pinellas Park, FL, 56-57

Port Jefferson Free Library - Port Jefferson, NY, 89-92

Public Library of Cincinnati and Hamilton County
    (TeenSpot) - Cincinnati, OH, 201-204

Rawson Memorial Library - Cass City, MI, 13-15
Rob Leominster Public Library (Robert Cormier Center
    for Young Adults) - Leominster, MA, 67-69

Santa Cruz Public Library (Garfield Park Branch) -
    Santa Cruz, CA, 105-106
Santa Cruz Public Library (Scotts Valley Branch
    Library) - Santa Cruz Public Library, 41-42
Schaumburg Township District Library - Schaumburg,
    IL, 53-55
Scott County Public Library - Georgetown, KY, 60-61
Seattle Public Library (Starbucks Teen Center) – Seattle,
    WA, 142-144

Shaker Heights Public Library - Shaker Heights, OH,
    109-111
Sno-Isle Regional Library System (Edmonds Library) -
    Edmonds, WA, 5-6
Southfield Public Library - Southfield, MI, 139-141
Swampscott Public Library - Swampscott, WA, 7-8

Wadsworth Public Library - Wadsworth, OH, 65-66
Waupaca Area Public Library - Waupaca, WI, 39-40,
    148-150
Wayzata Library - Wayzata, MN, 16-17
William K. Sanford Town Library - Town of Colonie,
    NY, 78-80
Worthington Ohio Libraries - Northwest Library; Old
    Worthington Library – Worthington, OH, 178-183

Author Index

Alessio, Amy, 53-55
Anderson, Kristen, 39-40
Anderson, Sheila B., 114 – 116
Ankney, Don, 21-25
Asher, Jennifer M., 109-111

Baltic, Sarah, 30-32, 201-204
Banks, Katie, 33-36
Bernier, Anthony , 107-108, 112-113, 188 – 192
Bevill, William, 170-173
Boddy, Brijin, 151-153
Booth, Sarah, 76-77
Branch, Nichole, 188-192
Brooks-Reese, Karen, 145-147
Burington, Peg, 148-150
Burnside, Patti, 60-61

Carty, Natasha Stocek, 11-12
Cofer, Sarah , 178-183
Cooper, Chris, 26-29
Coppell, Annie, 162-165
Cox, Helen, 119-121
Creel, Stacy L., 9-10
Czerw, Jeremy, 205-207

Daly, Emily, 70-72
DeLaughter, Maureen, 78-80
Dickerson, Constance, 58 – 59
Dilley, Patrice, 56 – 57
Duncan, Amy, 142-144

Eppinger, Monica, 174-177
Fesko, Shari, 139-141
Fiene, Jennifer, 21-25
Fiero, Angela, 93-96

Gallo, Mina, 3 – 4
Genett, Johannah, 93-96
Germano, Teri, 45 – 47

Hannigan, Jane, 21-25
Hansen, Genesis, 136-138

Hollingsworth, Arline, 56-57
Howerton, Erin Downey, 133 – 135
Imperio, Sandi, 105-106

Jackson, Frances T., 184-187
Jenson-Benjamin, Merideth, 62-64

Kendall, Karl, 125-127
Knauer, Jan, 50-52
Korn, Jennifer, 201-204
Kreutter, Lisa M., 81-84

Lombardo, Cindy, 48-49

McCabe, Ron, 193-196
Mercado, Mary Margaret, 170-173
Miller, Louise, 43-44
Moore, Nancy Jane, 117-118

O'Driscoll, Janis, 41-42, 105-106
Orr, Alison, 154-157
Ott, Valerie, 65-66
Owens, Theresa, 97 – 101

Paone, Kimberly, 174-177
Pechacek, Ann, 178 – 183
Pratt, Vicky M., 7 – 8

Ralston, Jill, 130-132
Reynolds, Tom, 5-6
Rockefeller, Elsworth, 208-212
Rosser-Hogben, Debra M., 21-25
Rummel, Jennifer, 166-169

Sanabria, Diane, 67-69
Schaarschmidt, Erin, 89-92
Scott, Karen, 130-132
Scott, Melody, 18-20

Thompson, Darren, 85-88
Toth, Frieda, 30-32
Tuccillo, Diane, 128-129

Tvaruzka, Kati, 122-124

Van Auken, Kate, 13-15
Van Dan, Rebecca, 73 – 75
Vandergrift, Kay E., 21 -25

Wagennar, Bethany, 16-17
Weinberg, Kathie, 197-200

Younker, J. Marin, 142-144

Zick, Medina, 158-161

About the Author

Anthony Bernier served as a professional young adult librarian for thirteen years (Director of YA Services for Oakland Public Library; nine years as YA Specialist Librarian), during which he was recognized for innovating a variety of outreach and programming models, including the original service and space plan for the first purpose-built YA library space: the acclaimed TeenS'cape at the Los Angeles Public Library.

Dr. Bernier is a trainer for the Young Adult Library Services Association's (YALSA) trainers bureau, Serving the Underserved (SUS); former chair of YALSA's New Directions Task Force; and current member of the *Voice of Youth Advocates (VOYA)* Editorial Board. He has published in *School Library Journal, American Libraries,* several essays and articles in *VOYA,* in addition to many scholarly publications.

A recently tenured Critical Youth Studies scholar at the School of Library and Information Science at San Jose State University in California, Dr. Bernier developed the introductory YA services course and teaches advanced courses in youth services research methods. His research concentrates on public space equity and the administration of library services with young people. His doctoral dissertation examined changing notions of public space in 20th century America. Dr. Bernier has received two National Leadership Grants from the Institute of Museum and Library Services (IMLS) to advance research on YA spaces and he continues to speak on and consult with architects and public agencies on public space design. As part of his work, Dr. Bernier coined the phrases "Geography of No!" and "After-School Apartheid" to characterize libraries, along with other public institutions, as marginalizing young people from being perceived as fully entitled participants in civic life.

Dr. Bernier's work demonstrates that we maximize our professional and ethical commitments to intellectual freedom when we facilitate meaningful connections between user access to content, information, and technology. This means minimizing space and service prohibitions that contradict these professional and ethical foundations.

Dr. Bernier lives in Oakland, California, where he is a proud Oakland Athletics baseball fan and rides both a BMW R1100RT and a Vespa named "Brother Guido."

CPSIA information can be obtained at www.ICGtesting.com
Printed in the USA
BVOW05s1942041213

338190BV00004B/8/P

9 781617 510113